To : ANGU

A BOY
CALLED
ARSENAL

To A TRUE FRIEND.

ARSENAL.

A BOY
CALLED
ARSENAL

ALAN J HILL

The Book Guild Ltd

First published in Great Britain in 2020 by
The Book Guild Ltd
9 Priory Business Park
Wistow Road, Kibworth
Leicestershire, LE8 0RX
Freephone: 0800 999 2982
www.bookguild.co.uk
Email: info@bookguild.co.uk
Twitter: @bookguild

Typeset in 11pt Minion Pro

Printed and bound in the UK by TJ Books Limited, Padstow, Cornwall

ISBN 978 1913208 660

British Library Cataloguing in Publication Data.

A catalogue record for this book is available from the British Library.

For Arsenal

Contents

Prologue

I FIRST MET ARSENAL IN THE CONFERENCE ROOM AT AUTISM
Wessex. I had been warned:

"Arsenal is on the spectrum."
"Be careful how you approach him."
"Make sure you give him space."

I think I was more nervous than he was when he walked into
the room. It was my primary experience of meeting someone
who was at the higher end of the spectrum. Someone who
comfortably held down a role in the organisation, not only
holding down a role but adding a first-hand unique perspective.
He would experience the empathy that someone not on the
spectrum could not.

He walked in; many people already sat around the conference
table. He stood at the front of the room, saying nothing, blinking
behind his glasses at the bright white lights like a startled owl at

night. He was looking around the room, up at the spaces above him, into the corners, counting the number of people in the room. He was literally an animal working out his territory.

I didn't understand and, ignoring all the advice I had been given, jumped up and stuck my hand out at him. "All right, Arsenal, my name's Al. I'm helping the CEO write the strategic plan for the business. Great to meet you."

I could see he wasn't sure of me and at the same time as grabbing my hand to give a firm handshake, he visibly took a step backwards and away from me. *Well done, Al, you've put your foot in it from the word go!* I was not to be deterred and said, "Not many Scousers in the south of England called Arsenal. Where are you from originally?"

Arsenal had only said a couple of words to me, but coming from St Helens myself, I had already identified his strong Liverpool accent. "Whiston," he replied.

"Oh, I know Whiston. Not far from where I went to school. West Park Grammar. Knew a bunch of lads who came from Whiston. Dad was in the hospital for a while."

At this point I knew I had pushed it too far. I was the strategic planning manager for Autism Wessex and we were having a session with the senior management to look at vision and mission statements. Boring corporate work but essential for Autism Wessex to decide the correct strategic direction for the charity. Our forward-thinking CEO wanted input from someone who had experienced first-hand the problems people with autism faced, hence Arsenal's presence. He worked in one of our residential properties, 'Penny Farthing', as a care worker.

This was my initial experience of Arsenal. He was obviously someone who cared. A good day to him was one where he was able to teach one of the service users how to clean their own teeth. A better day followed when a day later they remembered what they had been taught. He contributed well to the meeting with insights that only he could have (that we will hear of later) and I immediately thought it was someone I would like to get to know better.

A week or two later it was a Friday night in Southbourne, a hot spot of nightlife and a playground for decadent clubbers. I was at the 'let's-force-work-colleagues-together-and-make-them-enjoy-themselves occasion', the work's leaving 'do'. Except this was going to be a right knees-up as two people were leaving and hence double the pleasure. The hostelry was called The Brewhouse and Kitchen, and I had been before. It was a busy pub with live music and a selection of over fifty ales. Pretty much Friday-night heaven.

Some of us had been for something to eat first and shared a bottle of wine and then on to the pub, so people were getting into the party mood. It had been a hot week in August and the place was packed with revellers who spilled out onto the street, but all in a good-natured way. Into this atmosphere walked Arsenal. He had made a promise to one of the girls who was leaving that he would be there, and he had kept his promise. At the time I simply didn't understand or comprehend how tough a promise this was to keep.

I am obviously a person who has difficulty learning a lesson as I strutted over again to Arsenal, once more thrusting my hand out in salute. Not as quick to take my hand this time; he was obviously only just managing to stay in the room. Twitching at every sudden noise, standing a little away from everyone else and finding the social context difficult to deal with, he was far from his comfort zone.

Nevertheless, I got him a drink – no alcohol for Arsenal as he stopped drinking years ago. I stood with him and decided to try and find out more about him. He wouldn't sit down, not liking the thought of being hemmed in with his back to the wall, to which I offered an inane fact about the movie *Shane*. We took up a conversation, the conversation that precipitated the writing of this very book.

I asked him about living his life as a person on the spectrum. What was he doing so far south of Liverpool? We agreed there were not many people on the south coast with the accents that we have. Why was he called Arsenal? And then, what was a bloke from Liverpool doing as an Arsenal fanatic? I then pried a little more into his personal life and, to my astonishment, found out that he had only been diagnosed at the age of forty-nine. He had lived with an undiagnosed condition for so long.

It was then that he used the words that made me realise we had to get his story out into the world. When I pushed harder and asked him what had caused him to get diagnosed, he simply replied, "They knew I needed help when my daughter tried to kill herself." This is the story of a true-life hero. Not a role in an action movie, not an overpaid sports star – of which we will hear much more about later in this tale – but someone who through sheer grit and determination has managed to turn his life and that of his family around.

This is the story of a man on the spectrum, a person living with autism. This is the story of Arsenal Whittick.

Chapter One

The Early Years

27th April 1962

Without football my life is worth nothing.

Cristiano Ronaldo

THE WORLD HAD SPUN SO MANY TIMES THAT WE HAD reached April 1962. It was a time of change. Strange statement, as you can pick any period in history and apply the same thought. Even so, the sixties, especially in the UK and the USA, have since been looked back upon as a moment in history of upheaval and social and economic change, both big and small.

On April 5th 1962, a very young NASA pilot, Neil Armstrong, took the latest high-flying super plane, the X15, up to the altitude of 54,600 metres. A new record.

On April 9th 1962, Arnold Palmer won his fifth golf major by taking the Masters for the third time in five years, beating Gary Player into second place.

Also on April 9th 1962, *West Side Story* became the first musical to win ten Oscars, including Best Picture, Best Director for Robert Wise and Jerome Robbins, Best Supporting Actor for George Chakiris, and Best Supporting Actress for Rita Moreno.

On 27th April 1962, Operation Dominic, the atmospheric testing of nuclear weapons by the USA, continued apace on Christmas Island in the Central Pacific.

Also, on the 27th April, and on a lighter note, Elvis Presley was number one in the USA with the single 'Good Luck Charm'.

The thirty-fifth president of the USA in 1962 was John F Kennedy. Later in 1962 he would embark on a series of tension-filled months known as the Cuban Missile Crisis.

Closer to home, events were not nearly so serious.

Hot off the press in London – 2nd April 1962 – the first panda crossing was opened in the UK outside Waterloo Railway Station. Who needs the Cuban Missile Crisis with gems of news similar to this on our very own doorstep?

Harold Macmillan was our prime minister, although a survey released on the 27th suggested that less than half of voters approved of him as PM. A time of change indeed; the names change in politics, but it seems little else.

Performing at the London Palladium for a sell-out two-week spell was the one and only Shirley Bassey. Variety was still very much alive and kicking, and Shirley was supported by Mike and Bernie Winters, along with Ted Rogers.

In at number one in the UK charts on the 27th April was The Shadows with 'Wonderful Land'. It was to be at the top for eight weeks before being replaced on the 17th May by the infamous B. Bumble and the Stingers singing 'Nut Rocker'. Not a song that regularly pops up on people's all-time top ten!

That week The Shadows were topping the bill at the Liverpool Empire, supported by Jackie Trent and Frank Ifield.

Our journey through the early months of 1962 has finally brought us to Liverpool. Earlier that month on the 5th April, a small, yet-to-be-famous guitar band were playing at the Cavern

Club. The event was billed as, 'An evening with George, John, Paul and Pete'. At this point of their fledgling careers, Pete Best was on drums.

Football will never be far from this story and on the 28th April, Ipswich Town won the English First Division for the first and only time in their 141-year (as of today) history by narrowly pipping Burnley.

Arsenal (AFC) finished tenth!

The weather in the UK during April 1962 was cold, wet and blustery. Gale-force winds in Scotland, snow across higher ground in England and Wales, and the stormy weather of March spilled over into the first week of April. The temperatures were cooler than average, especially in the north-west, and rain fell steadily during the first three weeks in Liverpool and Manchester. It was a drab and dingy start to spring in Liverpool.

Then the sun came out for the long Easter weekend, so from Good Friday on the 20th through to Easter Monday on the 23rd, the people of Liverpool enjoyed the warmer weather and took to the festivities with a feeling that summer was just around the corner. For Mrs Flynn, heavily pregnant with her second child, the end of the month couldn't come quickly enough.

The day of the 26th was a tough one for her as her water broke and she went into a long labour. The day was cold with a thick fog in the morning drifting into the city off the North Sea, but this soon burned off and the Liver Bird sparkled in the early spring sunshine as the warming sun soon burned the fog away. It was a good day to come into the world.

After a long day of labour pains, Mrs Pat Flynn gave birth to a baby brother for her eighteen-month-old eldest son Edward, known as Eddie. On a cool, damp, foggy night at six minutes past midnight, a baby boy was born in North Cantril Avenue, West Derby, Liverpool, but it would be nine long years before he became Arsenal Whittick.

Alan: So you spoke last week in the pub about not remembering much about the first six years of your life. What exactly do you remember and is there anything you can tell me?

Arsenal: As a kid I can only remember negatives, unfortunately. The first thing, memory I have as a kid was – I lived opposite the school, the primary school. And the only memory I have of that school is one day, I was taken over to the bus stop, away from the school.

           I never knew at the time, but it was a 'special' coach I was going on. I actually literally got dragged as I was screaming. I didn't want to go on this coach, and no one had explained anything to me. I never got on it in the end.

Alan: Who was trying to put you on the coach?

Arsenal: Me mum. I was only thinking about this about a month ago and I rang me dad up to ask him about it and he said, "I don't remember stuff, I'm getting on now, lad." Because he's in his seventies now. But he did suggest to me that I ask me brother, so I've tried to contact him, but he works all hours, so I still have to ask him if he remembers anything about this coach. But, when I was diagnosed in 2011, I asked me mum if she knew anything and she said, "There was no health support for me back then," and that told me then that me mum and dad actually knew there was something wrong.

Alan: When you say special coach, where was the coach going?

Arsenal: I dunno. Never even got on it because I was fighting me mum. Because I didn't want to go on

	it. I was a kid. In junior school, so I was under ten. It was going somewhere, but…
Alan:	So who else was on this coach?
Arsenal:	I dunno. A couple of kids. I remember them looking out the coach window at me. Because I was hanging onto the railings by the bus stop because I didn't want to go.
Alan:	What was the name of the school?
Arsenal:	The school I actually went to was St Alberts Primary School. And the coach was over the road outside the school. The school had its own entrance and there were a row of cars, but this coach I was going on was at the normal bus stop.
Alan:	Someone must have arranged for you to go on this coach.
Arsenal:	It was arranged for me, but they'd never told me.
Alan:	Your mum must have been involved.
Arsenal:	Yeah, yeah. Because I just remember getting actually dragged to the bus stop and I was like, wow!

After forty-seven years and counting, Arsenal still has no idea where the coach was going. This event in his life would have been traumatic to any child. Dragged screaming to be placed on a coach, no information, no understanding why he wasn't going into school like he did every other day of his life. Now add to that the complexity of being a child with autism and undiagnosed. His parents were doing their best for him and whatever the advice at the time had been, it involved putting Arsenal on this 'special coach'.

No one in the early '70s made allowances for children with autism. It was a very new diagnosis even though it was first recognised as a condition back in 1908 by psychiatrist Eugen

Bleuler to describe a schizophrenic patient who had withdrawn into his own world.

Doctor Bleuler was using the word autism rather than 'diagnosing' someone with the condition. That didn't take place until 1943.

Autism was even then not a new condition. It didn't suddenly appear in humans in 1943. The first ever recorded case of autism was probably in 1800 and the condition almost certainly has been around for centuries before then.

In 1800, a Frenchman named Jean Marc Gaspard Itard wrote an account of a twelve-year-old boy (his approximate age), who had been living in a forest until he was captured on Wednesday 8th January 1800. Itard named the boy Victor, who made no direct communication and was very self-absorbed.

Itard assumed that Victor had grown up without any form of human contact as he never spoke. He would gesture if he wanted something. According to Itard, Victor would pull someone by the arm to gain their attention and wanted items to be in the same place constantly. He was also very unhappy unless the object was moved back to its former place. It's obviously impossible to be sure, but this could well be the first recorded example of a person with autism.

During the early '70s in the UK, interventions typically included removal from the family home. Many children were placed in institutions in order to receive care around the clock. Treatments included:

- D-Lysergic Acid Diethylamide (LSD),
- Electroconvulsive therapy (which as late as 2010 was still under investigation as a treatment for autism),
- Behavioural approaches that used aversives (punishment).

Autism was a misunderstood condition, and the misunderstandings led to unfortunate interventions and treatment therapies. Developments in the decades to follow led to fortunate changes.

For Arsenal at the age of nine, after not speaking for the first six years of his life (and then, because of his severe stammer, continuing to have incredible difficulty in making himself understood), there was very little compassion or understanding. Basically, he was a 'troubled lad'. A bad loser who was obsessed with football and always getting himself into scrapes.

I'm not sure we can find out where the coach was going that day it was parked outside St Albert's Primary School, but there's a part of me that feels very glad that Arsenal didn't get on it.

Through several interviews, it was very hard to find out any more from Arsenal's early childhood. Mrs Flynn had her third child in November 1964, another boy named Mark, followed by Jackie, the first girl on 12th February 1968. There is a memory of Christmas Day, either 1970 or 1971, that Arsenal tells.

Alan: *Do you remember any special events like birthdays or Christmas Days?*

Arsenal: *The only Christmas I ever remember was one Christmas we come down the stairs really early with me two brothers, and me parents had laid out our presents. And me brother had got a watch and I 'ad but the presents were like near together. So, me brother picked his up and all I can remember, like half an hour later, was he had these two new watches. He'd picked one up, because they were all close together, and then he's waving his arm about, saying, "Look, I've got two new watches."*

And it never clicked, like, that one of them was mine. Until me parents came down and that's

	the only Christmas I remember before I went to senior school. I think I was eight or nine, maybe.
Alan:	*Have you ever been told why you have no memories of your early childhood?*
Arsenal:	*You know what, no one's ever mentioned it. I never got told absolutely anything as a kid or as an adult. Me mum had me older brother and me younger brother by the time she was twenty-one and when she was having her third child, her and me dad split up, which I never knew.*
	And then she met someone else who I call Dad who's been there ever since. But I never got told that either. Tony was there from when I was one and a half, and his name is Whittick. My mum's name was Flynn.
	In junior school I was always Flynn.
	I was just always Flynn.

I am not surprised that Arsenal's memories of his early years are either lost or hidden away, or subconsciously supressed.

We are talking about a young boy who for the first six years of his life was non-verbal, until by his own volition he started making noises – not words, but noises. He was one of four children by two different fathers but didn't remember one dad going and another arriving. He only remembers Tony Whittick being his dad.

He has autism, but society hadn't got to that point of its own evolution whereby autism was commonly diagnosed or even suggested as a reason for unusual behavioural traits. People with autism live by their routines and procedures, and the seemingly one recognisable act to acknowledge his 'differences' was to force him onto a coach of which he had no prior knowledge.

Finally, after six years of silence, not only was Arsenal a person with autism, but he had such a severe stammer that when he learned his words, he couldn't then get them out. Plus, there was no help for his parents working hard to bring up four young kids in working-class Liverpool in the '60s and early '70s.

Is it any wonder Arsenal has no memories?

The next stage of his life was 'big' school. The seniors. With trepidation but a positive attitude, life for young Master Flynn was going to change forever.

On the 8th May 1971, it did just that!

Chapter Two

Becoming Arsenal

1971

If you do not believe you can do it, you have no chance at all.

Arsène Wenger

IT WAS A WARM SUNNY MAY DAY ON THE MORNING OF THE
1971 FA Cup final at Wembley between Arsenal and Liverpool.
It was going to be an even hotter sunny afternoon and the rich
turf of Wembley Stadium was going to provide a stiff test for the
stamina and legs of both sets of players.

Meanwhile in Liverpool, particularly the West Derby part
of Liverpool near St Albert's primary, the conditions were going
to be slightly better for the kids of Steers Croft (the Flynn family
had moved 'around the corner' in the interim years from North
Cantril Avenue) and its surroundings. Snotty-nosed urchins from
Dumbree's Road, Princess Drive and Haswell Drive were about to
play their own version of the FA Cup final on the hallowed turf
of St Albert's playing field. Not as salubrious surroundings as the
Twin Towers but not as hard on the legs either.

Every year the lads from St Alberts Primary grabbed their jumpers for goal posts and headed off to the school pitch, bunking over the fence, and playing their own version of the FA Cup Final. Everyone wanted to be their favourite players from the sides contesting the final. This year, with Liverpool being one of them, the allocation of players' names was going to be even more difficult. Young Flynny (yet to become Arsenal) was one of about twenty lads haring off down Steers Croft to get to the school pitches.

The two Wembley sides were lining up as follows:

Liverpool

1. Ray Clemence
2. Chris Lawler
3. Alec Lindsay
4. Tommy Smith (Captain)
5. Larry Lloyd
6. Emlyn Hughes
7. Ian Callaghan
8. Alun Evans
9. Steve Heighway
10. John Toshack
11. Brian Hall
Substitute Peter Thompson
Manager Bill Shankly

Arsenal

1. Bob Wilson
2. Pat Rice
3. Bob McNab
4. Peter Storey
5. Frank McLintock (Captain)
6. Peter Simpson
7. George Armstrong
8. George Graham
9. John Radford
10. Ray Kennedy
11. Charlie George
Substitute Eddie Kelly
Manager Bertie Mee

As you might imagine, the demand was certainly on the all-red side. Twenty Liverpool kids fighting for ten names was never going to work, and Flynny knew this. He played in goal, but the school goalkeeper was part of the gang that day and Flynny knew that the other kid would be Ray Clemence for the day. So, wanting to ensure his place in the side in his favoured position, our canny hero thought, *I'll be Bob Wilson,* and sped off to one end of the pitch, throwing two jerseys down to make the goal. He tried to shout over his shoulder that he would be Arsenal's goalie, but as for many other times in his short life, his stammer stopped him getting the words out.

Alan:	*How in God's name did a little Scouser running around the streets of Liverpool, surrounded by Liverpool, Everton and Tranmere fans, get the name Arsenal?*
Arsenal:	*Saturday 8th May 1971. It was the FA Cup final. All the kids from the area used to go over to the fields and put their jumpers down and that would be the goals. We would have the Cup final before the real Cup final. So, we all ran over to the field and I was always the goalie, so I thought, I know that kid's going to go in that goal, so I'll go in that [Arsenal points to one side of his living room] goal.*
	So, I went down to the Arsenal goal and put down two jumpers. There was about twenty of us there and when I turned around there was nineteen on the Liverpool side and just me on the Arsenal side in the goal. And everyone just started pumping their fists into the air and chanting, "ARSENAL, ARSENAL."
	And it just stuck.
Alan:	*And you were Bob Wilson for the day.*
Arsenal:	*And then I went home and told me mum and dad, "I want Arsenal to win today." I was just ripped. I was fascinated then. I remember Steve Heighway scoring and I could feel the anger. Then*

> *Eddie Kelly equalised and put the game into extra time.*
>
> *And then Charlie George got the winner, shot from outside the box, top right-hand corner. From that day I was fascinated and addicted.*

So Flynny left the house that morning and came back as Arsenal. His mates soon realised that if they called him Arsenal instead of his real name, they had a far better chance of receiving the ball. He stopped answering to his real name at home until all his brothers continued to call him Arsenal. There is a serious matter of identity to be considered here. Later on in his life he would actually change his name to Arsenal by deed poll and at one of our discussions he uses the expression, "All I ever wanted to be was Arsenal." (For the sake of clarity, when referring to Arsenal Football Club I will use AFC, when you read Arsenal, it is the person.)

Flynny was creating a new character or person that he could identify with and give him a meaning in life. To use both his and his parents' words, "He became addicted to Arsenal Football Club," but more importantly, he stopped being Flynny and became Arsenal. He no longer would answer to his given Christian name and today will not even tell people, including myself, what his first given name was. As far as he is concerned, he is Arsenal. At that point, Arsenal Flynn. It would be a while before he became Arsenal Whittick.

In September 1973, Arsenal started senior school; another traumatic day not just in the life of Arsenal but in the early years of any child. Everything is big. The desks and chairs are made for sixteen-year-old giants. The school is bigger, the classrooms and assembly halls are bigger, and there are people milling around everywhere. At the time as a child you feel like you've been dropped off in the centre of London and told to find your own way home! The onus is now on you to get to your classroom; the teachers no longer come to you. You have greater responsibility than ever before to keep time and be in the right place at the right time.

St Dominic's in Huyton, now no longer, was no different to any other '70s secondary modern. Arsenal was thrown into this cauldron of raging hormones with an inability to express himself because of his severe stammer and the added problem of being an undiagnosed person with autism. We cannot even begin to think how difficult moving to a new school can be for a child with autism.

Today, planned visits for the child would be made ahead of time. Visual aids can help the child to understand what will be happening and reinforce verbal communication – fine if you don't have a stammer. Nevertheless, these should be used more than once, particularly if the change is going to take place over a prolonged period of time, which moving school obviously is. There are lots of strategies that are used today: use of social stories, preparation in the child's current school, obviously prepping the new school about the requirements and needs of the new pupil, and then just talking to the child and managing his or her anxieties in advance.

Not in 1972! In 1972, Arsenal turned up on day one with about another hundred new kids ready, or not so ready, for the brave new world of senior school. So young Master Flynn arrives at St Dominic's Roman Catholic after a twenty- to twenty-five-minute dragged walk across the fields by St Brigid's infants and past Hope Primary. His new clothes were rubbing him and bought to fit so that 'he could grow into them'. Dark blue blazer, grey trousers, bright blue jumper and crisp white shirt with a blue and white striped tie. Flynny looked as good as he ever did, even if everything was made for a lad of a slightly greater stature and build.

Alan: *How did you find senior school?*

Arsenal: *In junior school I was always Flynn. That's something else I remember, always being Flynn. [At this point Arsenal pauses and takes quite a while, in conversational terms, to start speaking again.] When I was going to senior school, I gather me parents had decided, like, to have us all under one name and call us all Whittick. But they didn't tell me.*

So, I remember, first day at senior school, back then they used to do the register, and it's your first day, they used to do the register in the playground. They used to call just your surname. So Whittick was right on the bottom. But to me my name was Flynn. So, no one told me any otherwise. And then the teacher's going through the names and I'm not even thinkin', am I?

I'm just trying to hear Flynn, aren't I? And then they call out Whittick and I don't answer. In my head I'm Flynn and I didn't answer. From then I was known as 'The boy who didn't know his own name'.

Arsenal was building himself up to just be able to say, "Yes sir," or, "Here," or whatever everyone else was shouting out to notify themselves as all present and correct. His stammer was very bad and all he was concerned about was hearing Flynn and being able to respond quickly enough so as not to be a laughingstock. As it was, he became, 'The boy who didn't know his own name'. Children are quick and not a little cruel when it comes to forming a hierarchy and ensuring that they're not at the bottom of it. Not being able to respond to the name Whittick immediately singled Arsenal out as someone to be ridiculed and, to a milder degree, bullied.

Today when telling these stories, Arsenal does it with a smile on his face and a shrug of his shoulders. "That's life, isn't it?" he intones in his still-broad Liverpudlian accent. This was the day when he first became known as Arsenal Whittick.

By day three at 'big' school, things hadn't got much better. Arsenal was in one of his first history lessons with Miss Lamb, as he recalls. The teacher asks Arsenal to read out in front of the class. Again, this is something that would never happen under today's educational regime. That is, asking a student with a serious speech defect to read aloud to a group of his peers on their third day of being part of this group.

> Arsenal: *Because of me stammer back then, I couldn't get no words out. So, the class pretended to fall asleep and some of them even pretended to snore. I just thought, Oh God, this is horrendous. But that's kids for you, isn't it? So, when I couldn't actually read out, I gathered the teacher has mentioned it in the staff room.*

From what Arsenal says, that was it. No further help. Nothing but a mention of it in the staff room. This isn't necessarily any one individual's fault. I'm a year older than Arsenal so I was at senior school at exactly the same time as he was. In the secondary modern, also since shut down, that I went to in the north-west of England, not far at all from St Dominic's – every school year had a 'special class'. This was for everyone, for whatever reason, who had 'learning' difficulties. These kids were almost kept separate from the rest of the 'normal' children. There quite simply was no particular provision for students with learning difficulties.

So, the history teacher working with Arsenal, the boy who didn't know his own name, on day three of his senior education, had no idea of his stammer. Certainly no one at this time knew of his autism or his identity crisis. Arsenal had no real understanding why his name still wasn't Flynn. His autism would have prevented him from processing the fact he was being called by another name and what it meant to him. In other words, he had no idea that Tony Whittick wasn't his biological father or even why his dad had a different name to his mum.

This high-profile birth at St Dominic's made him the number one suspect for the bullies. Now this is a word that Arsenal himself doesn't use, but there were obviously forms of psychological bullying that Arsenal was living through every day of his life. Also, this is when I think his autism would have helped him. Arsenal still today has great difficulty in showing sympathy and certainly empathy, but at the age of eleven, this lack of understanding of other people's thoughts and intentions would have armoured him from the cruel tricks he endured.

The other shield that he had in his armoury was his undiluted, enthusiastic love of the game of football and particularly Arsenal Football Club. He can never remember his parents preparing a meal because he was never in the house. He was permanently kicking a ball with his classmates, or brothers, or kids from Steers Croft and the surrounding area. If he had no one else to play with that didn't upset him, he would take a ball out on his own and spend hours kicking it against a wall until one of his parents called him or found him and dragged him home for food. He was truly addicted, and this extract from an email received in November 2018 from his dad says as much:

> "You were a staunch Arsenal supporter sometimes
> this was annoying – you wrote your hero's players
> names on Electricity sub stations and in many
> other unusual places!

"Some people objected too your love of Arsenal you
wore the shirt sang their tunes you made one or two
enemies along the way!"

This addiction to AFC focussed Arsenal's mind above everything
else that was happening in his life and became his raison d'être.
As long as AFC won, nothing else mattered. He prioritised
the results of AFC above everything else, with the rest of the
footballing world a distant second. This behaviour is a regular
and recurring theme when looking at people on the autism
spectrum.

Arsenal Football Club became a protector to Arsenal
Whittick. He had something to keep him busy, to give him a
purpose and to provide happiness in his life; although as the
years go by, we will see how it also provided years of unhappiness
for Arsenal and his family.

His school years from eleven to sixteen were better than
his earlier experiences with the education process but were still
demanding on both Arsenal and his family. As suggested by his
dad, he was in and out of trouble on many occasions and his
love of Arsenal Football Club – don't forget, we are in Huyton in
the heart of Liverpool and Everton country – would be forever
providing reasons for bullying or clashes with authoritarian
figures at school and in a wider radius. He refused to be called
by any other name other than Arsenal Whittick and this was
the name used on the school registers. These senior school years
were when he became Arsenal Whittick.

His stammer was also as much fun as an adventure
playground to his 'mates' in the classroom.

Alan: *Were you ever bullied at school because of your
stammer or autism? Do you remember senior
school fondly or did you hate it?*

Arsenal: *I just remember playing football all the time. At lunch, at dinner, at break time, in the playground. I remember people used to just hit me for some reason. And then I always remember someone saying, along the lines of, "It doesn't hurt him."*

And I gather people thought it was fun to just hit me because I've got a really strong pain threshold.

And then I remember, I think we were playin' football, I hurt a lad. I was in goal and I came out to challenge for the ball at his feet and hurt a lad. But he had an older brother and he got upset, so there was going to be this fight after school. So, I come out of school and they were all waiting for me. It was horrendous.

But they all formed a circle and the blazers were down. But you know what, I don't know how it started, but the two brothers were there and me and we were standing in the middle of this ring of blazers. I went over to the older brother and I remember getting him in a headlock and just squeezing him. I felt like everyone was trying to get me off because I was just squeezing him and squeezing him.

I was choking and squeezing, and everyone was jumping on me and trying to get me off. I wouldn't let go, I was trying to kill him, really. But then after that, it just changed. [Arsenal clicks his fingers to illustrate this was a changing point at school.] Everyone stopped hitting me. I never got hit again.

They must have thought, Shit, he won't let go. If he gets hold of you, he'll kill you. I guess that's

*what I was trying to do. I knew I didn't want to
let go. I knew I just wanted to keep on stranglin'
him. And that is the only fight I've ever had in me
life and not one punch was thrown. Wow, it was
amazing. No one hit me again. I must have been
about thirteen.*

Other tricks that were played on Arsenal revolved around his
inability to speak properly due to his stammer. He remembers a
gaggle of lads calling him over in the school library. They were
huddled around one book in the centre of the table-like rugby
players in a scrum.

"Arsenal, look at this. Do you know what it is?" one of
them loudly whispered – normal etiquette for schoolboys in
the school library. The book that had captured their adolescent
curiosity was one about the human body, what else? The book
was opened to a drawing of the female torso and they were
pointing to the cartoon breasts on the page in front of them.

"What are these, Arsenal?" They all giggled. "Do you know
what they are?" Arsenal today tells how his mind was whirling
with the different words he could use. *Do I say breasts? Or
boobies? Or tits or titties?* Either his autism or his stammer
stopped him from saying what he wanted to say. So, to make life
easier for himself, he just shook his head and stammered, "No,
I don't know."

"Arghhh, he doesn't even know that. Do you know nothing,
Arsenal? You don't even know what a tit is!"

When telling this story, Arsenal laughs and talks about the
cruelty of kids and plays it down good-naturedly, but there is a
sadness to his words and around his eyes. He also pauses more
frequently between his words, as though re-examining this
episode of his life is difficult. These are my thoughts, nothing
that he directly says.

For him, the letter 'S' provided most problems as a child and he tells of another day, once more in the dreaded school library, when he was called over to read words from a dictionary. To me, forty-plus years later, it sounds as though it may be the same cauldron of bullies. The page was turned to one of the 'S' pages in the dictionary.

"What does that say, Arsenal? I can't read it."

After an age of spluttering and long, drawn-out 'sssss' noises, Arsenal managed to say, "Snake."

"What about this one?" Again, Arsenal struggled for what to him must feel like the length of a double maths lesson while all about him were rolling about with mirth.

Eventually, keen-to-make-friends Arsenal realised, "They were just taking the piss."

He walked away, another moment lost in the life of a stammering child with autism trying to find their way in life in the '70s.

With limited resources and no specialised training, plus undiagnosed conditions, how did the school educate someone with the difficulties that Arsenal obviously had? The simple answer was, they didn't. What they tried to do was keep him occupied. Hence, Arsenal only ever recollects taking classes during his O Level years for two subjects: woodwork and art. The rest of the time he 'helped' the caretaker.

Arsenal: *Me only memories of being in class in senior school are when I did woodwork, I done it for most of the day. And when I did art, I done it for most of the day. And for the other days, in me memory, I helped the caretaker. I used to go round the whole school every morning, used to pick up all the registers from the classes and take them to the office. Then I'd go and see the caretaker. I would put all the tables and*

	chairs out in the sports hall for lunch. Or I'd go and put the goals up and the nets on the goalposts.
	I'd just do stuff like that.
Alan:	*What about other subjects, maths and English?*
Arsenal:	*To my knowledge I don't have it. Because last January [2017] I rang up Alderney Hospital, I said, "Listen. You know what, I think I'm really stupid. Can I come and see you?"*

> *And they said, "It's not that you're really stupid, Arsenal, you haven't had an education." And that's what it is. I have no knowledge. I only found out two months ago that yoghurt and cheese come from cows. I never ever knew. I was actually in work [as a carer in a residential home for Autism Wessex] and we'd been to get the shopping and we were putting it all away, and the dairy was going into the fridge. And I was putting mozzarella cheese away and XXXXX said that comes from a different kind of cow.*
>
> *I was shocked and thought they were having me on. They had to take me into the office and google it for me because I wouldn't have it. I just never knew. Wow – I just don't have the knowledge.*
>
> *I did an IQ test and the average is about a hundred and mine was seventy-one.*

Since his diagnosis, Arsenal has been setting himself education goals – learning about the body being one of them – but reading is a problem for him. It's not that he can't read, it's just that he finds a part of a book that interests him, and goes over and over the same part of the book until he almost wears the page out. Again, a trait of someone on the spectrum.

Subjects have to make a connection with him in any form of media to keep his attention and focus. The one book he has read cover to cover is a book written by a non-verbal Japanese child with autism called, *The Reason I Jump* by Naoki Higashida. I have since read it also and it's a first-hand account of a child with autism trying to explain in a series of Q&As why exactly he behaves the way he does. It's a fascinating insight and clarified to me some of the less extreme behaviour that Arsenal had been explaining about himself.

I immediately understood why Arsenal had no issue reading the book as he identified with every page of it.

His love for Arsenal Football Club meant that he was recommended to read Paul Merson's autobiography, *Rock Bottom*. In the introduction, Paul Merson talks about how he wanted to break his own fingers to stop himself placing another bet. Arsenal cannot get past this introduction. Whenever he picks the book up, he starts it again. It resonates with him. He has self-harmed so many times in his own life and tried to keep it hidden for such a long time that Arsenal just rereads this section over and over again.

I read it out loud to Arsenal and offered to read the book to him, but it was an offer he never took me up on. I believe it was his pride that stopped him from saying yes, so I never pushed.

Arsenal is far from a stupid man and when I heard how he had turned his life around, I knew that wasn't the behaviour of someone with a low IQ. He may not have been educated and may be a person dealing with autism, but that does not make him stupid.

He only took the two O Levels in the end – today they would be GCSEs – as he never attended enough classes in other subjects to merit taking the examinations. His results:

- Woodwork – Pass – Grade A.
- Art – Pass – Grade A.

Chapter Three

Becoming Arsenal Whittick

Ongoing

You only stop learning when you quit.

Ruud Gullit

DURING THESE FORMATIVE YEARS AT SCHOOL WHEN Arsenal Whittick was slowly but surely creating an identity for himself, his life continued apace outside of school as well. The meaning of life to him was still a red-bodied shirt with white sleeves, but this passion drove him to exceed in spite of his natural failings. He lived in Liverpool, he was a child, he had no money, he had chosen to support a football team that was, especially for a kid, a long way away. To be exact, from 150 Steers Croft in Liverpool to Highbury, the then-home of Arsenal Football Club, it was, and still is, 191 miles. A bit of a journey on a pushbike!

Alan: How did you raise money to go to the games?

Arsenal: In school, in the morning, before school I used to help the milkman. And then after school I had a paper round, I used to deliver the Liverpool Echo. Then on Saturday morning I used to help at Scott's Bakery. They had a van that delivered cakes and bread and such. I'd do that after the milkman again. In the afternoon I worked for the Alpine man. Used to deliver pop and lemonade. Then after that at 5pm I used to wait for the Football Pink, the pink Echo on a Saturday night to be printed and I'd deliver that.

          Then on Sunday morning I would deliver the papers, then play football on a Sunday morning after the paper round. Then Sunday afternoon I had a Wall's ice cream round that was like a freezer on wheels. Used to knock on doors and sell ice cream. Once a month I would get all my money and go to Highbury. I used to work for it and that's how I done it.

Alan: How did you get to Highbury, as there wouldn't have been many coaches going from Liverpool down to Highbury?

Arsenal: Used to get the train from Liverpool Lime Street to Euston. Then from Euston, used to get the Underground to Finsbury Park from Victoria and then walk to the ground.

Alan: And who did you go with?

Arsenal: No one. I used to go on me own.

Alan: And how old was you then?

Arsenal: First game I ever went to was 1976, last game of the season, Man U away so I must have been fourteen or fifteen when I started going. [When I *researched this game it was the 14th May 1977, the last game of the 1976/77 old Division 1 season. Arsenal was in fact fifteen years old.] That was me first game and I started going regularly the following season. I just used to love it.*

I got the coach up there from Liverpool and the coach stopped outside Lou Macari's chippie right next to Old Trafford. Because it was me first game ever, I got there at ten o'clock in the morning. In those days, the coach was allowed right up to the ground. But after the game, because of the traffic the coach had to go somewhere else to get picked up. But I didn't know that!

I was stood on the opposite side of the road and there were loads of people coming out and because I was small, I couldn't get away. I think I ended up in Salford, I believe.

Because all these thousands of people were marching along, I just got carried along with them. The police had to ring me mum and dad. "Do you have a son called Arsenal? He's missed his coach and can't get home." I believe me dad was annoyed, for some reason? And then he just put the phone down on 'em. The police took me to Manchester Piccadilly, and they put me on a train to Liverpool Lime Street and that's how I got home. So, I went to me first game and I got lost!

Alan: *I know I shouldn't ask this but what was the score?*
Arsenal: *We got beat 3-2! I went in the Stretford End, there were seats back then. I was amazed there were seats. And I sat in the seats. Then I was addicted!*

Back then you used to pay on the gate so you could just turn up and pay. Birmingham, Wolves,

> Coventry, Man City, Man U, Oldham, two
> Sheffield grounds, I used to go to all these away
> games.

Alan: And now you say addicted, but at that age you
obviously never considered it to be an addiction?

Arsenal: No, no. It was when Alderney Hospital spoke to
me mum and dad when I was being diagnosed
years later and me mum put in the report that I
was addicted to football.

It was indeed years later that the word 'addicted' was first used to describe Arsenal's love of football, but it was during these years from the age of nine and the 1971 Cup final to the age of sixteen when he left home for the first time that Master Flynn became Arsenal Whittick. In one conversation I had with him he actually said, "All I ever wanted to be was Arsenal Whittick."

The memories that Arsenal has retained all revolve around either football or family events. He remembers the whole family jumping on a coach and going to Southport for the day, the closest Arsenal ever got to a family holiday. This was a big day out to the seaside town of Southport, with its funfair and beaches. One of Southport's most celebrated sights is Lord Street, a Victorian canopied boulevard, edged in scenic gardens. With a charming, unique style all of its own, Lord Street has been a favourite shopping destination for over a century. This is where the Liverpool coaches dropped its eager day-trippers off.

There must be something about Arsenal and coaches because once again he doesn't remember the brightly coloured horses bobbing up and down on the carousel. Nor does he remember the dodgem cars, big dipper, slides or paddling in the sea on the beach. What he remembers is being waved to by all the kids on the back seat of the coach, and waving back as it pulled out on to Lord Street to wend its way back to Liverpool at the end of the day. His autism wouldn't let him work out that he shouldn't be waving to them but actually should be sat next to them. It was only as the coach disappeared out of sight up Lord Street that he wondered how HE was going to get home.

To use his words, "It never clicked. They were banging on the windows and I was just shouting bye bye." Luckily someone told his dad that they had just waved Arsenal off and ten minutes later the coach returned. Arsenal was still stood where he had been left as he hadn't yet 'processed' what he was going to do. He said it seemed like a lifetime. Crack round the head, "Get on the bloody coach."

Arsenal used to play football every Sunday and the kids from his estate had a Sunday League children's side in the local League. His team was called Steers Croft, imaginatively named after the street he lived on, and they worked their way to the Cup final versus Roundhey. They lost 5-1 in the final and Arsenal was in goal. The opposition had a young lad called Mick Quinn who eventually went on to play professionally at the top level. He scored all five goals. The medals were being given out by a famous Liverpool player called David Fairclough who was known at the time as 'Supersub' as he invariably came off the bench and scored for Liverpool. Fairclough lived on Cantril Farm estate and was an obvious choice to be a guest of honour at a boys' Cup final. After the game the players received their medals and were getting snapped by their parents as mementos of the day.

Arsenal remembers getting a medal and a handshake, but the thing he remembers most about the day was that he was on his own. No one had come to watch him play: no parent, no sibling. It was his only sporting achievement and he had nobody to share it with and no photograph of the day to remember it by.

As well as playing for Steers Croft, effectively an 'estate' team, he played football at school all the time, although he never made it into the school team. He played kickabout with his mates whenever he could – although Arsenal says he never had any friends. He watched Arsenal Football Club whenever he could, either live or on telly, *Match of the Day* being his highlight of the week. When he couldn't find anyone else to play with, he kicked a ball against a wall on his own.

Even with all this football in his life – and let's not forget, from the age of fifteen he held down six or seven separate jobs to pay for his football trips – the highlight of the week was the Sunday afternoon kids and dads' game down at St Albert's school football pitch. Arsenal couldn't play every week, depending on his work commitments, but he managed to juggle his jobs around to be a regular Sunday afternoon player. He was Pat Jennings, the Arsenal goalkeeper in the 1977/78 season.

Arsenal: *Kids from our estate and dads and me dad every Sunday used to play a game. And every single Sunday I used to get sent off. From me dad. He'd say, "Arsenal, just go home." Every single week. I just used to be so angry if we were losing. And we used to play next to the school. The games were always up to twenty. First to twenty was the winners. They got to nineteen [the opposition] and most weeks I would be in goal. For some reason, as soon as their nineteenth goal went in, I started to feel the anger. So, when I got the ball in me hands, I'd kick it on the school roof.*

Alan: *Well, they can't score the winner from there, can they! [I cannot contain my laughter at this story.]*

Arsenal: *You're laughing now, but I used to get in so much trouble. And me dad would say, "Well you're going to have to get up there now and go and get it."*

	So, I'd scramble my way up onto the main roof, get the ball, kick it down. Then I would have to try and get back down meself. I had to hang and drop down. When you're a kid, it seemed massive. And then I'd finally get back down, and dad would say, "Go on. Off you go." And I had to go home.
Alan:	But I guess you learned your lesson and only did it once?
Arsenal:	I used to do it every single time we were losing. As soon as they got that nineteenth goal, the ball would be back on the roof. But I never lost because I never saw the winner! I was straight home.

On another time I was in goal and we were getting stuffed. We must have been losing 18-6. This lad called Pip, he was running towards our goal and in me head, all I'd seen, was the ball. And I have to get that ball. I must have been about fifteen/sixteen, virtually an adult. And Pip, God bless him, he was about nine and he was running towards me.

Now in me head I saw him as the opposition. I had to get the ball, he was coming towards the goal, and I'm a hundred per cent whatever I do and me mum says that in the report. I went out and I hit him so hard I broke his leg in two places and I remember me dad giving me a bit of a hiding on the pitch.

And then, do you remember Benny Hill? That's what it was like with everyone running after me. I could hear the music in me head as everyone chased me. At the time I was arguing me case on the pitch, claiming, "I got the ball." Because I did get the ball. But Pip's lying on the

> floor screaming with his leg broken in two places
> and all I can say is, "I got the ball." And then me
> dad belted me again around the head and said,
> "You'd better get home."

Alan: *Is that a symptom of autism? The fact that you
had got the ball, therefore to you it didn't matter
that you had broken Pip's leg?*

Arsenal: *I got the ball. His leg didn't matter. It's called
'theory of mind'.*

These are almost all the stories and tales that Arsenal Whittick
has to tell from the first sixteen years of his life. Not many
memories at all. During this time, he was becoming the person
he wanted to be, Arsenal Whittick, and erasing the persona that
was young Master Flynn totally from his mind.

The stories he tells reinforce who he wants to be and not
who he was when he was born. His mind is blocking out the
majority of his early childhood, plus all the years when he was
non-verbal, caused by both his stammer and his undiagnosed
autism. His better memories, admittedly as he was an older
child, are from his footballing days and times with his family.

His father, in a recent email I've read, suggested that Arsenal
was a very poor loser, but Arsenal talks about the anger and total
disregard for either his own safety or that of others around him
that made his autism a danger.

The next chapter of Arsenal's life was just around the corner.
He would leave home, get a flat and hold down his first full-time
job upon leaving school. But before then we are going to move
forward in time to 2011. Arsenal was forty-nine and another
life-changing event was about to happen. Someone was about to
recognise that he may be on the spectrum.

And what of Pip? There is an epilogue to that story.

Arsenal: *Pip has a permanent limp, even to this day. It must have been ten/fifteen years ago, and me mum and dad were on holiday in Spain, lying by the pool. Next minute, there's a lad wandering over to 'em and he's carrying one of his legs funny like. Dragging it slightly.*

    "Hello, Mr and Mrs Whittick."

    "Hello, Pip. How are you?"

    "All right." And then a look of fear and puzzlement came on his face. And he asked, "You're not with Arsenal, are you?"

    "No, no. He's not with us."

    "Thank fuck for that!"

And Pip turned around and limped away.

Chapter Four

Diagnosis

2011

For sportsmen or women who want to be champions, the mind can be as important, if not more important than any other part of the body.

Gary Neville

By the magic of writing we are now going to fast-forward thirty-three years and so much has happened in the intervening time. By knowing the extent of Arsenal's problems, caused by being on the spectrum and being unable to express himself succinctly due to his stammer, this will better inform the events that happened between the years of sixteen and forty-nine. Plus if this were a novel and not one man's true account of his life, you simply would accuse the author of being a little fantastical. Too far-fetched. An English fable or a folk story.

Except it's not a 'story'; it's not a work of fiction or a 'tale of the unexpected'. What we read are the memories of Arsenal Whittick and his immediate family.

Alan: *So how did you finally get diagnosed? I know it was through Samantha, your eldest daughter.*

Arsenal: *She was about fourteen and I thought this was how people lived their lives. Every time she came home from school, I would just pick up on stuff she hadn't done, all the time, every day. It was just getting too much for her and she started to cut herself all the time. So, she went to CAMHS [Child and Adolescent Mental Health Services] in 2009 for having suicidal thoughts and self-harming.*

           And then in 2010, when she was fifteen, it was just getting worse for her. I was just always seeming to have a go at her. It was just getting too much for her. And then in 2010, November, she tried to take her life. Because after cutting herself for over a year and harming herself for over a year and having suicidal thoughts...

At this point Arsenal is not looking anywhere near me but over the other side of his living room. The pauses between words are getting longer and he's having difficulty getting them out and when he is, he's repeating himself. I don't think he accepts or understands his emotions, but his eyes are filling with tears. At some point in the future we will discuss his ability to show either empathy or sympathy, but he is undoubtedly getting emotional talking about Samantha's lowest point.

Alan: *Did you know she was cutting and harming herself?*

Arsenal: *Yeah, but I never knew it was wrong, did I, because I was hitting myself every day. I just thought it was normal. I thought that was how people led their lives. And then after a year of cutting and feeling suicidal, she just thought that was the next step. And so, November 2010, she tried to take her own life.*

And then she was in hospital and then the next day, I'd stayed overnight. So, the next day because of her age they interviewed her [I would like to think that after a suicide attempt that age wouldn't come into it and anyone would have been interviewed] and because of her age I was allowed in the room. I was just sitting there and they asked Sam why she'd tried to take her life.

She just pointed straight at me and said, "Because of him." And everyone looked at me for some reason? So they asked her why and she reeled off all these things about what she'd been feeling. Unloved. Everything she was doing she thought she was doing it wrong because I had such high expectations and I thought everyone should do it like me. The things she would do different to me I would say to her, "You don't do it like that, you do it like this." And she would say, "No, you do it like this, Dad." It was just arguments every day about everything.

And then the hospital asked me, "Mr Whittick, in your opinion how much of what Sam has said is true?"

And I said, "All of it!"

"Really?"

"Yeah."

"So, you self-harm as well?"

"No, I don't self-harm."

The doctor then asked, "So, what are all those bruises up there on your head, Arsenal?"

I said, "Oh, that's where I punch meself and knock meself out."

"And why are all your veins on your cheeks prominent and fiery red?"

"Well, that's where I punch meself as well."

"Mr Whittick, do you not realise that is self-harming?"

And I replied, "Is it? I thought self-harming was cutting yourself." And then they explained self-harming to me, and I never knew I was self-harming. I was just hitting meself. Virtually there and then they said they wanted to have a meeting with me. And that's when I started under Kings Park Community Hospital. [Kings Park is a small community hospital based in Boscombe, near Bournemouth, that houses an outpatient's department and multiple community teams. These teams include Community Mental Health Teams (CMHTs) and CMHT social workers, Community Neurology Services, Bournemouth Intermediate Care Team and Bournemouth Central South District Nurse Team.]

Arsenal: I was there for a bit, but they wanted to put me on medication. They wanted to control me because my outbursts... they were just horrendous. Samantha said that my reactions to stuff was like if she'd burnt the house down. And that's how violent I would get to meself and the wall or just whatever was nearest. But for Samantha it was just that dread of every day coming home.

And she'll tell you, she was walking home from school and all her mates would be saying bye bye and have a good evening and Sam would say,

> *"I have to go and see me dad. I hope he's not in. I*
> *hope he's dead!"*
>> *And her friends would say, "Don't be like that."*
>> *"But you don't know him." She dreaded every*
>> *day coming home. In the morning time she would*
>> *be dreading that she had to get up as I'd be on her*
>> *for everything. Lateness, tidiness, everything.*

Alan: *Do you understand now why she felt that way?*

Arsenal: *I'm getting there. It just takes time. When I say*
          I'm getting there, I suppose I do, but, it'll be later
          on in the day I'll think about things and then I do
          get it. But, sometimes right on the spot it doesn't
          register and so it's later on when I do my negatives
          and positives from the day—

Alan: *Is that you processing?*

Arsenal: *Yeah, yeah. If I don't understand anything tonight,*
          I've got my dictionary down there and I'll think,
          oh, that's what that means or that's what she
          meant. Or I'll get the laptop out and after a while
          I'll realise and get it.

Arsenal never really answers the question here. He answers a different one, one which is easier for him to process. Instead of answering if he now understands how Sam felt or feels, he answers how he deals with understanding words or phrases that he hears during the day. One of his many coping mechanisms that he uses to get through every day. We will hear much more of these later.

I wonder if he still can't empathise with Samantha's feelings and instead of saying so, answers a question that I haven't asked him?

From this initial diagnosis, both Samantha and Arsenal were referred for further tests, assessments and treatment.

Sam's diagnosis from the Shelley Clinic in Boscombe is obviously vital to Arsenal's story, but not at this point. The most important fact to be taken from Sam's attempted suicide was that she sought help and at this point of her life, managed to get it. A secondary consideration, certainly at the time, was Arsenal's behaviour.

The doctors who were treating Sam saw something in Arsenal that they believed needed further investigation, especially as Sam's self-harm had been triggered by how she felt about her dad. Sam tried to take her own life in November 2010 and the first report Arsenal has in reference to these incidents are dated 23rd November 2010, not that long after the event and quite right too. For himself, the first clinical psychology report he has is dated 26th May 2011.

The first doctor that Arsenal saw at Kings Park is someone he doesn't have fond memories of. Apparently, she never lifted her head once to speak to Arsenal and he felt treated badly, with little or no respect. She just 'kept her head down and tapped at her computer'.

He was subsequently referred to the Shelley Clinic under the same doctor, Dr A, before transferring to the Community Adult Asperger's Service, part of the Dorset Healthcare NHS Trust in Westbourne. He was seen for an initial diagnostic assessment for autism spectrum disorder on the 13th and 20th April 2011 by Dr W. He was also referred to Alderney Hospital as an outpatient on the 19th May and saw a consultant clinical psychologist, Dr S, for further opinion.

During this time period, Dr W, who provided the original assessment, also spoke with Arsenal's mother, Pat Whittick, on the phone (as she still lived in Liverpool), to obtain developmental information. Arsenal's first report ever received on what until then was his perceived condition, was written on the 26th May 2011 by Dr W of the Westbourne Centre.

In order to diagnose someone with autism spectrum disorder, there must be recognised significant difficulties across several areas, including:

- Social interaction,
- Social communication,
- Restricted patterns of behaviour or interests,
- Repetitive patterns of behaviour or interests,
- Stereotyped patterns of behaviour or interests.

These problems should be life-long and not attributable to any other cause. In order to assess these traits, Arsenal took part in interviews, phone calls were made to relatives, he took specific autism recognition questionnaires, an informal assessment was made of his emotional literacy, as well as self-completed autism and empathy reports prior to his first appointment.

The analysis from the various tests, including specific examples of Arsenal's reaction to certain situations, occur later in his story and mostly in the intervening years from the age of sixteen to when this diagnosis was made so will not be included here. Nevertheless, the summary was as follows:

- Arsenal's developmental history, together with both past and current presentation, indicated that he was absolutely on the autism spectrum;
- Given the late development of language, he met criteria for a diagnosis of high-functioning autism rather than Asperger's syndrome;
- There are a number of factors associated with Autistic Spectrum Disorder (ASD) which predisposed Arsenal to his depression and distress of the time. Rigid, black-and-white thinking with no compromise, the need for routine and structure, being a perfectionist with

high expectations, and Arsenal's theory of mind skills meaning he couldn't take on alternative viewpoints and be confused by others' motivations and feelings.

The report finishes with several recommendations to a way forward that cover very important topics as follows:

- Identifying triggers to self-harm, from which strategies to cope can be developed;
- Different accommodation;
- An assessment on cognitive functioning;
- Employment;
- Local support organisations such as the Wessex Autistic Society, now known as Autism Wessex, and finally;
- A four-week programme offered to newly diagnosed adults to provide valuable education about the disorder and what services are provided locally.

I think the most important point here is that Arsenal now had a name, a handle, a condition for the way he had been behaving the whole of his life. He also had a goal. He had two daughters who had never believed they had a dad who loved or cared for them, one more so than the other due to the difference in age. He was going to do something about this. He could find solutions and mend his relationship with Sam while ensuring his relationship with Danielle never became as fractured.

What of his wife of twenty years? How would this news impact their relationship? As it turned out, that would be a very different story!

The second report from Dr W is written six months later on the 5th December 2011, from which we get an insight into how Arsenal is coping with his diagnosis. Arsenal had met the doctor at three separate outpatient clinics at Alderney Hospital to make a cognitive assessment. The tests included two psychological tests.

For the record, these were the Wechsler Adult Intelligent Scale (WAIS) and the Adaptive Behaviour Assessment System (ABAS). The WAIS is a psychometric IQ test. This test showed Arsenal to be 'below average range' based on the average for the general population of a hundred. These tests cover verbal comprehension, perceptual reasoning, working memory and processing speed.

The ABAS makes a complete assessment of the daily functional skills of an individual. His scores supported what Arsenal had been experiencing all of his life.

1. His ability to communicate with others was generally quite poor.
2. He lacked verbal expression, appropriate eye contact and didn't follow implicit rules of social communication such as pauses, smiles and nods.
3. Writing basic information was fine, but Arsenal never searched for information, not even reading advertisements when looking for a service.
4. Arsenal had few leisure activities and didn't take part in group activities.
5. He had no friends and poor relationships with family members.
6. He embarrassed or hurt people by not refraining and couldn't respond sympathetically by listening, sharing possessions and giving complements.

BUT NOW HE KNEW AND HAD A NAME FOR IT!

Alan: *You seem a very passive person and yet you tell me you were always angry?*

> Arsenal: *I am a very passive person now but didn't use*
> *to be. In 2011 I went to Kings Park Community*
> *Hospital and they wanted to put me on medication*
> *to control me because... wow, I was so angry. I*
> *used to harm every day and...*

Arsenal stops talking at this point and I offer to talk about his self-harming on another day. He is extremely open with me but still there are triggers that he is dealing with that makes him angry and he commences to put slides in his imaginary slide projector.

At the time, the family are also trying to come to terms with Arsenal's autism diagnosis and in one of her classes that she is taking at college, Samantha learns about a 'Sally-Anne' test. This was something I had never heard of and needed to educate myself.

The Sally-Anne test is a psychological test used in developmental psychology to measure a person's social cognitive ability to attribute false beliefs to others. The flagship implementation of the Sally-Anne test was by Simon Baron-Cohen, Alan M Leslie and Uta Frith in 1985; in 1988, Leslie and Frith repeated the experiment with human actors (rather than dolls) and found similar results.

After learning about the test at college and trying to understand her dad's recent diagnosis, Sam came home to see if she could apply the test to her home surroundings but with her dad rather than actors or dolls (the dolls were named Sally and Anne, hence the test name).

> Alan: *Because you got the ball, it didn't matter about*
> *Pip's leg? Is that a symptom of autism?*
> Arsenal: *Yeah, yeah. I think some of my reactions are called*
> *'theory of mind'. They did a test on me – and it's*

so simple. My daughter did the test, actually, and I told Alderney and that's your theory of mind skills. They told me, your theory of mind skills are really poor.

And what the test was. My daughter was in college doing psychology and they did a little bit on autism and she told the teacher about me and the teacher said, "When you go home tonight just try this test on your dad and if he's got autism this is the answer he'll give you." And she tried it and what it was, there was Samantha, me and Nicola, me wife at the time. We were stood in the kitchen and Samantha said to her mum, "I'm going to try something now, Mum." And what the test actually was, is that Nicola put her mobile in this drawer here [Arsenal opens a drawer in the kitchen to his right] and then she went out the room. Samantha got the phone out the drawer and put it in this one [Arsenal indicates a cupboard on the other side of the room]. Sam then said to me, "When Mum comes in, where is she going to go to, to get her mobile?"

And I went, "In this cupboard." [Arsenal indicates the second location the phone was moved to, the cupboard.]

And then Sam burst out laughing and said, "That's just what the teacher said you'll say."

And I go, "Yeah because it's in there. That's where it is."

"But Mum's been out the room, so she still thinks her phone is in the drawer."

And we nearly had an argument about it because I was shouting, "No, it's in here, in the cupboard not the drawer." See, I couldn't see that Nicola didn't know the phone had been moved. I knew where it was, so therefore she knew where it was. Because I had seen it moved from drawer to cupboard, I thought EVERYONE knew it was in here.

I think it's called the 'Sally-Anne' test.

So effectively, whatever is in Arsenal's mind, whatever he thinks, he believes everyone else, in the entire world, has exactly the same information. So, if he has decided that he is going to self-harm, for whatever reason, he can't understand why others don't do the same.

Alan: *Now you know this test, and have explained the results to me, does that help you put things into perspective?*

Arsenal: *I'm learning now that not everyone thinks like me because when I used to harm, a lot of it was because someone had done something different to me. And I couldn't work out why they hadn't done it the same as me. Then I would have the argument in my head and that would lead to self-harm. But yeah, so most of it is about when someone does something different. And I don't get it, do I?*

"Why the fuck did they do that?"

The clinical description of Arsenal's 'Why the fuck' is as follows. In order to 'pass' the test (indicating no autism), Arsenal must have answered the belief question by indicating that Nicola should have believed that the phone was still in the drawer and not the cupboard. This answer was continuous with Nicola's perspective but not with Arsenal's own. If Arsenal could not take an alternative perspective, he would have indicated that Nicola had cause to believe, as Arsenal did, that the phone had moved. Passing the test was thus seen as the manifestation of Arsenal understanding that Nicola had her own beliefs that may not have correlated with reality; this is the core requirement of theory of mind.

As we know from his diagnosis, Arsenal failed miserably. While this test is by no means fully conclusive, it is used in telling about social development trends in autism. But far more importantly to Arsenal, Nicola and Samantha, they had completed their own test or investigation and were starting to realise some of the issues that Arsenal had been enduring for the past fifty years. His perception of reality was black and white, and not only black and white but his sole source of reality. This was the whole family's 'What the fuck' moment. Not only was Arsenal starting to understand his 'condition', but so were his family, the people who had suffered the most through Arsenal's difficult years.

Now we can examine those difficult years from sixteen onwards with a greater perspective and some sympathy. Some of what is to come would simply be too unbelievable and while it's still difficult to have any empathy, understanding and sympathy should be at the forefront of our thoughts. As they started to move into the thoughts of Nicola, Samantha and Danielle. If only at the age of sixteen, Arsenal's family and friends could have had the same understanding!

Alan: *Was Samantha's suicide attempt the trigger for you to get your diagnosis?*

Arsenal: *It wasn't a trigger for me. It was a trigger for the hospital after hearing Samantha tell them why she tried to take her life – because of me.*

> *And right away, they say in my report, that they knew straightaway, I wasn't right. And then, I got interviewed and it just snowballed. I got diagnosed within six months.*

Alan: *But you agreed to have some tests done, so did you get to the point when you thought you were driving your daughter to suicide, and you needed to do something?*

Arsenal: *No. Somebody else made that decision for me. No, it never registered at all. It never twigged with me at all. It was all down to them saying this is what you got to do. I got signed off one hospital and went to Alderney Hospital and it was there that they told me if you keep on doing this you are going to hurt yourself and that could lead to death.*

> *Then they said, you're hurting your girls and you're hurting your wife. It was the hospital that had to tell me because I got nothing of that message coming down to say I've got to stop this. [Arsenal points to his head.] That's it, you see; people have to tell me stuff.*

It's one thing to be told 'stuff', but to be told everything that Arsenal was hearing at forty-nine would have been too much for most people. Not Arsenal. He talks about triggers all the time; well, this was the trigger to turn his life around.

Chapter Five

Liverpool Family

1976 Plus

You always go back to where you belong.

Thierry Henry

ARSENAL, BY HIS OWN VOLITION, BUT ALSO BY THAT OF HIS siblings and parents, was not an easy child or young adult to rub along with. It was difficult to have a conversation with him because of his crippling stammer, he seemed slower to learn than other people his age and his range of interests was limited, by any sixteen-year old's standards. He could talk about football all day, but he supported Arsenal in a football-mad city that predominately followed Liverpool and Everton and always did. He rubbed people up the wrong way, but as we find out thirty-three years later, he had no filter.

Along with having no filter, he had no sense of fear. So, when faced with a gang of angry Liverpool fans after Arsenal Football Club (AFC) had beaten them, he had no problem in telling them that 'Liverpool are shit!'

Nor having the correct levels of adrenalin produced by fear to generate 'flight' or also to generate 'fight'. So, he would make his decree on the quality of Liverpool's football excellence to an angry mob and then just stand there and wait to see what happened. He says he has only ever been in one fight in his entire life, and that was when still at school, but openly admits to taking some terrible beatings from opposition fans.

His love of AFC didn't sit that well with his own brothers either. His older brother Eddie, born 30th March 1961, was a Liverpool fan and Mark, born after Arsenal on the 25th November 1965, was also a Liverpool fan. Pat Flynn had three lads under the age of five. Jackie, his eldest sister, came along on the 12th February 1968, Anthony (known as Simmo) on the 28th November 1973 and finally Jeni was born nine years later on the 15th June 1982. Arsenal today doesn't have a relationship with Jeni and she herself said that Arsenal doesn't feel like a brother to her as they never even slept in the same house. I guess twenty-one years is something of an age gap between brother and sister.

More on the siblings later, but what kind of a relationship did Arsenal have with his parents? Arsenal's dad and his brothers particularly say that Arsenal was always Pat/Mum's favourite, a fact that Arsenal doesn't dispute but doesn't recall. Looking back, Arsenal being the favourite makes sense.

Who was always in trouble; who always needed extra help with school work; who found it difficult to make friends and never really had a best friend and who took until the age of six (Pat in the diagnosis report says this was four) to express themselves verbally and then through a frustrating spluttering of words? Any mother, while loving her children equally, would seem to spend more time on the neediest.

As in most working-class households of the 1970s, the father was the disciplinarian and that was the role worn by Tony Whittick in his home. He would be the one to give Arsenal a crack around the head if he wasn't behaving or 'being a sore loser'. We also now know that when Arsenal made that 'triple-X' tackle on poor Pip, he wasn't trying to hurt Pip but just take the ball. Although Arsenal's dad has a slightly different recollection to Arsenal, suggesting that his son ran half the length of the pitch to win the ball back, taking Pip with it. It was always his dad who had to deal with discipline after an event and with no autism diagnosis to explain why Arsenal did what he did, most disciplines involved a 'smack' or 'crack' of some form.

Arsenal's relationship with his dad was impacted by two major events that occurred within a week or two of each other. Arsenal believes they didn't impact him overly, but they could not have been easy for a young man struggling with his own identity to deal with. Or to use Arsenal's words, 'process'. He was only taught to process after his forty-ninth birthday!

Alan:	*So what about your parents? How was your relationship with your dad?*
Arsenal:	*Me real dad is still out there. I went to me cousins. He was called Popeye because when he went to sleep at a sleepover, he kept his eyes open. I must have been about fifteen, I think. I think so. So, we went to me cousins. There was a guy in the kitchen in the corner. Just sitting there. He never spoke to me or nothing. And when we come out, me cousin went to me, "You know who that is, don't you?"*
	And I went, "No."
	And he said, "That's your dad."
Alan:	*Good lord, what a way to find out who your real dad was!*
Arsenal:	*I know, and I went, "What? You're joking." And that's how I found out. This must have been, must have been… 1976. It was around that time. I*

must have been fourteen not fifteen because it was probably in the same week because me mum and dad got married on the 6th April 1976. And so, I was about fourteen and it was on a Saturday [the wedding] and I remember because I was getting ready for Match of the Day.

Subconsciously or otherwise, Arsenal brushed over his thoughts and feelings about finding out that Tony Whittick was not his real father as a throwaway line at a party. He tells me that even today no one in the family ever mentions this fact. It is a family 'secret' that isn't spoken about by anybody. Arsenal just moves on to a story linked to his understanding of who he is by talking about his parents' wedding.

Arsenal: *Me mum and dad come in with a group of people. There were loads of people, that's what I remember. And they come in and said, "Arsenal, you've got to go to bed now."*

And I said, "But Match of the Day is coming on."

"Sorry, but you have to go to bed." There were a few words. There wasn't an argument, but I needed people to explain it to me, not just say I had to go to bed when Match of the Day was starting. So anyway, I went upstairs into me room and I left me door open, it was a concertina door. And I had that open.

I was in me room lying there and a woman, me mum's mate called Pam Porter, she come upstairs to use the toilet. She come out the toilet and was at the top of the stairs, she went to wash her hands and then she come into the room. And she went, "Arsenal, what you doin' up here? Why don't you come down?"

I went, "No, no, I've got to stay up here."

And she said, "Come on down and have a dance at your mum and dad's wedding!"

"WHAT?!"

And that's how I found out. That they'd just been married. I was told absolutely nothing at all. Nothing at all.

Alan: When you have spoken to your parents since and you say what you've just told me, have they ever explained that, and why they didn't tell you what was going on?

Arsenal: No, no. You know what, to be honest, though, I think I've had one brief conversation and it turned into a bit of an argument and it ends then, doesn't it? Once you start arguing.

So, I wasn't told he wasn't me dad and I wasn't told about the wedding.

These are difficult recollections for Arsenal to make. His stammer gets worse and he has to pause on a couple of occasions to take a breath, but by the end of his story of the wedding he's angry again and almost spits his last sentence out. There, have that!

We all – well, most of us – love our parents very much. Unconditional love. Something in the DNA. We sometimes may not like them, but we always love them. Imagine being at a party at the age of fourteen and someone pointing out your real father to you across the room. Now that does take some processing, but for someone with autism, the processing can take years. Having spoken to Arsenal at length about this evening, even after being told by Popeye that, 'that bloke over there is your real dad', I'm not completely sure that Arsenal understood.

How would any fourteen-year-old understand? When Arsenal tried to discuss this 'new father' at home, it was a taboo subject, one that remains taboo right to this day. From Pat and Tony's perspective, this is also understandable. They were trying to pull together two different strands, DNA strands, into one family. They believed the easiest way to do this was to make three boys born of Mr Flynn to be boys born of Mr Whittick. They were all simply too young to comprehend it, especially Arsenal, who didn't take new information in very well.

Arsenal couples the two stories together, merging them into one. He describes them happening in the same week, which may well be the case, but to him they are one and the same story. He couldn't understand why he wasn't told about his mum and dad getting married. At fourteen he had been Arsenal for five years and Arsenal Whittick for three years. Tony Whittick was his dad and to Arsenal always will be, but Tony Whittick had a different surname because his mum and dad were not married.

So, within a week, his parenthood was doubted and then his parents got married. It may have taken Arsenal a while to process it, but he was starting to put two and two together. The final piece of this personality jigsaw was only fitted in several years later when Arsenal was twenty-three and had a bad accident at work.

As Arsenal is telling me the story of the wedding, he again, without prompting, runs into the third segment of this tale, which I'm starting to understand was his total path to becoming the person he always wanted to be. Remember his plea: "All I ever wanted to be was Arsenal Whittick."

Arsenal: *I had a bad accident in work when I just turned eighteen, I was. [Arsenal has it in his head that this accident happened when he was eighteen but as stated above, he in fact was twenty-three years* old, 1985]. I was in hospital but anyway, we went to hospital, me boss he took me. They asked me, me name and I went, "Arsenal Whittick."

And they said, "We have no record of you."

So, they then said to me boss, "Do you have his details?"

And he said, "Yeah. His name's Arsenal Whittick, he's worked for me since he left school." Or something like that. So anyway, when me mum and dad come in, next day, or the evening time, it was.

The nurse asked them for me name and they said, "Arsenal Whittick."

So, the nurse said, "We've got no records for him."

So, mum and dad went for a cup of tea and me dad said to me mum, "You know why there's no records? It's not his real name."

And that's when officially I found out I wasn't even Whittick. Me mum and dad had said when we were going to senior school,

"Right, all of them are Whitticks now." When I was coming out of hospital… [At this point Arsenal just stops talking.]

Alan:	So your mum had never officially, through the courts, changed your name. So, you were still Flynn?
Arsenal:	Yeah, I was still Flynn.
Alan:	So are you Catholic? Were you christened Flynn?
Arsenal:	Yeah, yeah.
Alan:	So what was your first name?
Arsenal:	Arsenal. That is my real name now.
Alan:	I understand that, but what was your first christened name?

Arsenal:	*I haven't told no one ever.*
Alan:	*Do you want it recorded in the book?*
Arsenal:	*Can I think about that one?*
Alan:	*That's fine. It's your book and you include whatever you want or don't want, but why would you not want it included?*
Arsenal:	*I've been Arsenal since I were nine. 1971.*
Alan:	*And have you now legally changed your name?*
Arsenal:	*Yeah, yeah. When I come out of hospital and they had no actual records of me name, I went to change it then to Arsenal, officially. So then, I went to a solicitor and I said, "I want to change me name. Is that OK?" and he said, "I need your birth certificate and I need that, and I need this." So, I thought OK and went to me parents and I said, "You know I've been called Arsenal since I were nine?*
	And they said, "Yeah."
	"You know at the hospital and no one knew me name?"
	And they said, "Yeah."
	"Well, I'm changing it, legally." Then, like, there was an argument again. And I said, "I don't see the problem."
	And they said, "No. You can't do it."
	"I'm doing it." The solicitor had given me a list of what I needed, and I showed me mum. "I need me birth certificate."
	"I don't know where it is. I can't find it." So, I went back to the solicitor and he said, "Tell your mum this is how you get copies of birth certificates if you've lost them." So, I went back again and told her. She was really against it. Really really against me getting this birth certificate. So eventually I got

it and on it was Flynn. That's when the penny sort of really dropped. And I thought, What Flynn, I thought I was Whittick? So that's why she didn't want me to see me birth certificate.

I was Whittick from senior school but not legally.

Alan: So when you saw the birth certificate and it said Flynn, what did that tell you? Did you already know the guy you'd seen at the party was your 'real' father?

Arsenal: I wasn't a hundred per cent sure of anything. I knew me cousin on the week of the wedding had said to me, "That's your dad," but it never registered.

Alan: Did you speak to him?

Arsenal: No, no. There was no conversation. And his name was Edward Flynn. That's all I remember. I never knew him, I never got introduced. But everyone in the room knew who he was apart from me. But you know…

Alan: Have you spoke to him since?

Arsenal: No. I've never seen him or anything. I've had no contact. Me mum has never explained it. Me dad hasn't. No one explained anything to me, so I've always been kept out, really. Of everything.

Alan: Do your brothers know the story?

Arsenal: I think me oldest brother does [Eddie]. And then me mum and dad had another two sisters and a brother. So, when I was eighteen and I went to change it to Arsenal and the solicitor said, "Your name's not even Whittick."

And I said, "What?"

"On your birth certificate it says Flynn."

> *And I'm going, "Me mum and dad changed it."*
> *"No, they didn't."*
> *So, I then went back to me mum and dad and said, "What's me name?"*
> *And again, they said, "Whittick."*
> *"But the solicitor said—"*
> *"Oh yeah, we never changed it at the solicitors."*
> *So, then I at last changed it to Arsenal Whittick."*

Alan: *The problems of identity you've described would be incredibly impactful on a young adult of any family, but then add to that the fact you have your autism to deal with. Do you think that impacted you or upset you more because of the autism?*

Arsenal: *I just wanted to be Arsenal Whittick, to be honest with you.*

So even after the traumatic events at the age of fourteen of meeting his birth father at a party and then being totally left out of his mum and dad's wedding – something that angers Arsenal to this day – it took another nine years and an accident at work to provide Arsenal with the required physical evidence needed by someone with autism to understand his own identity. Luckily for all concerned it was a Whittick that Arsenal wanted to be and not a Flynn.

Arsenal does not think of Tony Whittick as his stepdad; he thinks of him as his dad. He has never known anyone else and as far as Tony is concerned Arsenal is his own. He met and took responsibility for Arsenal when Arsenal was approaching two years old, and the bond has and still is a typical father/son relationship, albeit one stretched by geography and circumstance. To help us with this project, Arsenal has been talking to his dad and has received a couple of emails.

From: Anthony Whittick
Sent date: 22/11/18
To: Arsenal Whittick
Subject: About your recent letter!
               The life and upbringing of ???????? Whittick!!

My memory is not what it used to be but I have written a number of things about your growing up in the early years.

You were a staunch arsenal supporter sometimes this was annoying – you wrote your hero's players names on Electricity sub stations and in many other unusual places!

Some people objected too your love of Arsenal you wore the shirt sang their tunes you made one or two enemies along the way!

You where only young when your mum and dad wed.

You had several hero's in your life time like Gary Newman the singer – you painted his facial looks on yourself – sang his songs and then there was (blonde) your female legend even I loved her!

Your love for Arsenal got you into trouble on a number of occasions – when you didn't like getting beat on the pool table – a gang waited outside the pub me and Eddie Kane sent them packing but we were lucky they were easily put off – the manager of the pub at the time phoned us about your safety!

You were always mother's favourite child but mark was very quiet a bit too quiet – he was stubborn too!

Good luck with your book congratulations from all of us.

From me your Dad!!

These are not the full emails but extracts from them; what came across as I read them from afar – emotionally, physically and through time – was the simple, straightforward, unconditional family love that carried through in them. In the rest of the emails, Tony Whittick writes about Arsenal's brothers and what happened to them, his grandchildren, his wedding to Arsenal's mum, and how his son Anthony got the nickname Simmo which has been used all of his life.

I spoke to Arsenal about the love that bleeds in the letters for him, but he simply cannot see that himself. To Arsenal they are but words – he asked his dad a couple of questions and these are the answers. The answer it gives me is to the question that isn't asked: Arsenal was loved and raised as Tony Whittick's son just as Eddie, Mark and Anthony were, and Jackie and Jennifer were as his daughters. There was no differentiation in the Whittick household and while it was traumatic for Arsenal to find his identity, Tony and Pat Whittick simply wanted to raise their family as one and that was the Whittick family. All decisions were made for the right reason and that reason was love.

As already suggested, Pat Whittick had a favourite. Arsenal's dad says so in his email and Eddie, Arsenal's older brother, has recently corroborated this thought in communications for the book. This is something that Arsenal as a child never recognised. As Tony suggests, Arsenal was forever getting into trouble due to his love, infatuation, ADDICTION to Arsenal Football Club.

Arsenal: *Dad said I writ on the electricity substations at school – and I know I did that. You see, I put Arsenal FC on the substation about that big! [Arsenal stretches his arms – one up, one down – to suggest the writing was very large!]*

Alan: There weren't many Arsenal fans in Liverpool; everyone must have known it was you?

Arsenal: But I never knew, did I? I never twigged, did I, that there's only one person round here who's going to write that.

But when me mum was on her deathbed, she was talking about things. And I had me daughter there, me two daughters, and she told a story in front of everyone. And she told me daughters about me painting Arsenal FC on the substation and the school called her in. And I didn't know this until she was on her deathbed. Me mum actually went into the school for the whole of the week... and scrubbed it off.

Alan: Did she?

Arsenal: Yeah, and I never ever knew. WOW. I wonder why the school never asked me to do it [scrub it off], as I was the one who did it? And me dad told me – I used to write Arsenal on all the pillarboxes. And he said same as our Simmo [Anthony – Arsenal's younger brother] really – that I was a bit of a nightmare. I just used to put myself in dangerous situations.

How much was Arsenal loved as a child? It sounds as though he daubed paint over half of Liverpool, but when he did it at his own school, rather than humiliate him by getting him to scrub the walls, Pat Whittick did it herself. Then, so Arsenal didn't feel bad about it, she didn't even tell him. I think this says two things: one – her love for Arsenal was a very special love indeed and two – Pat knew that something wasn't quite right about the way Arsenal behaved; she didn't have the word autism in her vocabulary, but she knew he had some condition. Why else cut him the slack she did? She thought that Arsenal couldn't help himself. Sadly, Pat isn't here now to answer my questions, but she was when Arsenal was first diagnosed, and her input is in that report.

Mrs Whittick felt that she had to devote more time to Arsenal than her other children. He was very interested in writing and drawing and would practise his letters with her. However, if his writing was not perfect, he would rip it up.

Arsenal's eye contact is now good, but his mother discussed how this has not always been the case, and that when he was younger, he would not meet people's gaze and looked away when talking. She reported that his facial expression is generally blank and impassive and that only when experiencing extremes of emotion is Arsenal's mood apparent. She described how when he was a child he would often react inappropriately – such as smiling when something bad happened – which at the time, she construed as him being naughty. She also reported that he has never 'got too involved' with others and that he can be socially withdrawn.

With regard to peer relationships, Mrs Whittick reported that Arsenal did not really mix with other children – preferring to stay with his mother rather than going out.

As a young boy Arsenal did seek to share his achievements with his mother. For example, Mrs Whittick discussed how Arsenal made a wooden bird for her which used to hang on the wall. Even now [2011] when he goes home, he asks about the bird and Mrs Whittick believes that Arsenal still wants to know that she's still proud of it.

There was a difference in the reports of Arsenal and his mother in terms of how tactile Arsenal was. He reported that he was never hugged as a child and would not seek comfort from his mother if he was in distress. However, Mrs Whittick felt that he was a cuddly child who had to tell his mother if he was upset.

Pat Whittick supported most of what we have heard so far in terms of Arsenal's behavioural traits. When reading the above I think it's obvious that she knew that Arsenal was different but, like we all do in similar situations, girded her loins, got out her stiff British upper lip and got on with life. She had plenty to think of with at least four or five other mouths to feed as time went on.

Another point to note is the one about hugs and contact. I don't think anyone is deliberately misremembering here, but who as a mother will say that their child wasn't hugged enough? Plus, we know that Arsenal's memory is impacted by his autism and what his subconscious wants him to remember. My thought is that the truth lies somewhere in the middle.

Arsenal has mixed relationships with his siblings. The strongest connections are with Eddie, the eldest, and Simmo (Anthony) the youngest son of Tony and Pat. Arsenal hasn't spoken to his other brother Mark since 1989. He is on speaking terms with both sisters but has a stronger relationship with the elder, Jackie, born six years after Arsenal rather than the younger Jeni, born – according to Tony, Arsenal's dad – in 1982. In the diagnosis report, Pat Whittick is identified as saying, "Arsenal was much put out by the birth of his sister when he was nine years old and although they are good friends now, it took him quite a long time to reconcile him to her arrival."

Many of the dates of birth I've been given don't seem to match up. Pat says Arsenal was nine when a sister was born, but I have Jackie born in 1968 and Jeni born in 1982? Neither match up and Tony now openly admits that his memory 'is not what it used to be', so I'm not sure who can put this straight for me. Tony can't find his wedding certificate but believes he was married in either 1976 or 1977. Tony suggests Mark was born in 1965, but Arsenal thinks it's a year earlier in 1964. We will work with what we have and try and draw up the correct timelines.

Arsenal has strong memories with his varying family members and it's plain that Arsenal holds these memories very dear and family is very important to him. Nevertheless, he doesn't dwell on things and if someone says I don't want to see you or speak to you again, his autism allows him to accept these terms without much resistance. He easily accepts the fact that he and Mark have not spoken since 1989 and would not even put his arm around Arsenal to allow them to carry their mother's coffin together.

Is Arsenal much more affected than he shows? I know he doesn't believe so and shrugs his shoulders, saying, "That's life, isn't it."

Pat Whittick's funeral was a tough day for all the siblings, but Arsenal's autism stops him showing empathy or sympathy, and as Pat herself said, "Arsenal can sometimes act inappropriately at social gatherings." Her funeral was no exception.

Alan:	*So you had two brothers that lived with you, but you've spoken about sisters as well.*
Arsenal:	*Yeah, they all lived with us. There was me, our Eddie, there was our Mark. So, there was three by Flynn. And our Jackie, Simmo and Jeni are by Whittick.*
Alan:	*Oh, I see. So at some point there were six kids kicking around the house.*
Arsenal:	*Yeah. Now I, because I left home really early that I never grew up with my sister. She's only in her*

thirties. So, when she got married, she said to my wife [Nicola], "I don't think I really know Arsenal because when I was born, he'd already left home." But we never had that relationship.

Alan: Are you in touch with them all?

Arsenal: No. I'm in touch with our Eddie, he's a year older than me. But I lost… well, when me mum died, 2013, when she was buried, AFC had a big match that day, you know, and when AFC scored, I ran into the wake, didn't I, shouting, "Fuckin' hell, yeah, we've scored!"

So, since then I've not spoke to them, really. But since I done the hug video one of me brothers has been in touch. So…

Alan: So when you ran into the wake, had you been diagnosed at that point?

Arsenal: Yeah, it was two years later.

Alan: So all your family knew that you'd been diagnosed as autistic?

Arsenal: I think they knew, but I was just hypo that day because of the football.

So, relationships got frayed on this sad day as Arsenal couldn't link the events of his mother being buried, his family's reaction to the funeral and the fact that his beloved AFC were playing a big game at the same time as the wake. To him they were totally separate.

Mum has died, been buried, we are all sad – done.

AFC are playing a big game, score, Arsenal is elated – done.

These events happening on the same day, perhaps within the same hour, didn't matter to Arsenal. He didn't mean any disrespect; he loved his mum as much as any of his siblings, but that shouldn't be a barrier to him being delighted that AFC have scored. Not only that, but him being sad for his mum wouldn't stop him expressing his delight at the goal being scored. Or using profanity to express that delight. He simply has no empathy.

To his brothers and sisters, this was an act that was beyond what he'd done before, and bridges are still being mended. The search for information to get this project into print has helped him restart dialogue with his family. I hope when they read this book it will help give them some understanding.

Eddie, as his older brother, was his protector and probably closer to Arsenal than his other brothers. Whenever any questions come up in collecting information, Arsenal says, "Our Eddie will know," or, "We'll ask our Eddie."

He crops up in many of the childhood reminiscences that Arsenal has, especially around football. Arsenal never understood why everyone knew it was him writing the AFC graffiti on all the postboxes, even though Eddie tried to explain to him several times. He would be walking down the street with Eddie with his AFC top on, and people would be turning and looking at Arsenal as if he had two heads.

"Why's everyone looking at me, Eddie?"

"Arsenal, you're the only Arsenal supporter for fifty miles. When you write AFC in two-foot letters on the postboxes, who do you think people think it is?"

"But they can't know it's me cuz I do it in the dark when no one's around."

All Eddie could say was, "Fuckin' hell."

Arsenal was also a hundred per cent influential in Eddie's choice of a career.

Arsenal: When I was eighteen, I just wanted to get away,
             so I went for an interview for the army. I took
             me brother and the two of us were in the waiting
             room and I went in.

> *And the army officer said to me, "Sorry, but*
> *you're not fit to join the army."*
> *And I went, "What?"*
> *"Because of your stammer." Because, and they*
> *gave me an instance, and the problems in Ireland*
> *were really big back then, so if you and someone*
> *else are looking after one another and you can't*
> *get your word out, it might be too late. So, they*
> *walked me out the room and they said to me*
> *brother, "Come in. Next."*
> *And he said, "No, no, I've just come for the*
> *bus ride with him."*
> *"You're here now, you may as well come in."*
> *Twenty-odd years later, he came out. Yeah,*
> *our Eddie. He's suffering now for it, like.*

So, Arsenal took Eddie along for support to his army interview and Eddie ends up in the army for twenty-plus years.

Family, births, birthdays, weddings and funerals. They seem to be the only time when families get together to celebrate their own kinship and belonging in the world. To coin a popular phrase of the moment, 'this is me', or rather, 'this is us'. Eddie got married on the 2nd December 1978; Arsenal was sixteen and had started his martyrdom to Arsenal Football Club.

Arsenal Whittick's archenemy Liverpool FC were playing at Highbury on the day that Eddie got married. At the start of December, Liverpool were top of the League, the old 1st Division, with twenty-nine points, two points clear of Everton in second place and a full nine points clear of Arsenal FC in fifth place. In 1978, it was then two points for a win, not three, so this was a substantial gap.

Every day of his life Arsenal battled with Liverpool fans: one versus many, David versus Goliath. Not only did Arsenal choose to support AFC while living in Liverpool, he did it during Liverpool's rise to their greatest ascendancy of English football. Arsenal said that every single day of his life, "I got the piss taken out of me and I just hated Liverpool."

Even people who had no interest in football would seek Arsenal out on a Monday morning as the only AFC fan north of the Watford Gap and ridicule him mercilessly if AFC had been beaten over the weekend. So, when Liverpool/AFC games came around, they were even more important than the norm. Trust me, Arsenal placed AFC results at the very top of his Maslow's hierarchy of needs, even above the basic requirements of food, water, health, warmth, sleep and safety. AFC's results were more important than anything else in his life and results against Liverpool were more important to him than all the others.

> Arsenal: *Eddie got married on Saturday 2nd December 1978 and I was sixteen and he sent me an invite. And when I got it, I went, "Who the fuck gets married on a match day?" So, he was getting married at ten, ten o'clock in the morning. I went in, but I don't know, I could feel something in me. So, I knicked out and got the 11.45 Liverpool train to London. So, I got to Highbury at ten-past three, so I missed the first ten, but Arsenal won 1-0 and it was against Liverpool.*
>
> Alan: *Liverpool again, it always seems to be Liverpool on the big days.*
>
> Arsenal: *Alan [his first name was David] Price scored. And then I got, when I got back to the reception, in the evening, I got back to Liverpool at about half nine in the evening. So, I got to the reception about ten, and by that time everyone was really pissed so no one really knew.*

> *But then about two weeks later we got the wedding photos back. And you know what mums are like. Just having a look at every single photo, and she said to me, "Arsenal, how come you're not on no photos?" And I can't lie so I had to tell her that—*

Alan: *So no one knew? Did you just sneak off?*

Arsenal: *Yeah, I just went. I never got caught out until two weeks later when me mum had a look at the photos.*

Arsenal cannot lie. He may sometimes misremember, such as David Price's first name above, but then he knows the exact date and time of the Liverpool game and even what train he caught. On researching the dates and times, invariably Arsenal is always correct when it comes to the major events of his life, which includes most football matches. If you ask Arsenal, 'Does my bum look big in this?', do not expect a politically correct answer, or even a white lie, in response. If it looks big, you are going to be told it looks big. Memory is a fickle lover, though, and ask two people who ate together what they had for dinner last night and you won't get exactly the same answer.

Now cloud that answer with thirty years of perspective and trauma, and you can rest assured those two answers will now be very different. But in all these stories there is a consistency and honesty running through them that keeps their integrity intact. I believe every word that Arsenal tells me is what Arsenal believes to be the truth. If I get an alternative view, he will 'process' the view and come back to me with what he thinks, but as he always says, "I cannot lie," and if he cannot lie it will get him into trouble.

Jeni, who is the youngest of the six brothers and sisters, never lived in the same house as Arsenal when growing up because there was such an age gap between them and so feels that her and Arsenal never had a sister/brother relationship. Arsenal does remember her being born but is unsure of the age difference between them. Tony, his dad, says Jeni was born in June 1982, which would make Arsenal twenty years old when she was born.

Arsenal: *I don't have any dealings with Jeni, I don't have any memories of her actually being around as a kid and that. But I went to me mum's one day and she had just brought home Jeni from hospital. And I, for some reason, me mum's got this in her report [Arsenal is referring to his hospital diagnosis report], I just didn't take to her. I didn't want to know her.*

I remember them coming into the living room, it sounds horrendous this I know but, and she come into the lounge. And I had this paper, the Daily Mail, and when they brought the baby into the lounge, I just did that. [Arsenal now mimics holding a newspaper up close to his face so that he couldn't see what was happening around him and he laughs nervously.]

And me mum said to me, "If you're not going to look at the baby, you can go." So, I went!

Alan: *Oh, dear.*

Arsenal: *And I think that could stem from. On our block where we lived, I remember a neighbour called Mrs Savage saying to me, "Are you pleased about your mum having a baby?" And that's how I found out. So, I think, I don't know, that might have been my way of… [Arsenal doesn't finish his sentence.]*

Alan:	Could you not tell your mum was pregnant?
Arsenal:	[Whispers with a nervous laugh] No. I never even noticed. But how early it was when Mrs Savage told me, I don't really know, see. It could have been a couple of months, couldn't it? But, Mrs Savage was the first ever one to tell me that my mum was expecting. So, I gather that might have something to do with me might not wanting to know her because no one told me. So, I thought, I don't know, I'm guessing there so I don't know.
Alan:	You don't remember particularly why you reacted the way you did?
Arsenal:	No, no. All I remember is hiding me face from the baby. And me mum said, "If you're not going to look at her, you can go." So, I got up and left and that was it.

Arsenal had strong relationships with his siblings when he was younger, and they were all living under the same roof. His current relationships are with Eddie and Simmo (Anthony), but he doesn't currently speak to Mark. That relationship went wrong in 1989 and initially started through that great sport of social importance, football! They haven't spoken since 1989 because of a disagreement over football and we will come to that later. Remember, Mark was a Liverpool fan and Arsenal – well, we all know who Arsenal follows.

At his mother's funeral, Arsenal upset all the family, but especially his sisters, and he is still trying to put that wrong right – easier with Jackie rather than Jeni, who admits she doesn't know Arsenal.

When it comes to his mum, Pat Whittick, there is the unconditional love to and from his mother. She doted on Arsenal to the extent that she would try and put his wrongs straight at the school without telling him until her deathbed. Arsenal speaks fondly of her, as much as his unsympathetic autism will let him.

Tony Whittick took on three young lads who were not his birth children and then added three more kids of his own to the clan. From everything I've heard, they were all treated exactly the same. Tony didn't treat any of his six children differently. With Arsenal that was tough. Communication problems arising from his stammer and then autism on top of that must have made him a frustrating child to raise. Then, when I read the emails from Tony to Arsenal, all I read is the love of a father for a son.

Engaging with his family has always been an issue for Arsenal, acknowledged in his diagnosis report by both the doctors and his mother, and we have other examples to bear that out later. If you have no 'condition' such as autism to explain some of Arsenal's actions, you are just going to think he is an uncaring idiot who doesn't deserve your love or support. I think his family and Arsenal himself have behaved as well as any family would in their environment.

So, at sixteen, with problems to deal with, Arsenal set off into the world of employment and self-dependency. It wasn't going to be an easy journey, but it was going to be entertaining.

Chapter Six

Working Life

1978 to 2002

*I never comment on referees and I'm not going to break
the habit of a lifetime for that prat!*

Ron Atkinson

I HAD TO ASK ARSENAL TO LIST ALL THE OCCUPATIONS AND
the years he had them for me, as it was almost impossible from
our discussions to work out the timeline and the roles. Even
with the list in front of me it's still like knitting fog!

Apart from wanting to be a professional footballer – that
Arsenal realised was beyond him if he couldn't get in the school
team – he wanted to be a jockey. He watched *World of Sport* on ITV
every Saturday with Dickie Davies, and the horses and colours of
the running silks fascinated him. He was also small for his age and
therefore decided that this could be put to his advantage for once.
If there was one prerequisite for a jockey, they had to be small and
light, and so after week upon week of watching racing on the telly,
he put together a letter himself and sent it off.

Not one to be easily deterred, Arsenal sent it to one of the best horse trainers and stables in the country, that of Henry Cecil. In 1978, Cecil had only won two classics, but by the time of his death in 2013 at the relatively young age of seventy, he had won three 2000 Guineas, six 1000 Guineas, eight Oaks, four Epsom Derbies and four St Legers. He was also champion trainer ten times. Young Arsenal could obviously spot a winner.

Amazingly, Arsenal got a letter back offering him a six-week trial at stables in Longborough (although Cecil never trained out of Longborough, his stables being in Newmarket). Unfortunately for the budding Lester Piggott, Arsenal's mum put a stop to that avenue of a career saying it was 'far too dangerous'. The closest Arsenal got were the donkeys at Southport Beach! To quote Arsenal, "I just wanted to get away."

Instead of being an international sportsman, he finished school on the Wednesday and started work on the Thursday. I asked Arsenal for a copy of his CV so I could follow his route through his career, but he doesn't have one and has never had one. Every role he's ever had has been through word of mouth and interviews. Not bad for a bloke who can't speak very well because of a terrible stammer, certainly as a younger man.

Alan: *So you left school at sixteen and you left home at sixteen as well? Is that right?*

Arsenal: *I left home in that first year after leaving school. I worked in the fruit and veg market in Edge Lane, Liverpool.*

Alan: *How did you get that job?*

Arsenal: *Me mum's brother, I think he had a fruit and veg shop for years and he used to go there [Edge Lane Fruit and Vegetable Market] to buy his stock. He knew all the stall holders and he got me a job there. And then I stayed there for a while actually, well, about a year, I think, and then I moved out.*

I moved to Edge Lane, so I was nearer work. And then I stayed there for a couple of years.

Alan: *And what was your job there? What exactly was you doing?*

Arsenal: *I was a barrow boy. We opened at six o'clock for the customers, but we'd get there at four o'clock [4am] and lay out all the displays. So, for those two hours that was like overtime, but it was a bit of extra for me match money. So that's what I used to do, I used to go for 4am and set it all up. And then, customers used to come in and have a look at your stuff. If it was up to standard, they might order a couple of boxes of apples, or bags of potatoes or anything.*

I would put it onto me barrow and then take it to their vehicle and load it. We were supposed to finish at 2pm but we always got off about twelve because everyone was done then. It was dead after that. After about 10am there was no one coming in because all the shops open at nine so all the good stuff's gone.

So, I done that, and I was on £16 a week then. And then I went up to £25 a week because I was driving the forklifts.

And where I lived, I was in a flat, but I ended up going back home.

Alan: *And why was that?*

Arsenal: *The reason was the guy above me in the flats had his electric, I don't know how he did it, don't ask me, but he'd wired his to mine. And I was paying for his electric.*

Alan:	*Cheeky bugger. And how did you find out?*
Arsenal:	*Because of me bills. But I never realised that I think it was me oldest brother who realised [Eddie]. And when he looked into the boxes because it was all in one, there was a film negative from a photo. There was a strip of negatives stuck in his electrics to stop the wheel from turning. And me brother noticed, and he noticed this thing and he went, "God, he's fiddling his electric."*
	And I said, "You know what, my bill's really high, funnily enough."
Alan:	*How long had you been paying his bills for him then?*
Arsenal:	*Probably since I was there. Twelve months. We rang the police. He got arrested and that.*
Alan:	*So why did you not stay if he had gone?*
Arsenal:	*I don't know. I went back home. I was too upset.*

Arsenal went back home, tail between his legs, and stayed at the market for another few months. Timelines are a little hazy now, but he remembers his next couple of jobs well as they lead to a terrible accident that precipitated the legal change of his name to Arsenal Whittick.

In 1980, at the age of eighteen, after moving back in with his mum and dad, he changed roles and left the market to join Dams Furniture. They still are a manufacturer and wholesaler of office furniture that have been in business since 1967 and are still trading today in Liverpool. Dams originally was an acronym meaning 'dictating and adding machine service' and was a one-man band ran by Barry Scott to do repairs on business machines.

By the time Arsenal started there, they had their own workshop and were making and distributing their own office furniture. Arsenal trained as a 'chippie' or carpenter, utilising one of the few work skills he had developed at school: woodwork! After three years learning his trade, he moved to Gostins of Halewood, then a highly reputable cabinet makers who provided furniture for the royal family.

Gostins' Arcade has been a fixture on Liverpool's Hanover Street for more than twenty years, but originally Gostins' name was associated with a furniture store and warehouse. Popularity dwindled after customers chose bigger retailers instead. Arsenal moved there, making period furniture in 1984 before the accident in 1985.

Alan:	You said you had a bad accident at work. Where were you working then and what happened?
Arsenal:	I was working for a company called Gostins of Halewood. They used to do reproduction furniture, like for the royals. If we made a four-poster bed, it would take about ten weeks. Or, if we made a Welsh dresser, I'd probably take a bit longer. But you know what, after we'd made it, the French polish guy would get like a rock and damage it and then spray it. And after about a month it looked a hundred years old. It was brilliant. It was fantastic.
	I went to work on the first, err, I never used to work on a match day. I've never worked on a match day. And for some reason or unbeknown it was the first day of the season and we were playing Liverpool. [This means the date was the 17th August 1985. Everton were the previous season's champions with Liverpool as runners-up. AFC had finished seventh.]
	We had to get a job out. And they said, "Arsenal, can you work?"

And I went, "We're playing Liverpool at Anfield."

"Can you come in for two or three hours then and you can go the match afterwards?" So, I thought, OK. But I was on such a high for the football I made a mistake. I cut me hand with a circular saw. I was on such a high, wasn't I?

Alan: How bad was it?

Arsenal: It was bad, but I don't know. You might be able to see this? [He shows me his scar and then Arsenal stands up in his living room and starts to mime what he was doing on the day. He leans over as though pushing a piece of wood lengthways through a spinning circular saw.] So, as I pulled the saw towards me and pushed back, when I went to pick up me wood the blade wasn't completely behind the fence. And when I went to get it, the blade just went shwooo through me hand.

And you know what, when I picked up me wood, to put it on the bench and I noticed all this blood. I looked up at the ceiling for some reason. I thought it was dripping from above. Then I realised and these two fingers [index finger and middle finger], sounds mad now but, they were hanging on what looked like a corkscrew. They were like down there. [Points to the floor.] Them two fingers were just hanging off by what looked like a corkscrew of skin. [Arsenal indicates a point about a foot below where his fingers are now, indicating that they had almost become detached and were hanging loose.]

It sounds stupid now, I know, but I had all bits of white skin on the back of me hand and because

I was shaking, I thought I had maggots on the back of me hand. I thought, Where the fuck have they come from? And I think it was me skin. And that's the time when I went to hospital and they asked me name and I said, "Arsenal Whittick."

And my boss said, "Yeah, Arsenal Whittick. Been working for me for twelve months."

At this juncture I make the point to Arsenal that all his knowledge and memories revolve around these major events in his life. Nearly chopping his hand off, Mum and Dad's wedding, when he became Arsenal it was FA Cup final day. All his memories are attached around big events. He accepts this but with some reluctance. I wonder what his subconscious is still hiding.

The injury that Arsenal says was his own mistake, in my view is clearly a result of his autism. It was the first game of the new football season and Arsenal's raison d'être had come around again. Not only that, the football gods had given him the best opening fixture possible, Liverpool at Anfield. He didn't have to travel, and he was going to see his archenemies as well.

He was hyperactive due to the excitement building up in him, not only on the day but the several months' waiting for the new season. He should never have been working such a dangerous instrument as a circular saw in this mental state. Nevertheless, he had no diagnosis. He was simply a football-crazy fan who worshipped at the altar of Highbury. I'm certain that under today's health and safety regulations, knowing Arsenal's condition on the spectrum and his history, he would not be allowed near a circular saw on match day.

In 1986, Arsenal returned to work after a long layoff. He was lucky in that the surgeon managed to save his fingers and today they seem to be functioning normally. Gostin decided that they and Arsenal had to part company due to a redundancy programme they were running to cut costs. Strangely enough, only one employee lost their job on the programme: Arsenal Whittick. Arsenal was about to join the world of the unemployed for the first time.

On the 1st February 1986, Arsenal became a dad. Now this may come as a shock, as we've yet to mention any women in Arsenal's life, but we will devote whole chapters to that part of his history. Suffice to say, he had met his first serious girlfriend, L, in 1984, and their son was born into a small back bedroom at Arsenal's mother-in-law's.

He was out of work in 1987, had a young baby and was living at his mother-in-law's. The term is used loosely, as Arsenal and L had not married. He managed to find work again in 1988, which was just as well, as in 1989, along came another addition on the 15th May: another baby boy. Arsenal said to me that he wasn't really interested in girls up to the age of twenty-three (this would have been 1985), as football and work were all-consuming for him. He certainly started to make up for lost time as he had two baby boys by twenty-seven.

The job he managed to secure was with Nouveau Security in Speke Industrial Estate, Liverpool. They manufactured aluminium doors and windows and once again Arsenal's dexterity with his hands was put to good use. He split up with L in 1992 (that's worth a chapter all to itself), and then he met Nicola Swift. Samantha was born 14th June 1995 and in 1996, Arsenal moved lock, stock and barrel down to Bournemouth. He stayed with Nouveau Security until they went bankrupt and re-emerged as TGS Doors in 1993 in Aintree and are still there today. Arsenal had to give this job up when he moved south with the family.

Let's just take a moment to think what an amazing achievement this was. Arsenal had no CV. His stammer was so bad that he struggled to get through an interview. He had identity issues racing around his head with the Flynn versus Whittick situation and to top it all, he was an undiagnosed person with autism.

Yet from the age of sixteen, when he started as a barrow boy, to the age of thirty-four, when he headed south for a new life, he had only been out of work for any length of time in 1987 when he had been made redundant at Gostins. He was now in a new town, with a new baby and partner, with two more dependants living in Liverpool, and out of work again. So, what did he do – he went for a fish and chip supper!

Arsenal:	*So we come down here Sunday 5th February 1996, Samantha was seven months old. We came down to get away from all that shite and Samantha's health reasons tipped it over.*
Alan:	*Did you have a job or somewhere to live?*
Arsenal:	*We stayed in Nicola's mum's as she'd moved down twelve months earlier, I didn't have a job. Then a got a job in the matter of two weeks. I went down to Harry Ramsden's and it wasn't open. But the doors to the restaurant upstairs were open and they were having a morning meeting with the managers.*
	And luckily enough for me, Alan Simpson, who owned it, because it's a franchise, just happened to be there that day. And I walked in, passed the bar into the restaurant, the general manager [GM], I didn't know he was the GM at the time, Jez, don't know his second name, and he says, "Can I help you?"
	And I said, "I've just moved into the area and I'm looking for a job."
	And he said to me, "No, mate. I haven't got anything for you."

"I'll do anything, mate."

"I'm sorry, I haven't got anything."

So I said, "I'm willing to work for a week for nothing and at the end of the week you can see how I am."

And he said again, "We haven't got nothin'."

And Alan Simpson was listening to this and said, "So, you're willing to work for a week with no pay so we can see you?"

And I said, "Yeah."

He said, "We'll see you tomorrow."

And that's how I got into Harry Ramsden's. So, I was there from then for four years.

Alan: What exactly was your job?

Arsenal: I started in the potato room. I was just doing all the potatoes, all the chips. Then I went in the fish room, skinning the fish and cutting it. Then I went in the takeaway. Went on the tills. Then, I went behind the range in the takeaway. Then I went upstairs in the kitchen, doing all the bread and butter and puddings and that. Then, I went on the hot plate. Then I was made senior of back of house, so I'd worked in every department, hadn't I? So, I knew what I was talking about and I was into my timing, wasn't I? [One of Arsenal's obsessions was being on time and knowing exactly how long it took to do something, anything!]

So, I used to time people and say, "Can you be quicker?"

And I used to write them on the wall and the managers would say, "What's that on the board?"

And I'd say, "That's what time people can go for their breaks. And that's what time they have to be back."

And then they'd go, "But they're only allowed twenty minutes for break, why have you given them twenty-four minutes?"

And I said, "Well, it takes them two minutes to get downstairs and two minutes to get back up."

"What? You're timing them?"

And I went, "Yeah."

So, at least everyone knew exactly what times their breaks were, but I added on the time it took to get down and get back. You know what, though, I never had a problem. I never had a problem with anyone because everyone knew I'd done every job so they knew they couldn't bullshit me.

Then I went front of house, I done the bar, I done the waiter stuff and that, then I become duty manager. Then I went over to Southampton, Ocean Village. Went there to manage that for about, I wasn't there long, for about a year or maybe less and that closed down. I went back to Harry's for a bit, but then I didn't like it, going back there.

Alan: It had changed?

Arsenal: Yeah, yeah. They had a new... When Alan sold Ocean Village, he sold Bournemouth to a massive company, Compass. They'd just changed the tradition of it. Say that, I know it's like little things, but they changed the tablecloths. They had been brown and white checked like the original Harry Ramsden's, so it was all original stuff in there. They'd changed that to just white and in the bar. Imagine there's like a three-hour wait or something like that, people would wait in the bar and they would be alcoves so they could have a chat and catch up. But they started putting tables in the bar. I don't know it just seemed to be changing it to just the normal fish and chip. And they took the piano out and that. They had a piano there.

Alan: So it lost its originality?

Arsenal: There's a guy there who's on the scene in Bournemouth, actually. He's now called Matt Black. He used to come in, he played the piano, and it was really good. And they used to do all different events so if you were going the BIC [Bournemouth International Centre] you could come to Harry Ramsden's first and get a pre-show meal and you'd get like a lot of discount. It was really good, and they used to do the boat trips and that, but when Compass arrived, they stopped everything, just like that.

It just lost its appeal to me. In the takeaway and the restaurant, they had pictures of Harry Ramsden opening up his first shop in Guiseley, up in Leeds, up that way. And there was all Harry Ramsden stuff up and they took them all down. They redecorated and it just lost it for me.

I went in last year and the menu is just really massive now. Back then it was more straightforward. And now it's got all sorts. It's just mad.

How many people do you know who would give a job up because they changed the tablecloths or the menu, or took pictures down and changed the decorations? Change is something that all people with autism have varying levels of difficulty with. It can be obsessive; if you left your coat on the back of a chair, Arsenal would 'explode' and self-harm because he, at the time, couldn't understand why you hadn't hung it on the coatrack. He now copes and we will come to that, but on this occasion, Harry's had changed too much for him to want to cope. He had no idea he was on the spectrum, so he just walked. At this point he had no coping strategies and so the easiest thing to do was to leave.

Just like he couldn't cope with being left out of the communication of his mum's pregnancy with Jeni. He couldn't cope then, so when his mum gave him the option to walk out the door, rather than face a new baby, he walked.

Modern life is full of change and many people, autistic or otherwise, do not like the speed of change or the speed of life today. So how do we cope? We plan and prepare. That is also the best way to deal with change for a person with autism – let them know well in advance, give them chance to mentally prepare and then introduce the changes in small increments. Arsenal came back to the Bournemouth 'chippy' in the year 2000, at the age of thirty-eight, a full eleven years before someone would first suggest he was autistic. So, he dealt with all the change by putting it behind him and moving on to the next role. The difference being that it was himself who was instigating the change and not someone else imposing the change upon him.

Arsenal went to work at a branch of TJ Hughes in Boscombe for two years, starting in 'pot wash'. He says that at every company he worked for, he had to start at the bottom as it's the only job he could get without a CV or interview. But then Dave Whelan of JJB Sports fame bought the company and Arsenal's branch made changes. This was 2001, and Nicola gave birth to her and Arsenal's second daughter, Danielle, on the 24th July. Arsenal decided he'd had enough of other people telling him what to do and would open his own business, and so in 2002 he decided to take an intensive driving course with the British School of Motoring (BSM) and open his own taxi-minibus company.

Arsenal had no job and had paid for the course himself; it wasn't cheap, especially when he had no income at the time.

Alan: *So what happened at BSM?*

Arsenal: *Well, with the BSM stuff, I was doing a course there every week and at the end of the week there was a folder and your instructor would tick it off and comment how you was doing. It was only until I went to court, I looked at everything and realised anything about speech they never ticked nothing.*

        So, I thought, Yous knew there was going to be an issue, and instead of saying from the start something like, "This isn't the right job for you," they let me pay them every week and then I'd left me job for it and everything. The fucking shits. I'd rather somebody have said, "Arsenal, mate, you won't be able to do it." And then at least I'll know.

I researched and found the tribunal details.

Whittick v British School of Motoring Employment Tribunal, April 2002

The tribunal stated that Arsenal had a stutter; they used the word stutter not stammer. BSM agreed that Arsenal had a disability within the Disability Discrimination Act.

Arsenal made his case saying that he had paid for and attended several training courses and meetings and was assessed as to his ability to apply for a franchise to manage a driving school. His complaint was that he was prevented from completing the course, hence not becoming an instructor and therefore unable to start his own business.

The tribunal held that it had no jurisdiction to even consider the complaint, because Arsenal was not employed by BSM nor intending to be an employee of BSM.

Arsenal had paid BSM for a training and instruction course. On his successful completion of the course he would be able to obtain a franchise from BSM but was never going to be an employee of BSM.

The *London Evening Standard* also had the following headline:

Stutterer turned down as driving instructor

The article outlined that a man with a stammer, again the word they used was stutter, had been refused the role as an instructor due to his inability to say "stop" at the speed required for an emergency stop.

They went on to say that Arsenal had spent his own money to go on the course for 10 months but due to his speech impediment had failed it.

The solicitor acting for BSM said that it was only when Arsenal got to the third stage of the course, the one requiring verbal skills did his stammer become a problem.

Unfortunately for Arsenal he had told BSM that he didn't believe his stammer was a disability but the Southampton tribunal found this not to be the case and as Arsenal didn't work directly for BSM he hadn't been discriminated against. Arsenal paid £2,600 for the course and gave up his £15,000 a year job to study.

Arsenal is adamant that the BSM knew what they were doing. They spoke to him every time he went, and they didn't need to wait for the verbal skills part of his course for them to know he had a stammer. They just wanted the money. Arsenal couldn't win his tribunal as he was never an employee, but the article in the *Evening Standard* did once again change his life for the better.

We will now take a slight detour from Arsenal's employment history and talk about his stammer and how he managed to overcome the last forty years' difficulties. Someone read the article in *the Evening Standard* and volunteered to pay for Arsenal to go on a course to help him with his stammer. The organisation is called the Starfish Project.

Chapter Seven

The Starfish Project

2003

Reading FC won't have the confidence to be confident.

Paul Merson

THE BEST WAY TO DESCRIBE EXACTLY HOW THE STARFISH Project helps people with speech defects is to understand what causes stuttering and stammering in the first place. Firstly, stammering and stuttering are two different words to describe the same condition, so as Arsenal always refers to his condition as 'stammering', we will use the same word.

We do not know what causes stammering, but research shows that a combination of factors is involved. Stammering affects four times as many men as women. Statistics show us that approximately 500,000-plus adults in the UK stammer, which is about one per cent of the adult population.

It is vital to recognise that everyone who stammers is different, and stammers differently. Everyone is an individual and any therapy or training must respect the individual. Therefore, every person who stammers is potentially an expert on their own stammering. Recognising and always respecting these very important facts is the foundation to the Starfish Project and its success in helping people in their recovery from stammering. Arsenal, for the first time in his life, believed he had a chance to do something positive about his stammer and threw himself wholeheartedly into the project.

As a child he had taken some speech therapy lessons but to no avail. Either he or his therapists had given up at an early stage of the therapy. Plus, in the '70s, the approach to helping people with speech defects was a long way from the sophisticated methods being used today and in 2003.

Stammering is a disorder of fluency that is characterised by various behaviours that interfere with the forward flow of speech. While all individuals are disfluent to some extent, what differentiates stammerers from non-stammerers is the frequency of their disfluency and/or the severity of their disfluency. However, the other factor that differentiates stammerers from non-stammerers is that almost invariably the disfluencies that the stammerer regards as 'stammering' are accompanied by a feeling of loss of control. It is this loss of control, which can't be observed or experienced by the listener, that is generally most problematic for the stammerer.

Stammering, however, is not simply a speech difficulty; it is a serious communication problem. It can undermine a person's self-esteem, affect their interaction with others, impede their education and seriously hamper employment potential.

At this time, all leading experts agree that, unfortunately, there is no cure for stammering, and people who stammer should beware of and avoid any therapy that offers a cure, but what the Starfish Project offers the individual is 'stammering control training'. The sessions Arsenal enjoyed were not just theory, they also equipped him for everyday situations: role-play sessions like telephone work, ordering a drink in a pub or a meal in a restaurant, addressing a group, etc. To a life-long stammerer such as Arsenal, this must have seemed like an incredible and impossible situation. (Arsenal told me he never went to a bar in a pub but always sent someone else.) Finally, the course would end by preparing Arsenal for his 'new' life and how to handle some of the possible challenges he would face.

All this in three days and paid for by the generosity of a member of the *Standard* reading public who read between the lines of Arsenal's plight in the newspaper report and saw that here was someone who was trying to improve his 'lot' in the world but was being held back. I stress again, though, a three-day course to put right a life-long problem. I don't think you can overstate the impact this had on Arsenal's life.

Alan:	*You mentioned that you only started communicating verbally at the age of six or seven…*
Arsenal:	*Yeah, I used to make noises.*
Alan:	*How did you actually learn to speak then?*
Arsenal:	*I don't know, but there's a lot of people, well, not a LOT of people, but if you're non-verbal no one actually knows why you're non-verbal. Even to this day, all the experts don't know why people stammer, even to this day. They just don't know. Because everything works and if anyone with a stammer sings, they don't stammer.*
Alan:	*I know, I think I've heard that. So, was it the stammer that was causing you to be non-verbal? Was it the autism or was it the stammer?*
Arsenal:	*The non-verbal is first [stammer] and then the autism. The difference between autism I have and Asperger's syndrome is language. And that's*

the difference between the two. I didn't have no language until I was six and then made noises and when I tried to speak it was then 'they' realised I couldn't speak. And then I just struggled all the way through until 2003.

So, I went to speech therapy probably until I left school, and then after school I never. Then I went again in 2003 on me speech course, but I don't remember any of me speech lessons [as a child] apart from one.

When I went in, I was living in Liverpool, I couldn't speak and the woman, the speech therapist, said to me, "Do you like football?"

So, I couldn't get a word out. Eventually I did and I said, "Yeah."

And then she said, "What football team?"

And again, I couldn't get me words out and she was trying to help me, and she said, "Do they play in blue?"

I shook my head.

"Do they play in red?"

So, I nodded. So, in her head I was supporting Liverpool, wasn't I? [AFC and Liverpool play in red.]

So, she said, "OK." She was trying to get me to say the team I liked. So, she thought it was Liverpool. And she goes, "What you need to do is get your tongue and just put it up there," [indicates roof of mouth] and I'm going, "ARTHENAL, ARTHENAL." And that's the only speech lesson I ever remember. All the rest were just… [Arsenal stops speaking.]

Alan: Were you ever asked to sing?

Arsenal:	*No, no. I just remember pictures they were showing me with two letters in, that's all I remember, really. Trying to say Arsenal with me tongue stuck to the roof of me mouth, up here.*
Alan:	*Were you trying to improve your speech in these lessons, or did you just want to get out?*
Arsenal:	*I don't recall, to be honest. But when I went to the Starfish program I kept in touch with people and the one person I've kept in touch with since 2003 he doesn't costal breathe no more.*

At this point it may be worthwhile understanding the term 'costal breathing'. The medical definition of costal breathing is, "Inspiration and expiration produced chiefly by movements of the ribs." According to the British Stammering Association, 'costal breathing' as a treatment for stammerers is an 'alternative approach' and they particularly reference the Starfish Project. This method of breathing is taught on the course, sometimes aided by the use of a belt, one that Arsenal has always used. A strong belt is utilised to restrict your ribcage and force the diaphragm to be the main breathing muscle using the following technique.

A belt is placed around the lower ribs and tightened until it's difficult or impossible to breathe in, inhale, using the ribcage or chest. Arsenal's body therefore uses the abdomen to take breath into the lungs. The belt can then be worn for minutes or hours and eventually Arsenal reached diaphragmatic breathing.

This breathing technique helps both stammerers and opera singers to speak/sing on an exhale rather than an inhale and helps to 'get the word out'. It is not a solution for all stammerers which is why it's an 'alternative' solution, but it did work for Arsenal.

Arsenal: He's gone back to having a stammer because it's too much for him. The costal breathing. It's what opera singers do. That's the breathing what the opera singers do, it's from the diaphragm.

Alan: So where was the Starfish Project?

Arsenal: A hotel in Eastbourne. I'll have the details in there somewhere. [Arsenal points over his shoulder to another room in his flat.] We went to a hotel for a week and then every morning they'll all come down for breakfast at the same time and that. We had our own room for breakfast and then after breakfast we would go in like a hall and then each day, we'd have to get up in front of everyone and speak and we would be videoed.

And then at the end of the week or the week after you get the video in the post and you watch it; and it's amazing. It's very good. And all the stories you hear from the people who have a stammer and it's just an eye-opener. And that's what made me work hard on it actually to just improve your life. Because I never realised how much it affected me really. [Arsenal is now speaking in a low, melancholy voice, almost living the realisation all over again.]

I never really twigged. [He goes quiet.]

Alan: Do you think your stammer plus your autism was making you angrier and angrier because you couldn't really communicate?

Arsenal: I don't know because... I know there's a lad in work [one of the Autism Wessex residential homes], and he's non-verbal. And when he, when staff, don't sort of do what he wants or expects, he gets angry – hits himself. That's because he can't tell 'em, can he?

So, I don't know, I've never thought about it,
actually. Wow! I don't know.

The Starfish Project was founded by Anne Blight, who had been working worldwide for and with stammerers for many years. She had successfully trained many hundreds of stammerers who now knew the joy of being able to control the stammer that controlled them for so long.

Feeling frustrated at the lack of in-depth therapy available for stammerers within the health service, Anne got involved as a volunteer for the British Stammering Association.

She was excited by the potential of diaphragmatic retraining (costal breathing), and some methods that are believed to have been used by therapist Lionel Logue, notably with the late King George VI – or for those more familiar with movies rather than history, the Best Picture Oscar-winning *The King's Speech* tells the story. However, she became very disillusioned by the way that diaphragmatic retraining (costal breathing), was introduced into the UK by expensive franchised multi-level marketing.

Believing strongly, as she still does, that it is wrong to take financial or psychological advantage of the misfortune of others, or, as some therapies do, give false hope or a promise of a non-existent cure from stammering, Anne founded the Project in 1998.

The Project is non-profit making, maintaining a cost-covering basis, and Anne pledged to keep the course fee at £250, the same as it was fourteen years ago, for as long as they could, to ensure that they made courses available to as many people as possible. Anne also pledged, and still offers, FREE lifetime support and no-fee refresher courses.

It remains Anne Blight's dream that one day Starfish therapy will be available free to anyone that seeks it.

Anne's work was recognised in 2005 when she was awarded the Celebrities Guild of Great Britain's 'Unsung Heroes Award' after being nominated by many recovering stammerers.

I continued to probe Arsenal about his stammer and the Project, and we were actually talking about the movie *One Flew Over the Cuckoo's Nest* when he seemed to remember something that annoyed him.

Arsenal:	*It's strange like where stammers are. There's a song and it's a classic song, and he pretends to stammer in the middle of it. And I thought, wow! I get so angry when I hear the song.*
Alan:	*I know which song you mean. 'My Generation' by The Who.*
Arsenal:	*It is, yes. [Arsenal laughs loudly as I think he finds it strange that I know exactly the song he means, but that's the only song I can think of with a stammering lead singer; then I see him trying to control the anger building up inside of him.] It really annoys me. I just don't understand why you would try to have a stammer. When he doesn't understand for people who have a stammer how hard their life has been.*
	If you go the Starfish course, some of the stories I heard are just amazing. And you just go, wow, even I didn't think of that happening and that. I was sent on this course and I gave it absolutely everything and as me dad said in his email, it changed me, didn't it?
Alan:	*Turned your life around.*
Arsenal:	*Yeah, yeah, yeah. There was like – have I told you the stories about the Starfish course?*
Alan:	*No, please do.*

Arsenal: *Because some of them are funny. Well, not funny, but, they were like, wow. There was a woman there in 2003, who was buying a house for £300,000. And back then everyone was going, "£300,000?" That was a lot of money then. And she pulled out of the deal because of the name of the road was something like, 'Six Penny Lane', and she couldn't pronounce it and pulled out of the deal. Because every time someone would say to her, "Where do you live?" That would be a block for her so…*

Alan: *Is the letter 'S' particularly difficult to pronounce or…*

Arsenal: *I find 'S' and 'F's and some words, well, a lot of words. There was a girl, she was about eighteen, she was in tears telling the story that… She had all these roots in her hair. And she was explaining that her mum and dad had gone on holiday, and it was the first time that she hadn't been to the hairdressers to get her hair done. Because when she goes in, what do hairdressers do? They talk to you all the time. And they ask you stuff.*

So, her mum had always gone with her and she never had the bottle to go on her own. So, she had all these roots coming through and she was sat there all distraught wearing a hat. And she said, "I don't want to live. Look at me." And her stammer was affecting her appearance. She was worried about her appearance.

There was a lad who was in university for four years and every weekend he had a job, a Saturday job. And every afternoon he used to go to this sandwich shop. And he's be in the queue and the staff would say to him, "Is it your usual?" And he would nod. So, for four years he had the same sandwich, but he didn't want it. He would have picked something off the board, but it was so easy to just nod. That's someone actually being affected to what they eat.

So, there was a girl, it [a stammer] affected how she looked; a woman where she lives and Darren, who I keep in touch with, he was, his mum and dad and wife had a joint B&B in York by the Minster. It was like two in one, actually. They had two different names and when you go in you register for two different hotels but then they join up. His parents had one and him and his wife had the other. But he never worked in there, he was a long-distance lorry driver. And he admitted on the course that the reason being was that he didn't have to speak to no one all day long.

Alan: So every single person who was on that course, their whole life was affected by having a stammer to a far greater extent than people would think?

Arsenal: Yeah, yeah. And when he went onto the course, he changed his job to, he was still driving but, he was local, so he was getting home each night and he wasn't doing any weekends and it was better for him. But then they moved up to Scotland, him his wife and the kids and they got a B&B up there. But he doesn't help out still. He's got his own business cleaning carpets and that's what he does. And he's on his own so doesn't have to talk. And you think, wow.

He's the one who, if I ring him up, I always go, "Arsenal Whittick speaking."

> And then he'll say, and there's a pause of about thirty seconds and he'll say, "Darren XXXXX speaking." Because on our course, that's one of the first things we had to do. Introduce ourselves all the time. Even when I text anyone, I introduce myself.

Alan: I know. [I now have hundreds of texts from Arsenal and they all start with, 'Arsenal Whittick texting'.]

Arsenal: Or if I message someone on Facebook, 'Arsenal Whittick messaging', or do you know if the kids ring me? But it used to annoy them but now it doesn't because they understand now why I'm doing it.

> I'll answer my phone even to them: "Arsenal Whittick speaking."
>
> And they'll go, "I know, Dad, I rang you."
>
> And when my phone rings I'll let it ring a couple of times and then I'm getting me costal breathing ready and then I go, "Arsenal Whittick speaking."

To anyone without a stammer this is a little thing of no significance whatsoever. To Arsenal, and many other sufferers like himself, there is a real sense of achievement on picking up that phone, or shaking someone's hand, or standing up at a meeting or at a family dinner or even going to the bar and ordering himself a pint. Being able to announce to the world: here I am and I'm Arsenal Whittick is very important. Probably more important to Arsenal than most other stammerers as I paraphrase, "All I ever wanted to be was Arsenal Whittick." There is a real sense of pride that can be heard in Arsenal's voice as he proudly exclaims that he now uses a phone properly or interacts socially with people better than ever before. Listening to him, one can only imagine what it was like the first time he started to use his 'new' voice in public. Some of his relationship problems caused by his autism were just exacerbated by his inability to speak.

As his diagnosis set out for us, he has, or now had, real problems forming close relationships with family and had 'no close friends'. These problems emanate from his autism; that reluctance is embedded in his DNA. Then add to that the reluctance to speak due to the stammer and it's no small wonder that he couldn't forge relationships with family and friends as the forge was never lit. Even when he wanted to speak, he couldn't get his words out and often gave up. It is therefore doubly important to him that his daughters especially can now pick up a phone and ring him knowing that, 'at least Dad can now answer the phone'.

Arsenal: *I have strategies for absolutely everything, mate.*
Alan: *And they're working brilliantly for you.*
Arsenal: *And they work, so I can live with that. And when, if, Danielle is with any of her mates, and she rings me, she puts me on speakerphone, and I go, "Arsenal Whittick speaking." And I can hear all her mates laughing. [Arsenal bursts out laughing himself at the thought of this happening.]*

They'll go, "Why did he say that?"

And she'll tell 'em. "He has a stammer, so he has to control his breathing." And then it goes silent because they're thinking, Shit, we've just been laughing at him. But I'd rather be having a laugh and her not be scared of me no more. I'd rather have that all the time, so…

Alan:	*So how did they teach you to breathe differently because you speak as you exhale?*
Arsenal:	*They give you a book, I'll find it for you, and it just teaches you how to do it. And I just practised and practised until I could do it. I followed the pictures because I don't really understand the body, do I? You started off by... You haven't seen me put me belt on, have you?*
Alan:	*No, I've not.*
Arsenal:	*So when I was on the course, we had to put a belt on. [The belt can best be described as a thick, white cotton belt, not dissimilar to one that would be worn by someone wearing a judo jacket to tie it tight. Arsenal indicates a place around his lower ribcage where he would tie this belt.] And then you can feel you're breathing inside; you can feel it. I don't know why, but you can just feel your breathing a lot better. [It seems to a layperson that you talk as you exhale and the word comes out with your breath, Arsenal confirms this, but it's my interpretation, not his.]*

Arsenal now uses this belt as a sensory overload for himself when he gets angry. For example, when he used to watch football and was waiting for the AFC game to kick off, he would get uncontrollably angry if the phone would go just before the start. By tying the belt very tightly around his diaphragm, he could better control his breathing, which would aid him in taking control of his temper. Just one of his many coping mechanisms. As I write this today, Arsenal hasn't gotten angry or self-harmed since 2014.

The Starfish Project is a philanthropic organisation that is a lifeline to people like Arsenal. As I have learned – and Arsenal did as well when he met fellow sufferers on the course – the impact of having a stammer is much more far-reaching than people without one could ever imagine. As one person who Arsenal met in Eastbourne stated, "I just want to kill myself." It is so difficult to empathise with that level of soul-destroying frustration, but when every waking minute of every day can leave you in tears, it can obviously lead to the levels of self-harm that the young girl was experiencing. I don't know the answer to this, but I'm starting to think Arsenal's anger may well have been borne as much from his stammer as it was from his autism.

It's time to close this chapter. We leave it knowing that Arsenal is now better equipped to deal with day-to-day life than he was when we started it. He now has a process and methodology to deal with his speech; as we know, it will never be cured and it's testament to Arsenal's fortitude and providence that he has continued with his costal breathing to improve his life and that of his family.

But why Starfish; where did the name come from?

Here is a beautiful story that explains the origin and meaning of the name the Starfish Project.

An old lady was walking along a beach when in the distance she spotted a small girl, aged about 8 years old. The girl was picking starfish off the beach and throwing them back into the sea. The sun was setting and the pretty girl began to move faster and faster to increase the number of starfish she could help by throwing them back into the deeper water so they survived.

The old lady approached and asked the girl what did she think she was doing? "I'm helping the starfish by getting them back into the sea so they can breathe". she replied.

The old lady said, "Do you not realise there are hundreds of starfish on this beach and hundreds on the next and the next so there are thousands of starfish out there. What you are doing simply won't make a difference."

The girl smiled, bent down, picked up another starfish and threw it back into the sea before replying, "It made a difference to that one."

Chapter Eight

More Work

2003 Onwards

Arsène Wenger asked me to have a trial with Arsenal when I was seventeen. I turned it down. Zlatan doesn't do auditions.

Zlatan Ibrahimović

AFTER THE FAILED TRIBUNAL WITH BSM AND THE KINDNESS of a stranger, plus the stoic approach to making his life better for himself, Arsenal was now better placed to interview for roles and found himself working for Bournemouth Borough Council, or as they are better known in Dorset, the BBC. This wasn't any ordinary role, though, as that would be too easy for Arsenal. No, he had decided to become a parking attendant, or as you or I like to call them, a traffic warden!

Another job, another tribunal. From 2003 to 2006, Arsenal patrolled the streets of Boscombe and Bournemouth, applying his own brand of common-sense parking restrictions. He never gave out hundreds of tickets, but instead showed a leniency and empathetic nature that was at odds with his still-undiagnosed autism. But what he now had was better communication skills. If he saw someone parking up in a restricted zone, he would offer them ten minutes to move the car and find another spot before handing out the ticket.

His literal nature would put him in awkward situations. There is a hill in Boscombe that leads down to the pier and beach at the bottom, and the pier is situated close to a very popular public house called The Neptune. Directly on the beachfront, close to the best surfing area and about two miles from Bournemouth Pier, it's a very popular spot and parking is at a premium.

> Arsenal: *Things don't really register in me brain and I come out with some stuff. I hurt people all the time.*
>
> Alan: *Can people hurt you mentally? Can people say bad things to you that hurt you?*
>
> Arsenal: *No, you can say anything to me at all and it doesn't hurt me. This is like that; it was in the summer and I was working for the council as a traffic warden. These lads had parked on the hill running down to Boscombe Beach. But I seen them parking up on there as I was walking down the hill. And there was five lads in the car, and I went up and I said, "Mate, I'm going to give you ten minutes to sort out somewhere else to park because you can't park on here."*
>
> *And they went, "Yeah, OK, all right, mate. We're just sorting something out." So, about an hour later I was coming back down the hill, and there was this car all parked up and I thought, The little shits. I'm giving the ticket out and they come out the Harvester. They'd been in the pub. They'd parked there and been for a couple*

of pints and a meal and there's a car park just on top?

Anyway, I gave a ticket and the driver was fuming with me. And he was just trying to be really leery in front of all his mates and he went to me, "You're a fucking parasite."

So, I said, "No, I'm not. I'm a Scouser." And all his mates were laughing at him. And he was ranting and raving. And that's the way I… I didn't even know what it was. So, I went home, and I went, "I got called a parasite today. What's one of them?"

"It's like an insect, it's a horrible creature."

"Well, I got called one today."

And Nicola said, "What did you do?"

"I told him I wasn't – I told him I was a Scouser."

And she just said, "Fuckin' hell."

When we discussed this, Arsenal and myself laughed for about ten minutes. This is another example of how far he has come. When this happened in 2003/4, he couldn't exactly see the funny side of the story, but now he laughs away at this previous version of himself. I explained to him what parasite actually meant and he took a little umbrage and defended traffic wardens.

Arsenal: *Everybody thinks you get more money the more tickets you give, but you don't. That's only if it's run by a private company. If it's run by the council, you get paid the same no matter how many tickets you give. There were people who used to give out fifty tickets a day, I think the most I ever done was about eight. And I'd think, how can they do fifty* tickets? *They're doing dodgy tickets and I know how they do them, but that's down to them.*

At least every eight I did, and that's me most in a day, at least I knew in my notebook, it will say, "They arrived back, and driven off," or something like that. At least if anyone ever appealed any of my tickets, my tickets always stuck. Pristine all the time. Whereby the ones who were doing fifty/sixty a day, if anyone appealed them, they'd probably get off because they may have gave it a minute or something like that. I gave everyone ten minutes, all the time. There's loads of scams they can do.

Alan: *But why would they do that if they didn't get paid any more money?*

Arsenal: *Power, I think? There was one guy there, his nickname was Bosh. Because that's what he was. [Arsenal laughs to himself as though he remembers Bosh fondly.] Bosh, ha ha. He's booked a bus at a bus stop; a hearse; he's booked an ambulance… But he gets everyone else in trouble. Because I was in Boscombe once and Bosh had been doing the rounds the day before. So, all the shit he causes, the next day I cop for it.*

So, one day, there was a garage, and you know when garages have all the cars on the forecourt, and they're changing them about because they have to make them look different. Well, this garage had put a couple of cars just on double-yellers as he's moving them about, and Bosh come booked four of them and fucked off. So, next day I was coming round, and this guy shouted, "Hey, I want a fucking word with you, what are all these?"

> *And I went, "I haven't gave them." And I went over to him and said, "Can you just calm down a minute? Do you see that number? Is it number forty-nine? Can you see my number there [indicates his shoulder], number fifty-six? They're not mine. I'm on today. When did you get them?"*
>
> *"Yesterday."*
>
> *"OK. You'll have to appeal them. What was you doing?"*
>
> *"I was moving me cars about."*
>
> *"Move your cars about again. Take evidence of what you was doing…" And he did and he got all of them cancelled.*

Arsenal has always had a very strong sense of right and wrong. There is no grey. It's either legal or it isn't; fair or not fair. This belief is strengthened when dealing with himself or his family. On many occasions he has called the police or involved authority figures of some description to settle disputes. If he feels unfairly treated at work, he challenges and invariably wins. Even if that means resigning his position and going to court. In much the same way he cannot lie, he also cannot deliberately break the law. This must have developed as he got older, as the young Arsenal Whittick had no problem scrawling AFC in six-foot letters on electricity substations.

Bosh also ticketed a hotel and on one occasion a mosque, causing all the worshippers to run out into the street in stockings or bare feet. Arsenal wouldn't have done this but roars laughing when telling the tales. Apparently Bosh had another side to him and also helped out local charities, invariably dressing as a stormtrooper to raise money at galas and fetes. In Arsenal's words, "When he put that uniform on, he changed."

Below is a *Daily Mirror* headline from the 27th May 2006. What could possibly have caused this headline and where in the country was this heinous crime taking place? Why don't we hear some more about Arsenal's time as a parking attendant?

WARDENS ISSUED ILLEGAL TICKETS
FOR FOUR YEARS

Arsenal: *I was a parking attendant, a traffic warden. I used to go into a meeting each day and it would be like… Imagine there's ten areas in Bournemouth, there'll be a folder on each area of Bournemouth. So, on this day I was in Boscombe, so I got the Boscombe folder and it had all the updates, roadworks, or anyone who's applied for a permit. There's a list of roads we're not allowed to give tickets on because even though there's yeller lines, the council don't have the permission to put the yeller lines there so they're invalid.*

Alan: *No! That can't be true.*

Arsenal: *Yeah, it's called a TRO [Traffic Regulation Order].*

Alan: *So how are we supposed to know as drivers?*

Arsenal: *If you ever got a ticket, you can go down the town hall, and you can ask for the TRO book. And in the TRO book it will tell you every line and sign that they've got orders for. So, it's like planning permission, you wouldn't believe how technical it all gets. But, in this room they have a big whiteboard, and there's hundreds of roads you can't go down.*

And one day we had this meeting, with our deputy manager, and she said, "As from today, we're going to wipe clear this board, and we're going to take all the sheets out of the file and you have to go down every road, and if there's cars there you have to give a ticket. Any questions?"

"I've got one: why?"

I think she said something like, it's her job to worry about that and it's my job to just do it. But I can't knowingly give a false ticket. And I said, "I'm not happy."

And she said, "Right, I'll go and get the big boss." So, the big boss come in. He sat down, at the end of an oblong table, I was this end, he was that end. [As Arsenal is relaying this story his stammer is getting worse; not massively worse but noticeably so. I think that even though Arsenal is smiling and seems relaxed, the memory is not pleasant for him and must have been stressful at the time.]

And he says, "Do you have a problem?"

And I says, "I don't have a problem."

So, he then says, "It's your job to put the ticket on and it's my job to worry about if they're going to pay it."

And I said, "But I can't knowingly give a false ticket."

And he said to me, "If you're not going to do that, there's the door."

So, I said, "Tell you what, can you put that in writing for me?"

Next minute, mate, he banged the table and he flew round, and he went to me, "Do you know who I am?" [Arsenal is now openly laughing at this recollection.]

And I went, "What?"

"I've been knighted by the Queen and I've served my country in the Commandos."

And I went, "And?"

He went... People had to restrain him and everything. Anyway, I took it to an employment tribunal because I resigned the next day. Because I said, "If I'm in Boscombe, and those people have been parking there for twenty years, and you're asking me to go and give those twenty cars tickets, tell you what, I wouldn't even get out the end of the street, because I'd be lynched."

He went, "Don't you worry about that."

[Arsenal then shows me a copy of the tribunal papers.] It's not very long but you can read it. There were seven parking attendants and two managers against me. But you know what, I paid for a barrister because I knew I was right. And I won.

Alan: Did you get all your expenses back?

Arsenal: In total I got about £24,000. And I named every road, the council had to pay back £275,000 for fines what were illegal. I blew it, didn't I? Am I a liar, right, right? So, I asked, where's the TROs? In here *[holds up the paperwork]* is the judgement and I got all the information from the Freedom of Information Act.

In the room, we had the meeting in the morning, two parking attendants and we have notebooks, so say we had a meeting on Tuesday, they'll write in their books, 'On Tuesday, blah, blah'. And then at eight o'clock the meeting. And that's all they normally put because you have a meeting every day because things are changing all the time. *[Arsenal's thoughts are jumping all over the place as he remembers what to him was a significant victory of the little man versus the system. He is getting excited again several years after the event at the prospect of proving that he isn't a liar, a moral trait dear to him and his coda for life.]*

Two parking attendants in their books had written down that, 'He'd lost his temper and threatened me'. So, under the Freedom of Information Act I got the pocketbooks. But the council had put all black lines through everything. And I went, "You can't do that."

"Yes, we can under the Data Protection Act."

So, I went, "You're just fucking with me now."

So, I went to a barrister and he said, "I'm not havin' that."

So, he done it all and we won.

Alan: I guess you didn't go back to your job then?

Arsenal: They offered it to me, but I said, "No, thank you." You know what, in his statement [the big boss], denied that he banged the table. In the judgement they say, "Two parking attendants who gave evidence to the effect that Mr XXXXX had spoken very strongly to the claimant but did not state that Mr XXXXX had banged the desk."

So, I thought, Shit. But it then says, "We find on the balance of probabilities, having heard and seen the witness give their evidence, and with regard to their demeanour, that we prefer the evidence of the claimant that Mr XXXXX did raise his voice and hit the table. Indeed, while giving evidence on this point Mr XXXXX hit the witness table." Ha ha ha ha. [Arsenal roars laughing.] Honestly, he hits the table giving evidence. He lost it.

Alan: [Reading from the statement] "It was not denied by Mr XXXXX that he had stated that employees that were unhappy with the instruction could 'look for alternative work' and he also stated that he considered that to be an appropriate thing to say to staff."

Arsenal: He had no remorse. I was in Asda and I bumped into the manager. And you know what, he was so rude and disrespectful for me in Asda. And I thought, you know what, I said, "Listen. We went to the tribunal, I won. That's it. You don't have to be so rude like that." And he was so rude.

Alan: In what way was he rude? Did he swear at you or insult you?

Arsenal: Yeah, he called me a little shit and that. And he said all the things I've done for you and that. I said, "It doesn't matter what you do for me. It doesn't mean you can cross that line." He was really rude and just threatening again sort of thing. So, I thought, you know what, OK, you've had your say, I'm going to have my say.

    And he went, "What do you mean?"

    "You'll find out soon."

    So, I walked away and next day I went down the Echo and I went, "I got a story for yous."

    "What's your story?"

    "Bournemouth Borough Council are giving parking tickets and they're not actually legal."

    And he said, "Have you got any evidence of this?"

    So, I took all me court documents and the next minute they said, "Can you come upstairs?"

So, this bloke, a director or something, looked at the evidence and said, "Just need to ring a solicitor." [Arsenal mimics making a few phone calls.] "Yeah, we're gonna run it." It made page one for ten days running in the Daily Echo. Page 1, a couple of pages, Sky got involved, Sky come to the house, done an interview for Sky, done radio interviews and everything. I thought, Don't treat me like that, mate, because it can come back and bite you on the bum. A month later it was announced he was leaving his role.

All the traits of Arsenal's autism were at show here. But yet he was still undiagnosed. Here is an extract from the diagnosis.

- There are a number of factors associated with Autistic Spectrum Disorder (ASD) which predisposes Arsenal to his current depression and distress. Rigid, black-and-white thinking with no compromise, need for routine and structure, perfectionist with high expectations, and Arsenal's theory of mind skills meaning he can't take on alternative viewpoints and be confused by other's motivations and feelings.

The fact that he couldn't give a ticket if he knew it was illegal was 'rigid, black-and-white thinking'. He cannot live with being called a liar, almost to an obsessive level. 'A perfectionist with high expectations' – once he had decided to challenge, he was going to carry this through to its absolute end. Plus, when Mr XXXXX tried to call on favours past, it cut no slack with Arsenal. They were two totally unrelated incidents – all he could deal with was the here and now of being asked to break the law followed by threats.

I do believe that Arsenal's autism enabled him to 'do the right thing', when the majority of us not on the spectrum may well have let it go and almost certainly would not have ended up in a tribunal. One thing I have learned from my time with Arsenal is that people with autism may think differently to many of us, but they are far more straightforward and have a far straighter moral compass. There are many plus points as well as negatives from thinking like someone on the spectrum.

Eventually the *Daily Mirror* did get wind of Arsenal's plight in Bournemouth from May 2006.

WARDENS ISSUED ILLEGAL TICKETS FOR FOUR YEARS

The article said that it was claimed the council had been handing out illegal tickets for four years and when this was pointed out to them they refused to give refunds. That was before Arsenal came along and won his tribunal. Apparently, the chairperson of the tribunal described Arsenal as a *"man of principle"*.

Arsenal is described as a 'man of principle', but at no time does anyone actually hear what Arsenal is saying. He told everyone on numerous occasions that he 'cannot knowingly give a false ticket'. He never said that he chose not to, or his morals wouldn't let him, or even that he 'couldn't turn a blind eye' to such proceedings. What he actually said, was that he 'cannot' issue a false ticket. Once again referring to his yet-to-happen diagnosis:

- There are a number of factors associated with Autistic Spectrum Disorder which may predispose Arsenal to the depression and distress he is currently experiencing. Amongst these is a rigid, black-and-white thinking style which does not allow for compromise, in himself or others.

Simply put, Arsenal would make himself ill or depressed if he 'compromised' his black-and-white thinking of what is right and wrong. Therefore, the constraints of his own thinking process stopped him from issuing an illegal ticket knowingly because it would make him very ill. His own mind was protecting him by refusing to bend on legality and Arsenal's very words indicates this. He never said he wouldn't give an illegal ticket; he said he cannot.

After this setback to his career – not that Arsenal saw it as a setback – he went cleaning cars for three years from 2007 to 2009. He founded a new company called Waterless Car Valeting in Bournemouth; an advanced car valeting service that, as suggested by the name, doesn't use water. The waterless process 'uses Pro-Dry, a plant extract-based product that emulsifies dirt and cocoons it which is then wiped off, leaving your paint work cleaned, sealed, polished and protected. This advanced cleaning system provides a protective glaze and a UV guard against oxidisation, resulting in a long-lasting shine'.

Arsenal always works and every role he takes he has to start at the bottom. He still doesn't have a CV, but at least now since the Starfish Project he can conduct an interview. Nevertheless, he felt at this stage of his life he didn't want to work for anyone else but wanted to work for himself.

> Arsenal: *Waterless was my business. I wanted a business and I just wanted to be on me own, really. I wanted a business on me own so I could do it, everything's a hundred per cent then isn't it. Down to me. The buck stops with me. So, I done that, and it was Waterless because I knew I just wanted to graft and do a hard day's work, but I knew there was loads of valets out there.*
>
> *There's hundreds of them, so I needed a unique selling point, so I went waterless. And I bought a*

yellow Renault Trafic Bus in bright yellow, like a banana. I had all yellow tops, same as the van, and I wore black trousers and shoes, so I was a bit more noticeable. I had it for three years and it was amazing. Some of the cars, oh, wow. Ferraris, Rolls Royces, Porsches, I was right up there, judge's cars and everything. It was amazing.

Alan: *So you finished that business to go to the Co-op?*

Arsenal: *I did me knees. I did that for three years and then had a couple of knee operations and while I was waiting, I did the charity work for Barnardo's and the stroke victims. I wasn't supposed to be working, see.*

Alan: *Did you sell the business afterwards?*

Arsenal: *I sold it off in bits. I sold everything off separately. I didn't sell it as a going concern, I just sold the van, then I sold the Gala tent. I had a Gala tent, it was massive. You'd probably get two Range Rovers in there. What I done was, if it rained, I used to put it up on me drive, that way I never lost business. So, it worked like that.*

Alan: *So did people come to you or did you go to them?*

Arsenal: *Nicola done the one on the driveways, so they used to bring it to the house. Nicola would do the one there. And I used to be mobile. I'd go to their houses… What I used to do, I'd take them into work in my crew bus, treated them like royalty, opened the door for them an everything. So, everyone at work would see how they were getting to work in this big 'banana car'. And I got loads of business out of that and then when the car was ready, I'd ring them up and tell them their car was ready.*

Alan:	And what product did you use to clean the cars without water?
Arsenal:	What I used was from a plant extract and it was called Pro-Dry. It was from a company called Pro-Dry and I used to buy the stuff from them.

So, Arsenal had an entrepreneurial bent that came to the fore as his confidence grew as he mastered his stammer. Plus, as he says, he wanted to work on his own. Then in 2010 he needed a knee operation. As often happens with men of a certain age who have been active most of their lives, Arsenal's cruciate ligaments ruptured in his knee and he required a complete rebuild. As Arsenal has already told us, though, he needs to keep busy or, "I have to be busy or I can go down so quick. I like to be busy." So even though Arsenal could no longer run Waterless, as the operation on his knee left him totally debilitated, he undertook charity work to keep both his body and, more importantly, his mind active.

Arsenal:	I was in Winton in Barnardo's there for a while. I was there for about six months or more. Just because I wasn't allowed to work, see, but I needed to be doing something.
Alan:	And what were you doing?
Arsenal:	I was just on the tills. I was putting everything out. I was just a volunteer there, so I'd go in there, and say we had a load of new stock and stuff and I'd put it out.
Alan:	OK, so it was a high street charity shop?
Arsenal:	Yeah, yeah.
Alan:	And the stroke unit, what did you do at the stroke unit?

Arsenal:	*I went every Wednesday and I… I've got a letter off them in there, actually. And, what I'd do, I'd go in and there was about six tables, yeah, six tables. At my table there were five guys who'd all had strokes. And we all had a table each. And in the first half we listened to someone who come in and gave a speech. Then we'll have a break and then second half, say our table would do activities, or board games and stuff.*
Alan:	*So you were working and helping stroke victims?*
Arsenal:	*Yeah, yeah. To recover.*
Alan:	*And how long did you do that for?*
Arsenal:	*It must have been over a year. I've had two or three operations now on me knee. I think I first did me ligaments in 1992 and then two more operations, so for over a year I helped stroke victims. When I did me fingers in Liverpool, they used to bring me a big load of work at home. Although I wasn't allowed into work, because I was an estimator, they used to bring work to me home and I'd read it and that.*

Apart from when injured and the one year in Liverpool after he was made redundant, Arsenal has in some way or form worked his entire life. In 2011, the year of his diagnosis, he started his final role before he joined Autism Wessex in November 2014. He started a role working for the Co-op bakery in Bournemouth. At this point in his life he was coming to terms with the fact that he now had a name for his 'odd' behaviour of the last forty-nine years and was undergoing treatment with Alderney Hospital. He was also trying to understand why Samantha had tried to kill herself. Pointing the finger firmly and directly straight at Arsenal as to the reason why!

Arsenal: *I worked in the Co-op and we had a delivery day on my day off and I was the baker so I used to get in an hour earlier than the manager so I used to open the door for the manager and he'd go in the office and I'd go in the freezer to get anything out to put in the ovens.*

I went in one day and opened the freezer and we'd had a delivery and we had croissants and on the box was a big arrow saying, 'THIS WAY UP'. And someone had put it the other way round. [Arsenal is regaling this story as though he's telling a joke and talking about someone else, almost as if he can't recognise himself in the story; he laughs as he tells it.]

And I was like, "What the fuck!" And you know what, I was arguing with myself in the freezer. We had a trolley still in there from the delivery. And I was punching this metal trolley. See that knuckle there? [Arsenal shows me the middle knuckle on his right hand.] See it's further down from the others, well, I broke that knuckle. I was punching it and my manager could hear noises. When he opened the freezer, I'm punching the trolley. [Arsenal mimes full-blooded swings with his arm, showing me how hard he was hitting the metal trolley. I can only imagine the damage and pain he must have caused himself.]

And when he seen me, he ran to the office and locked himself in. Because I'd gone. And he thought if I'd got hold of him, I'd kill him as well. [When I first heard this tale, I didn't hear the 'as well' at the end of the sentence. I should have been paying better attention.] And then I had a meeting?

Alan:	And how old was you then?
Arsenal:	This was 2000 and, and, and—
Alan:	Was you in your thirties or forties?
Arsenal:	No, this was in me fifties. This was possibly 2013.
Alan:	So even five years ago, after diagnosis, you could still react this way simply because a box was upside down?
Arsenal:	To me, it tells you on that box. That's why the arrow's there.
Alan:	But what makes you get angry about it? A box is the wrong way up. Is it because you couldn't change it?
Arsenal:	No, it's because I couldn't understand why someone had done it. And that's where a lot of it comes from. So, what happened [again, Arsenal stammers more when he recollects something which he considers 'bad'] was we had a meeting and I thought I was going to get the sack. I really did. But the clinical psychologist was told by him and he went, "Arsenal can't be doing that in work, self-harming, everyone is scared of him."

And Alderney Hospital said, "But Arsenal can't understand them simple things in life. And that's why we're giving him help on CBT [Cognitive Behaviour Therapy] to train his brain to think differently." And I went there every Monday in 2011 and 2012 for CBT. And I went every Wednesday to learn about not to self-harm.

But in the Co-op, the clinical psychologist from Alderney Hospital said to them, "But Arsenal's brain is so simple – it's black or white. If that box has got an arrow, then a hundred per cent that's the way it's got to be. And if you differ from that,

that's where he gets angry. Then that will take him into self-harm."

Alderney Hospital came up with a suggestion. They said, "OK, so what days are there deliveries?"

"Monday, Wednesday and Friday."

"Right, can Arsenal work Monday, Wednesday and Friday and he can put the deliveries away?"

And they said, "Yes."

So that's what happened. "Arsenal will put the deliveries away and it'll all be perfect."

Then I done it and the boss thought it was amazing. He asked, "Can you do all the ordering?"

"Yeah, that'll be good for me." So, I took over all the ordering. So just by adjusting me rota to take over the deliveries—

Alan: *And everyone wins. You win, they win, the storeroom is perfect—*

Arsenal: *Even when I'm at home I can tell you where everything is in that freezer because I put it there. I put it there. Or on days off I could get a phone call saying, "Where are the donuts?"*

And I'll say, "Go in the freezer, go to the right, third shelf down, that's where you'll find them."

And they'd say, "How the fucking hell do you know that?" And that's what it's like.

Alan: *But that outstanding memory contradicts the fact that you can't remember so much of your early life? Perhaps we can explore that at a later date.*

There are several points to make at this juncture. Firstly, even though Arsenal was diagnosed and receiving treatment and conditioning for his status, he could at this point still not control his anger brought on by his autism and specifically his black-

and-white thinking. In fact, his anger, if anything, was escalating and this could be because he now knew that Samantha had tried to kill herself because of his behaviour.

Secondly, how does one cope with finding out so late in life that they could have been helped so many years earlier if only someone had either noticed or bothered and tried to get Arsenal diagnosed at a younger age? Again, did this fuel Arsenal's anger?

Thirdly, there are many skills that people with autism have that when harnessed and utilised properly with recognition of the condition, that people without autism don't have to the same levels. The example of utilising Arsenal to control the stockroom, including all deliveries, ordering and organisation was a success for all concerned and was being managed to a previously unseen level of efficiency.

Finally, Arsenal had been diagnosed, and by his own volition was working as hard as he could to 'improve' himself and to become the father that his daughters had always wanted. He was undergoing treatment weekly, but, as his behaviour at the Co-op shows, was still a long way away from controlling his anger and therefore his self-harm. So, in the next chapter let's look at how autism had impacted Arsenal's adult life.

Chapter Nine

The Impact of Autism

A football team is like a beautiful woman, when you do not tell her, she forgets she is beautiful.

Arsène Wenger

ARSENAL HAS MANY TALES AND STORIES TO TELL, AS DO HIS family, to best illustrate the impact autism has had on his life. Not only to illustrate the impact on Arsenal, but we can also glean some understanding for other people with autism. The story that for me personally has the most shock value or, alternatively, encapsulates how people with autism behave under certain sets of circumstances is to listen to Arsenal and his family explain about Arsenal's behaviour at his own mother's funeral. Behaviour that caused such a rift between siblings that even this week, the last week of February 2019, Arsenal is trying to mend and with some success as he collects information for the very pages you are reading now.

The tale actually starts before the funeral in 2013, post-diagnosis, when the Whittick family had gathered around Pat

Whittick's deathbed to pay their final respects and to say their last goodbyes. All her children were there, many of their partners, her grandchildren and of course her already-grieving husband of over thirty-five years, Tony Whittick. Everyone was taking their turn to hug Pat one last time and have one last conversation with her before she literally died. The room was full of tears and sadness but also love of a woman who had lived her life well and brought her family up to know right from wrong, good from bad; and not always in the easiest of circumstances.

Arsenal took his turn and spoke to his dying mum and she told him the story about cleaning the school walls for him that he'd covered with AFC graffiti. His dad said to him, "Give your mum a hug now, lad."

No move from Arsenal.

"Come on, son, give your mum a hug. There's others waiting." Still no move from Arsenal. He couldn't do it. He got brushed to one side before the situation became too difficult and someone else took his place at the top of the bed. He still could not hug someone; not even if it was his own mother with not long to live. This is the part of the diagnosis that people without autism simply cannot understand. What condition causes a man to not hug his dying mother?

When asked, the best explanation Arsenal can give is that it's like someone shoving a knife into his body. As he prepares to walk forwards to give someone a hug, he feels as though if he takes that stride forward, he will impale himself on a large knife. We will hear more about this difficulty with social interaction later when we hear about 'hug day' and the first time in his life that Arsenal manages to hug his own daughters.

> Alan: *This is a personal question, Arsenal, but here goes, how have you got kids if you can't even hug someone?*

Arsenal: *You know what, people have asked me that before.*
But you see, in my head, for some reason, I always
thought I could only hug the girl I was with and
no one else. So, when I had to hug everyone before
that in me brain, I was doing wrong.

And when me mum, I went to see me mum
in hospital, and the nurses would say, "She's going
to go today. She'll go today." So, we're all round
the bed and that, and then we had to leave, so
everyone went up to me mum and she's sitting up
in the bed and gave her a hug. [Arsenal smiles to
himself almost ashamedly and his voice lowers.]

Me dad said to me, "Come on, hug your mum."
And I said, "No. I can't."
And he went, "GO and hug your mum."
And I couldn't do it. Because to me, I could
only hug Nicola. And I couldn't hug me mum.

These are not happy memories for Arsenal. He is starting to understand that not everyone thinks like he does and therefore he needs strategies to cope with certain situations, but there is a forlornness to his words when he talks about his mum. His mum, who openly exclaimed that she had more time for Arsenal growing up as he needed her time more than the others did, which was then interpreted as him being the 'favourite' by other family members. Arsenal still does not fully understand but acknowledges that today he thinks he would be able to hug his mum when he couldn't then.

Days later at the funeral, Arsenal's behaviour is not what you would expect from a grieving son at his mother's burial and wake. Unfortunately for Arsenal and all his family, AFC had a Champion's League game that night. On the 6th November 2013, the day of Pat Whittick's funeral and wake, Arsenal Football

Club were playing an away leg at Borussia Dortmund in a Group F game of the Champion's League, 7.45pm kick-off.

Even though Arsenal had been diagnosed at this time and was twelve to eighteen months into his treatment, he was still utterly and completely obsessed with Arsenal Football Club, AFC. On match days, all Arsenal did all day was think about the coming game. His levels of excitement meant he could hardly work, and an evening match was the worst as he had all day to think about the game. He knew the players' routines, where they would be and what they would be doing at any part of the day.

He even knew the names and addresses of the match officials and where they would be travelling from and what their schedule for the day would be. He had nothing in his head apart from the potential line-up that AFC would have that night; who may or may not play well. He would read and listen to anything about the game pre-match, invariably with an earpiece tucked away, plugged into a radio of some sort. This wasn't just listening to the game; this was an all-day ritual. He could hardly speak with anticipation and excitement. Now put this person with autism at his mother's funeral – to quote Pat Whittick herself, "He wasn't obsessed with football – he was addicted to it."

Danielle, Arsenal's youngest daughter, was at the funeral. She was aged twelve.

> Danielle: I remember a few things from the day. Everyone was getting ready for the funeral, I think. It was something to do with my nan, so I think it was the funeral. Everyone was getting ready, me, my dad, my sister, and all my dad's brothers and sisters. Pretty much all my Liverpool family. And I remember as everyone was getting ready, all the guys came in and gave my dad what he was supposed to wear.

And I remember it being a black suit and a light pink tie. Like the cancer colour, pink. As a tie. And I remember my dad at the time, he didn't kick off, but he made a fuss about it, saying he didn't want to wear that colour. And I remember it creating a bit of a, not an argument, but a bit of heat on the day because everyone was following what the rules of the day were with what to wear and what my nan wanted everyone to wear. But because my dad couldn't get his head around it and didn't want to, he didn't... It made everyone feel like... I don't know, angry, I suppose, at the fact. If I remember, my dad ended up doing it anyway and that was fine.

I also remember on the day, we were saying goodbye to my nan, I remember everyone in the room was crying, a few people got up to put flowers on the coffin. Obviously, they took their time, walked slowly and it was really emotional. But then, when it was dad's turn, he literally stood up, went straight over, put it down, and went to go and sit back down. Kind of like as if it wasn't anything. It took seconds and it looked like as if he was getting up, putting a book down and going into another room.

Everyone wasn't too focussed on it because they were thinking about my nan, but people were a bit like feeling he wasn't bothered. But obviously, he was he's just not very good at expressing empathy and his emotions. Back then. It's definitely there now.

Alan: *He's told me that AFC were playing that day?*

Danielle: *Yeah. I remember everyone being focussed on my nan for the whole night but my dad kind of just...*

> *All he had on his mind that day was the football. I remember I think we went to a pub after, for a few drinks, and I remember my dad just there, trying to watch anything about the football. Everyone was obviously having a bit of a downer but, my dad was just stood there watching the football. Like just completely focussed on that. It upset everyone.*

Danielle is very protective of her dad, and rightly so. She shows a great deal of empathy with him as she has had mental health issues of her own to cope with and tells the stories accordingly. She has a soothing, measured voice and what she signals is her unconditional strong love for her father and what he means to her. She recognises his autism and the strength and sheer hard work Arsenal has had to harness to get to where he is today.

Arsenal has his own recollections of his mum's wake.

Arsenal: *Did I tell you about me mum's funeral? When me mum died in 2013, when she was buried, AFC had a big match that day. And when AFC scored, I ran into the wake shouting, "Yeah, fucking hell, we've scored." [Arsenal clenches his fists, raising them to the sides of his head and makes the age-old signal that sportsmen and sportswomen use across the world to signal their pleasure at scoring or winning.] Since then no one has spoke to me, really. But since I did the hug video, one of me brothers has been in touch.*

Alan: *When you ran into the wake, had you been diagnosed at that point?*

Arsenal: *Yeah, two years earlier.*

Alan: *So your family knew you were a person with autism?*

> *Arsenal:*   *Yeah, but I was just hyper that day. Because of the football.*

Today there is undoubted recognition that how he behaved isn't socially acceptable by any normal standards, but Arsenal has only watched AFC in a live game either on TV or in person, once in five years. He has weaned himself off the drug of AFC just like any other addict has to do in order to get well.

Arsenal also has real identity issues. We found out that early in his life, age fourteen, he was told at a party that the man who had raised him and, more importantly to Arsenal, the only father figure he had any memory of, was not his real father. Add to that the impact of autism and his inability to communicate, and he was always trying to find who he was in life. This peaked when he injured his hand, saw his birth certificate for the first time and legally changed his name to Arsenal Whittick. As I write this on the 6th March 2019, Arsenal will not tell me the name he was christened with; Flynn is all I know.

His dad, Tony Whittick, sends him Christmas cards with Arsenal's birth name on them and Arsenal blacks them out so no one can see the written word. Also, on the recent emails received from Tony Whittick, his dad jokingly refers to the book as *The Life and Times of XXXXX Whittick*, but Arsenal has again blacked the first name out so I can't read it. Only his family in Liverpool and perhaps Nicola – I haven't asked and won't ask – know the name he was given at birth. If Arsenal tells me and allows me to use it I will, otherwise it won't be in this book. I won't betray his confidence. If Arsenal chooses to tell me and use the name in the book, then so be it; it may even be cathartic for him. But if he doesn't, then you'll have to ask him yourself.

Alan: I know you have expressed the opinion that you don't want to tell me your birthname, which I obviously respect, but can you tell me why you don't want to tell me?

Arsenal: You know what, this might sound really stupid, but it's the only answer I've got.

Alan: Whatever you say is fine, Arsenal. This is your book and your answer can't be stupid. [Arsenal considers his next words for a long time.]

Arsenal: I relate, I don't know, it's negatives and everything. That was like a really bad part of me life back then.

Alan: Which is probably why you shut it out and don't remember much about it.

Arsenal: Yeah. That was a really bad part of me life, getting things done and stuff. I don't know, I look at my deed poll that I've got in there when I changed it. Even when I see it written down, I can just feel that anger in me, for some reason.

Alan: In that case, I don't need to know.

Arsenal: No, but that could... Over time, yeah. For some reason I just get real anger inside me.

Alan: I guess from what you're saying is you started to recognise a person that you felt was your real self and real personality when you became Arsenal?

Arsenal: Before Arsenal I have no memories at all. Apart from pulling onto the coach. And that's the only memory I can really have as a kid. [I notice for the first time Arsenal's choice of words here; he says it's the only memory he CAN have, not the only memory he has.]

Alan: And yet all you associate with your previous name is anger and badness. So, there must be something

	there? Some memory must be causing the anger?
Arsenal:	*There's a memory there, but my daughter's in the next room so I can't tell you. I'll tell you Monday. Danielle's in there. No one else knows about it apart from Alderney Hospital.*
Alan:	*Let's take it one step at a time. I'm just writing your book. I don't want to take you to a place that you don't want to go.*
Arsenal:	*No, I'll tell you. Maybe that [telling me] would release that anger. It's in there because I can feel it. As soon as I see my birth certificate, wow. Anger.*
Alan:	*When you had your one and only fight as a child, did you feel that anger? Have you ever felt anger since when you felt you could do some damage, either to yourself or someone else?*
Arsenal:	*No, because I've never had a fight, ever ever again.*
Alan:	*You are a very placid person.*
Arsenal:	*I am now. Now I've had treatment for me anger.*

There is something in Arsenal's past that is stopping him from acknowledging his original name, but for now he's not ready to share.

For as long as Arsenal can remember he has self-harmed. But until the age of forty-nine when he was diagnosed, he never personally acknowledged his behaviour as self-harming. To him, self-harming was someone cutting themselves or trying to kill themselves, perhaps suicide tendencies; but I don't think even then he would have classed this behaviour as self-harming. He never thought of himself as a self-harmer.

Now when I ask him how often he self-harmed, he recognises the fact that he harmed virtually every single day of his life. Something would trigger his anger, such as the box in the storeroom placed upside down on the shelf, and away he would go, punching away merrily until he either did enough damage to stop or physically 'punched himself out' to exhaustion.

For years and years, he hid this away from everyone, even his closest family. To hide away his actions meant he knew it wasn't right, whether he attributed the label of self-harm to it or not. In the years leading up to Samantha's suicide attempt, he got worse and worse, and became unable to control himself, either out in public or in the privacy of his own home. He was a man with autism, but no one knew.

Whatever was nearest to him he would hit himself with no fear of pain or damage. He had many triggers – that we can go through in detail – but until he started to get treatment, he had no way to deal with these triggers. It could be something as simple as a box upside down or the sudden barking of a dog. It would all lead to the same outcome: Arsenal would beat himself around the head or punch the wall until he blacked out with pain or exhaustion. Can you even imagine for a second how difficult it is to do anything until you are too exhausted to raise your own head? Now apply that thought to punching yourself in the face.

Alan: *So you hit yourself with your fists?*

Arsenal: *I used to use anything, mate! Whatever was the nearest thing to me. [Arsenal mimes holding something in his hand and hitting himself in the face.]*

Alan: *Goodness, you must have done some damage to yourself over the years?*

Arsenal: *Yeah. I had to go for this test to test me to see if I'd damaged me brain. It's in the report. They done this test on me. Just like… It wasn't like any wires on me brain or 'owt like that… They were asking me all this stuff, and I gather from the replies I*

	gave there was no damage there. But I've got like bruises up here still [Arsenal indicates an area of his head above both temples] and there's one here that's just permanent [forehead].
Alan:	*But if you hit yourself with an iron you will cause permanent damage. Let's be honest.*
Arsenal:	*Yeah. [We both laugh. One thing you can say about Arsenal is he has a great sense of humour.]*
Alan:	*When is the last time you self-harmed?*
Arsenal:	*Tuesday 19th August 2014. [This is a date literally imprinted on Arsenal's mind.] Over four years. In 2011 when I was diagnosed, I was self-harming every day. I used to get angry…*
Alan:	*You must be very proud of yourself?*
Arsenal:	*Not really, no. But when I was under the hospital, I had to keep a diary for a year. And every time I harmed I writ in it. Like the time, the date, and what I was doing, what I done. What they could do, when they looked at it, they could see all me triggers, every single trigger. When I had a meeting, they could tell me what all me triggers were.*

Before this diary, before any treatment, before working out coping mechanisms, Arsenal did not see any pattern or trends to what made him angry and then self-harm. He believed it to be the norm.

"I thought that's what everyone did." Yet at some subconscious level he tried, and managed, to keep it hidden from his family for years, or at least he thought he did. When we speak to his daughters and ex-wife, it wasn't as well hidden as Arsenal would have liked to have thought. Even so, there must have been some part of Arsenal's thinking that knew it was wrong, or at least not the norm, for him to try and keep the behaviour hidden away.

Alan: So, I'm going to go back to self-harming, at what age did you actually start self-harming?

Arsenal: To me I can always remember harming. It's just that I didn't identify it as harming. I just thought, *That was life.*

Alan: So, even as a child?

Arsenal: Yeah, I might headbutt a wall. Or I might punch a wall, or I might give meself a slap. And then it just seemed to be getting worse and worse. I used to do it... I used to go downstairs into the Arsenal room.

And then I'd be listening to the football and that's where I used to do most—

Alan: The Arsenal room?

Arsenal: Yeah, where I used to live, when I was married, I lived in a townhouse so, downstairs was a utility room, but it was really big. So, I had all my memorabilia in there. I used to listen to the football there and that's where I'd give meself a hiding. But over the years it's actually moved on to me doing it out in the public. If something happens to me, I just do it. [Clicks his fingers.] I've just gone. I could go, just like that. [Clicks.]

I'd give meself a smack in front of everyone and they'd go, "Whoaaa!"

Alan: Yes, I can imagine it's quite frightening when someone starts hitting themselves. I've never witnessed it—

Arsenal: My neighbour used to say to me the next day, "How's your weekend been, Arsenal?"

And I'd go, "Yeah, it's been all right. Until..."

And I'd go to tell her the score and she'd say, "I know, Arsenal. I could hear the thuds of you hitting yourself."

"Can you, Karen?"

"Yeah, I can hear you." [No stutter from Arsenal here, merely a deep sadness in his voice.] And she said, "In the beginning, me and Simon used to think it was, not funny, but we could hear you, throwing things against the wall and getting angry. 'Arsenal's off again.' But then when we started to hear the thuds of you hitting yourself, it's horrible."

And I was, wow, I never knew nothing. I thought no one could hear me, I just didn't know.

There were times, I think in the Champions League, we were playing Bayern Munich, and they scored just on the stroke of half-time. I give meself a hiding, blood up the wall and everything. I caught meself on the nose and it just went 'splurgh'. I never knew, I'd cut meself. And I went in the kitchen to make meself a cup of tea and the kitchen was like an L-shape, and I went in, put the kettle on in the corner.

And in this corner [points to the diagonally opposite point of the room] is Samantha, Nicola and the dog. They were huddled together. I never noticed their expressions, but the dog was shaking like a leaf. He was shaking and Nicola and Samantha were just looking at me. Staring at me. To me, as if I'd done something wrong? To me, I hadn't because I thought that was the norm.

I was making a cup of tea and when I was stirring it Samantha said to me, "Dad, are you OK?"

"Yeah, I'm OK."

And she said, "Are you sure?"

And I said, "Yeah, yeah. We'll get a goal back in the second half." [Arsenal laughs to himself wryly.]

"Sorry, Dad, but are you really sure you're OK?" And as I'm stirring the tea she says, "You're dripping blood into your tea." And it was from me nose. And I wasn't aware of it as I'm making the tea and I looked round and there was a trail of blood and I thought, Wow.

Alan: Did you ever frighten yourself?

Arsenal: No, no.

Alan: Never thought, I'm going to do some real damage here?

Arsenal: No, because I've never, hand on heart, knew I was going to do it. I don't think, AFC are playing today so I'm going to hurt meself, because in my head AFC are going to win, aren't they?

Alan: When you were covered in blood and still bleeding, did you not then think, Fucking hell, I can do some real damage here?

Arsenal: No, because the second half is about to kick off. Let's get back in there. And that's what I was like.

I remember when Man United beat us 8-2. The kids had two pink hand-made leather chairs. They were only about that big. Little chairs they could sit in and they'd had them for years. I remember that day I just picked them up... I must have threw it down just on the corner and it must have broken the wood across the front. And every time United scored, those two chairs got it.

And I was hitting meself and I remember when the seventh goal went in I remember being on the floor and I just never had any energy left to

> *do any more damage or hit meself. Physically just*
> *drained, I think.*
>
> Alan: *That doesn't feel that long ago. [It was the 28th*
> *August 2011 – nine months after Samantha tried*
> *to take her own life and at the start of Arsenal's*
> *treatment. I would think this was just about at his*
> *lowest point.]*
>
> Arsenal: *No, I just remember that being a very bad day. I*
> *had beaten meself to a pulp.*

It is incredibly difficult for anyone who hasn't lived Arsenal's life to be able to empathise with this level of self-harm or, indeed, this level of anger. We all get angry from time to time, but our minds allow us, on the most part, to control our actions. We sometimes may shout and, as we know only too well from reading and watching the news every day, it's a violent society that we live in. Even allowing for the everyday violence in society, the violence that comes from Arsenal, is, for the major part, directed at himself. If not himself then an inanimate object, such as a wall, door, chair or metal storeroom trolley!

The next point to consider is the sheer horror Arsenal's wife Nicola and two daughters, Sam and Danni, had to live through on a daily basis. The outcome, ultimately, was divorce for Arsenal and Nicola, and both the girls have, and are still dealing with, mental health issues of their own. If Arsenal had been born in the '90s or 2000s instead of the '60s, his condition would have been recognised much earlier in his life and much of the impact of autism could have been controlled and, to a certain extent, mitigated. At least we know in this story we have a happy ending.

Another impact on Arsenal of being a person with autism is his obsessive behaviour. His addiction, as we know only too well, is AFC and that will merit its own chapter, but he has others, less intrusive and damaging ones, that we can discuss. For example, Mr Gary Numan.

Gary Anthony James Webb was born on the 8th March 1958. He became better known as Gary Numan, initially the lead singer of Tubeway Army before striking out on his own in 1979 with the album The Pleasure Principle.

His music was classified as *"electronic"* in the early 80's and he also created a name for himself by developing different characters and looks for himself with every new album he released. He won an Ivor Novello award in 2017 from The British Academy of Songwriters, Composers and Authors.

Arsenal is drawn to outsiders. He likes people, characters, roles in movies that stand out as outsiders and that he can himself identify with. Something a little bit different or out of the norm. Exactly the situation Arsenal experienced growing up. He never had a 'best friend'. He was always on the edge of social groups at school and even on the edge of his family. His brothers and 'dad' maybe resenting his 'favourite' tag with his mother. Not exceedingly so, but enough for Arsenal to always feel on the outside. If there was an inner sanctum somewhere, Arsenal would be on the outside of it. He had a sense of belonging with his fellow AFC supporters, but because he lived in Liverpool this was an experience he only ever felt when going to the matches. Sometimes not even then, as he would often be stood with the opposition spectators.

Gary Numan and the fans of Gary Numan were different. In the late '70s, Numan began developing his style. According to Numan, this was an unintentional result of having bad acne. Before an appearance on *Top of the Pops*, he had, 'Spots everywhere, so they slapped about half an inch of white make-up on me before I'd even walked in the door. And my eyes were like piss holes in the snow, so they put black on there. My so-called image fell into place an hour before going on the show'.

His 'wooden' stage presence was, in his words, a result of extreme self-consciousness and lack of 'showmanship' and often referred to as being 'like an android'. During this period, Numan generated an army of fans calling themselves 'Numanoids' – not a word or description I have ever heard Arsenal use – that provided him with a fanbase which maintained their support through the latter half of the '80s, when his popularity started to wane.

Numan later said that he 'got really hung up with this whole thing of not feeling, being cold about everything, not letting emotions get to you, or presenting a front of not feeling'.

There is an obvious link to Arsenal and how he behaves. The coldness, the black-and-white thinking, being the outsider, the dressing up and being someone else; all of these characteristics attracted Arsenal and appealed to his own nature. Add to that, he also loved the strangeness and odd style of the music. Arsenal adored Gary Numan but, 'couldn't get into Bowie', another candidate for outsider and alien, rather than 'android' or 'Numanoid'.

Arsenal:	*I was always getting into trouble back then. Just for different things. Football or Gary Numan and that. Me dad mentions me Gary Numan days and that [Arsenal has commenced swapping emails with Tony Whittick about his time in Liverpool for inclusion in the book], because I used to dress up, so whatever image Gary Numan had, I would dress up. So, back in 1979, '80, '81, so from '79–'84, all his images were make-up images.*
Alan:	*Everybody did in the early '80s. Spandau Ballet, Human League—*
Arsenal:	*Yeah, so I used to wear the make-up, didn't I? Every time I went to town, I used to get a hiding,*

or I'd get chased, or, yeah. Once a month I used to go to a club, and downstairs it was just a normal nightclub, but upstairs was called 'Scene 2'. So that was Ultravox, Gary Numan, Human League, Soft Cell, all them bands who used to wear make-up and that. So, we all used to go and afterwards there'd be a gang waiting for us, just because we were different.

Alan: Did you wear the 'New Romantic' outfits, double-breasted shirts, big trousers…?

Arsenal: No, not really. I was just into Numan. I used to have him on me wall and I used to copy the images. 1983 it was, the 'Warriors' tour. He's all in black, harness on, baseball bat and knuckle dusters. And I used to go into the pub [dressed as described] and I remember the manager going, "Arsenal, can you take those knuckle dusters off, mate?"

"No, no, it's part of the image."

"Take them off or I can't serve you."

"All right then." But I'd sneak them back on. That's the way it was back then. It was just mad, just mad. There would be days when I'd go to the toilet, in that '83 image and someone would go to me, "Do you think your hard with that baseball bat?"

And I'd go back, "No, mate. It's just an image of Gary Numan." [Let's remember how difficult it was for Arsenal to get his words out at this age. Also adding to the stress and danger of the situation.]

And they'd go, "What?" And there'd be an argument or something.

But then I could wear the image of '84 and that would be blue hair, white face, blue make-up and that. And then people would go, "You gay bastard."

And I'd say, "Two months ago, I was hard and now I'm gay?"

"Are you the same fella?"

"Yeah!"

"Fucking hell. You weirdo!" [Arsenal finds this very funny and laughs out loud as he remembers his Gary Numan days.] I was always getting into trouble back then but just because it's different. That's all I put it down to.

Alan: *I think you're absolutely right.*

Arsenal: *I went the Royal Albert Hall last Monday to see him. First time I've ever been there. First time he's ever played there.*

Alan: *What did you think of the place, disregarding the concert?*

Arsenal: *It was all right. I looked on the internet at all the different surroundings of it and all the inside and all the halls and the different levels. I seen all these on the internet. We got there as soon as the doors opened. We were in the disabled section, so you had more room. You're allowed to take a carer with you, so it was all right. I had loads of information before it, got there early.*

We were high up but on row one so it was really good, and we could see. I really enjoyed it, actually. I'd done all me homework so that was good.

He done all the new album and he did maybe four, maybe five old ones. He was famous for 'Cars' and 'Our Friends Electric', but he only did 'Our Friends Electric'. He didn't do 'Cars'. But he told everyone that. 'Cars', the music he's doing today, you can't really change 'Cars', do you know what I mean? It's not like the music he's doing today.

He's changed a lot; he has a proper band and that.

A person with autism will get fixated on one artist or one type of music, just like Arsenal has with Gary Numan. He has every single song he's ever released on vinyl, special edition vinyl with coloured discs, CDs, and he's been to see him well over twenty times and has all the ticket stubs framed and in a picture. He has met him and had dinner with him. He dressed as him and still to this day follows everything he does. He even followed his exploits as a pilot and the display team that Gary Numan used to perform in. But Arsenal doesn't have any other recordings of other artists apart from Hayley Westerna. He simply isn't bothered about any other artists. He is obsessed with Gary Numan. And autism impacts his life once again.

Arsenal likes to be on time. Not only does he like to be on time, he would like you to be on time too. Not only that, but he would like every single solitary person in the whole world to be on time. Not once, ALWAYS. He couldn't work for British Rail! Being late is not an option. Even taking longer to undertake a previously timed task is not acceptable. It takes Arsenal twenty-two minutes to have a shave. If it took him longer, he would ponder this fact for hours, or as he puts it, "Arguing with meself until I'd lose my temper and give meself a hiding." Thankfully he no longer resorts to self-violence, but it still irritates him. I found myself stuck in traffic on one journey to Arsenal's flat, panicking that he wouldn't let me in when I got there. Eventually the traffic eased up and I sped there and ran from the car, making it with seconds to spare. A week later, making the reverse journey, Arsenal also hit the same traffic issue, but he had left himself much longer to get to my house. He wasn't late that time. He arrives, or used to arrive, for football matches several hours before kick-off to ensure he covered all possibilities. He was late once by ten minutes but as we've heard, that was because he sneaked out of his brother's wedding.

Alan: *I was running five minutes late today because the dual carriageway is blocked, someone had broken down and I was sat in bumper-to-bumper traffic. I was coming towards Hurn and I was thinking, Oh, shit! Arsenal's going to go ballistic when I turn up late.*

Arsenal: *You see, that's the improvement I've made. In the past, lateness would be a trigger. I used to take the kids to school, and I like to get everywhere ten minutes early. So, we'd leave at 8.20am. Then, I'd be downstairs by the door, and the girls would be upstairs, on the third level. And I'd be going [mimics looking at his watch on his arm], "Oh, shit." And I could feel meself ready to explode. And I'd go to the girls, "It's 8.20."*

And they'd go, "Dad, we're not ready yet." And bang, I've gone. I'm kicking the door; I'm screaming at them. I'm calling them bad names and everything. And then that causes them to not want to come down because they're that scared. And then they can hear me hitting meself and everything.

And then Samantha was trying to say to me, "But we're only going to be another minute, we've

	got another nine." Because I get there ten minutes early but, in my head… It'd gone over that time and I'd flip. I'd flip, ohh.
Alan:	*So, I was thinking, in the car this morning. Right, now what I'll say to Arsenal is I'll be there between 9.45am and 10.15am.*
Arsenal:	*That's one of me strategies [more to follow]. I had to time everything. When I iron stuff, takes me four minutes an item. And in the past, I might iron something, and then I might just… Imagine how, say I had five items. I'd go, I've got twenty minutes of ironing. And then I'll iron, and I've taken half an hour. And I go, "So, why has that taken me half an hour?" And then I start getting a bit angry in my head and I take the iron and I give meself a smack with the iron. I'm just mad, mate.*
Alan:	*[Aghast] So you hit yourself with the iron?*
Arsenal:	*I used to use anything, mate, whatever was the nearest thing to me.*

Can anyone who hasn't experienced working with someone with autism imagine smashing themselves on the head with a hot iron because they've taken ten minutes longer than they thought they would? It is beyond most of us to empathise with this, but the more I speak with Arsenal, the better attuned I'm becoming to the rules in his world. He talks of all the normal aspects of life that he applies time limits against. I suppose we all work to tight timelines and deadlines imposed on us by work, pleasure activities and the fast pace of modern life. We just don't literally beat ourselves up if we're slightly late.

Arsenal:	*I used to scream at the kids all the time. Or if Nicola said to me, "Tea's at six o'clock."*

I'd go, "OK." At a minute past six, I'd go in the kitchen and I'd go, "Where's tea?"

And she'd go, "Oh, just doing it now."

"But you said six o'clock?"

And she'd go, "Fucking hell, Arsenal, it's only a minute past." Phew, I've gone. By then I've gone. Because it had gone past six o'clock. So—

Alan: And that would kick you off?

Arsenal: Yeah.

Alan: You would self-harm because of that?

Arsenal: Yeah. There'd be an argument and then the tea's ruined then because I've ruined it. Because, no one's going to sit at the table with me because I'm so angry. I'm harming meself at the table going [using an affected whispering voice], "Where's me fucking tea?"

Alan: Anything else you time?

Arsenal: When I come home from work, before I do everything, I've got to get out of me uniform. And that might take at least nine minutes. So, for them nine minutes it doesn't matter if Danielle is shouting, "Help, help."

I'll go, "I'm just getting changed." Because that's the structure.

Alan: And you're still doing that today?

Arsenal: Yeah, yeah. But Danielle... I'm getting better at stuff. I'm definitely getting better. But that's the CBT, they tell me because I always think if I, if I move away from that I'm doing wrong. And that's where the arguments start because I think I'm doing something wrong. I'm not actually doing nothing wrong and that's what I'm learning and that. Even a shave takes twenty-two minutes.

Alan: But what you are describing and the structure that you have to your life, we all have that structure. The alarm goes off at 6.30am. I immediately know I have to get into the bathroom for a shave and shower. Then I dress and go downstairs, and I know then that it will be about five to seven. I put the kettle on, I get my sandwiches and put them in my bag ready for leaving. I will have already packed the rest of my bag the night before. And I'll sit down with my cereal at about five past seven. That'll give me fifteen minutes to eat breakfast and drink a cup of coffee. At twenty past seven I'll put everything away, get my shoes on, get my stuff, sit in the car and invariably it's bang on 7.30am. We all have our time constraints and routines.

It's just that when I miss the timings, it doesn't bother me that much. Because I have to be in work for 9am but like to be there at 8am. So, five minutes doesn't really matter. Which is exactly what you do! Except, you give yourself those leeways and still get upset with yourself when you don't hit them. In fact, if you don't hit them, you hit yourself.

Arsenal: It's like when I get into work on lates, I get in early. So, I go in our office, I go through the office into the staff room. Put me stuff away. And then I go and then I go in the office and I tidy up all the manager's desk. And they say to me, "What you doing?"

"Tidying up." And everything's got to be tidy before I start. And that's what I do. And then no one talks to me until I've done me little routine. I'm in a different, like a different zone. If I'm in the office and I'm on the computer having a look at me emails, people can be saying to me, "Arsenal!

AFC are shit and Chelsea are the best team in London." And you know what, I don't even hear it. And they give me abuse and everything and then when I come off everyone's looking and laughing at me. "It's great when you just zone out, Arsenal."

"Why?"

And they say, "We'll tell you one day." And then they tell me they've been calling me such bad names and for some reason I just zone out. But you know, it's me little routine. And then as soon as me routine's done, I go, "Right, who have I got today?" [Arsenal is asking which of the service users in the residential home he is working with one to one.] And then I look after them for the day and I'm so happy. And when there's only one user in the house, on a Sunday sometimes, so I know I'm going to have them. I say to the manager, "Can you do that allocation sheet?"

And she'll go, "But there's only you twos in?"

"But can you do it?"

So, she'll say, "You're working with XXXXX today, Arsenal."

And I can move on then.

There are two illustrations of the impact of autism here. The one we are referring to is Arsenal's hang-up with time and timings, but also the routines he gets himself into. Even though he knows there is only him as a carer and one user in the building, therefore he must be working with that person, he cannot start work with them until the 'allocation sheet' has been completed by the manager and he has officially been told who he's paired with. We know it doesn't make sense to wait but to Arsenal he 'can't' move on.

There is that word again that Arsenal has used all of his life, not won't or shouldn't or isn't willing to do something; Arsenal CANNOT move on until he's been told.

One of the therapies that Arsenal refers to is 'his CBT', cognitive behaviour therapy, that he started using not long after his diagnosis.

CBT is a treatment used for many modern-day mental health issues such as, eating disorders, post-traumatic stress disorders, *(PTSD)*, borderline personality disorder, obsessive compulsive disorder, *(OCD)*, panic disorder, substance abuse, chronic fatigue syndrome and chronic pain, sleep problems, anxiety and depression and of course autism.

Behavioural Therapy has been in existence as a therapy since the 1900's and works on the simple principle that behaviours can be measured and changed. Outside influences or 'stimuli' are identified and subsequent reactions to these are tracked and changed. It became popular post World War II for treating returning combat victims.

In the 1950's an American psychologist, Albert Ellis, based a new treatment on the concept that it was the thoughts of something that had happened to a patient that was causing emotional distress rather than the actual occurrence of the incident itself. Others took this thinking so these unrealistic concerns could be identified by patients and then once recognised could be challenged to achieve long term improvements. This was considered the first steps in Cognitive Therapy.

In the 1960's the two approaches were brought together and CBT was born. CBT attempts to identify all the negative thoughts and ideas that lead to mental health issues and helps the individual to create *"coping mechanisms"*, an expression that Arsenal continually uses, to address them. In fact, Arsenal says he has *"strategies for everything"*.

We will devote a chapter to what changes Arsenal made in his life and how CBT helped him to become a better person and to improve his own life and that of his family. Arsenal uses the terms used in the medical definitions above and regularly talks of his coping mechanisms and strategies to deal with the triggers that cause him to self-harm, to deal with the sometimes-crippling, both for him and those closest to him, limits he puts on his life with timings and routines, social difficulties and ultimately driving his daughter to attempt suicide. CBT may sound complicated, but it isn't.

An example below simplifies what CBT is trying to achieve. The diagram depicts how feelings, thoughts, and behaviours all influence each other. The triangle in the middle represents CBT's tenet that all humans' core beliefs can be summed up in three categories: self, others, future.

There are thousands of published papers on the topic, but we will continue to focus on Arsenal Whittick and the impact of autism on his life and then look at how CBT personally helped him and changed his life forever. A final quote from Arsenal on CBT and his treatment: "Alderney Hospital taught me EVERYTHING I know."

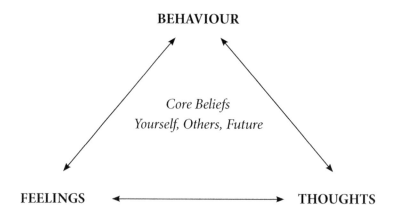

Another impact is that of Arsenal taking everything that anyone says to him absolutely literally. For example, when in an argument with one of his brothers when discussing football, he was told 'to go and eat some humble pie'. Arsenal spent the next thirty minutes in the fridge and kitchen cupboards looking for the 'bloody pie'.

As we already know when called a parasite, he responded with the fact he's a 'Scouser'. His current partner has told him to always make the bed when he gets up in the morning. The next morning after arising, he starts to make up the bed – his partner is still in there asleep. Argument commences!

"But you told me to make up the bed when I get up!" These are amusing little anecdotes, but Arsenal has taken these requests to extremes and holds with them for years (not just on one or two occasions), which have affected how he led his life. Now his CBT training kicks in and the literalism doesn't happen as much as it used to but, as with the bed incident, it still happens.

In 2014, he was in the pub one weekend with his eldest daughter, Samantha, and some of her friends who had come down from the Midlands to visit and watch a game of football. Arsenal didn't go to the live game but stayed in the pub and watched on the pub television.

Arsenal:	*I don't drink any more. I haven't drunk since Tuesday 28th October 2014. I can still go into pubs and everything.*
Alan:	*It's coming up to your anniversary, mate. I've not drank since ten o'clock last night. We can all remember our last drink.*
Arsenal:	*[Laughing] Yeah, I was in a pub with me daughter. Her friends had come down, they were supporting West Brom and they were playing Bournemouth. So, they went the match and we*

stayed in the pub. And at the end of the evening I went to me daughter [Samantha], "Are you having a drink?"

And she said, "Yeah. I'll have a Coke, Dad."

And I went, "No, come on, have a proper drink."

And she went, "No, I just want a Coke."

Then, there was nearly an argument. I was going, "Come on. Have a proper drink with your dad."

"No thanks, Dad. I'll just have a Coke."

I'm pushing and pushing and pushing and she said, "Dad, I need to talk to you. Sit down." So, I sat down, and she said, "So, why do you drink, Dad, if you can't taste it? Because, you've had a Guinness, you've had a bitter, you've had a lager tonight. So, why do you drink if you can't taste it?" Because I can't taste stuff.

And I thought, when I was eighteen, that was the first time, I had a drink. And me dad took me out for a drink, and he went, "This is what you can do now, all the time. And you can drink every weekend, you can have a drink." And I took it literally, didn't I? And that's why I started drinking. And I couldn't actually answer [Samantha], I said, "Me dad told me I could have a drink every weekend."

And she said, "But, why do YOU drink?"

And I said, "Because me dad said I could."

"But you can't tell the difference between the bitter, the Guinness and the lager, can you?"

And I said, "No."

"So, why do you drink it?"

> *And I just stopped like that [Arsenal clicks his fingers]. But Nicola [ex-wife], will say to me to this day, "Why don't you have a pint no more?"*
>
> *And I'll say, "No, it's all right, I'll just have water."*
>
> *"I think you're taking it too far the other way now. When your dad said you could drink you did, now you're not drinking? You can drink. You used to love a little drink and stuff like that."*
>
> *"No, I'll just have me water."*
>
> *So, who knows? I don't miss it or anything.*

Alan: *So what happens if someone says to you, "Arsenal, you can have a drink, a pint, whenever you want? It's up to you. You don't have to 'not have' it, you don't 'have' to have it, it's your choice? You can have it, when you want." Is that something you can do?*

Arsenal: *I just like me water now. That's the way it is. Who knows? At the moment that's what I do.*

Black or white, yes or no, even today after all his CBT work, sometimes Arsenal cannot budge from this way of thinking. I pushed him a little here about trying to go halfway – grey, if you like – and he changed the subject and started talking about something else. The topic, for now, was closed! The point is that an off-the-cuff remark from Tony Whittick, albeit a very important figure in Arsenal's life, some thirty-plus years ago, had caused Arsenal to behave in a particular way until 2014 when challenged by Samantha, another very influential figure in Arsenal's life. That challenge by Samantha stopped Arsenal from drinking alcohol, full stop.

When later I was speaking to Sam about the same incident, she has a slightly different take on it. She was nineteen at the time and didn't drink unless she was going 'out-out', and Arsenal and a couple of Sam's friends were teasing her as she wouldn't have an alcoholic drink. She tried to explain that just because everyone else was drinking didn't mean she had to have one. This made Arsenal think about his reasoning for drinking, which was, 'because at eighteen that's what everyone does'. A slightly differing version of the story but with the same outcome. It stopped Arsenal from drinking alcohol, ever!

There used to be a comedy character in the '90s on Saturday night television called 'Dangerous Brian'. This was Brian Conley's alter-ego stuntman. He would perform stunts that would often vary in danger and ludicrousness, some of which he'd often not perform. Stunts varied from bungee jumps to riding pizza delivery scooters. He was occasionally joined by his scrawny helper, Nearly Dangerous Norris, who dressed in a pink costume and often had no idea what he was doing.

Well, meet Very Dangerous Arsenal. I know that this is far from a laughing matter (Arsenal does have a great sense of humour), but from an early age Arsenal had no sense of danger for himself or inflicting pain on others or putting them into dangerous situations.

When contacting his siblings about this book and asking what they could remember about his childhood, Simmo (Anthony, his younger brother) came back with (on text), "You made my childhood a nightmare!"

Arsenal: *Our Simmo has told me some stuff and I've gone, "Wow, really?"*
Alan: *What's he told you? Can you tell me?*
Arsenal: *Yeah, tell you anything. I just text him to say sorry I deleted your date of birth. Because I delete everything at the end of the day, but I forgot to*

make a note of his date of birth. So, I asked him for it again and I said to him, "Plus, have you got any stories, good or bad?" [For Arsenal, stories are either good or bad, nothing in between.]

He gave me his date of birth and then he text me to say, "You basically made my childhood a nightmare." Wow, didn't know that. [Arsenal says these words very quietly, thoughtfully, you can almost see his mind ticking over trying to comprehend what that last sentence means. Lights are coming on everywhere for him. There is a long pause and Arsenal stops speaking.]

Alan: *But it doesn't say why?*

Arsenal: *I just... In another text he says I just used to errr... I hang people over the bannister. For some reason, I've done it to me kids, me brothers and sisters, visitors. For some reason I tip them upside down over the bannister and I get hold of their legs—*

Alan: *And pretend to drop them?*

Arsenal: *Well, yeah! Leave go and then catch them. We talked about it last night and Samantha, people were laughing, but at the time we lived in a town house, and we were three levels up.*

Alan: *So you used to do it with your kids then?*

Arsenal: *Yeah, I'd go, one, two, three. And then catch them. So, the kids remember it, Simmo remembers it, he said I was a nightmare!*

Alan: *Do you know why you did it?*

Arsenal: *No, no.*

Alan: *You don't do it anymore, do you?*

Arsenal: *No, no. And Simmo told me about how many times we almost got beat up at football games and that, but—*

Alan: Because of what you said?

Arsenal: *Just because I never used to see danger. So, I always wore an Arsenal top to every match, doesn't matter what part of the ground or whatever so, me an' him were always nearly getting beat up.*

Alan: Did he used to go with you then to watch AFC games?

Arsenal: *A couple of games I used to take him and that.*

Alan: So, you were eleven years older than him so if you were sixteen/seventeen/eighteen he would have been a little one.

Arsenal: *Yeah, yeah. And he remembers getting chased at Manchester Piccadilly by the Man U fans and so it's traumatised him I think [laughing]. It was a good day out for me but for him it was like, wow, I'm going to get beat up. But for me…*

When we talk about Arsenal's obsession with football, we will hear of the many, many times he put himself in harm's way at football matches; after all we all know what a considerate, fan-friendly atmosphere is created at a top partisan football game. The following tale happened throughout Arsenal's life as a football fan and again I stress the normally short lifespan an Arsenal fan has living in Liverpool; especially one without danger filters.

Arsenal: *Me dad sent me a text saying I was 'over-loyal to AFC'. What that means is I was too into them. I was always getting into trouble supporting AFC.*

Alan: You were bound to in Liverpool. There weren't too many other AFC fans living in Liverpool.

Arsenal: *And he [his dad] said that, "I writ on the electricity substation in school." And I know I did that but…*

You see, I put Arsenal FC on the sub-station, about that big.

Alan: Well, they were going to know who that was, weren't they?

Arsenal: I never knew that, did I? I never twigged. They said, "Look at that. Arsenal done that."

And me dad said, "I used to write AFC on all the pillar boxes." And he said same as our Simmo, really, that, "I was a bit of a nightmare." I just put myself in dangerous situations.

And he mentioned about the pub manager having to ring me dad up a couple of times, saying, "Your Arsenal's in the pub, but there's a gang waiting for him outside to kick his head in." So, he would have to come round with a couple of his mates.

Alan: So you were old enough to drink and this was football-related?

Arsenal: Yeah, yeah. If AFC won and that, I used to give it to them.

Alan: No filter?

Arsenal: [Arsenal mimics whooping it up and sticking two fingers up with both hands at imaginary Liverpool fans.] Whoo hoo, have it!

Alan: So what did your dad do in that situation? Would he come down to the pub and bail you out?

Arsenal: He would haul me out or once, there was about twenty guys and him, and Uncle Eddie said, "Come on then." And half of them ran and half of them stayed and he laid them out. Dad was about six foot two, black belt in karate [Arsenal impersonates some karate moves], just like that. But yeah, I was always getting in trouble back then. *Through different things. Either football or Gary Numan and that. Me dad mentions me Gary Numan days and that.*

So that was Arsenal 'Very Dangerous' Whittick. Tony Whittick in his email to Arsenal raises another impact of having autism. Arsenal didn't know how to lose. Anything he competed in he expected to win, plus anything he undertakes – a piece of woodwork or, as a child, some written homework – has to be perfect or he would rip it up and start again.

Tony describes this as 'always angry and a sore loser', but that's because no one knew that Arsenal was on the spectrum.

Arsenal: *If I lost at anything, I would lash out at myself, no matter what it was. And in the report that me mum done [for Arsenal's initial diagnosis], and she says, "If I was writing something, and it wasn't straight or I made a mistake, I'd rip it up and start again." I'd get angry. So, anything I had to do had to be perfect. And if it wasn't, I couldn't understand why it wasn't? Or how come I'd made that mistake and that. So, I'd get angry then and harm meself over it.*

Alan: *And when you say harm as a kid, did you used to punch yourself or slap yourself?*

Arsenal: *Yeah, bit of both. Or headbutt something. Or I was always… In me dad's letter he's going to send me, he's going to send it on email so if I go the library on Monday morning I'll see if I can print it out for you. But he says just like me mum says in there, actually. Just no matter what I done, I had to win at everything I was doing, or I'd kick the nearest person to me. Or do it to myself.*

And our Simmo said that, and he mentioned Pip [the young lad whose leg got broken by Arsenal in two places]. He said when I tackled Pip it was a triple-X challenge. He said it was horrendous. He said I nearly broke him in half. [Arsenal's pitch and tone is getting lower and lower. He's not proud of this action from his past and that manifests itself in his speaking voice.]

So, I text him back, saying, "But I remember getting the ball." And he text me back and said, "And there's the problem." You see, that's all I'd seen, I thought I'd got the ball fair and square. I'll have to see how old he was, actually.

Alan: *You told me you were sixteen/seventeen at the time and he was about nine?*

Arsenal: *Might have been, yeah. I'll get it confirmed. But to me, I'd won the ball.*

Alan: *But that wasn't a case of self-harming, was it?*

Arsenal: *No. Our Simmo says he repossessed the ball off me and I sort of grunted and chased him halfway across the pitch to get the ball back.*

Alan: *So when you say you got the ball, it doesn't sound as though you got much of it?*

Arsenal: *I got the odd stitch.*

Alan: *But what probably did the damage, and you couldn't process this, was the physical difference between you both if you were sixteen/seventeen and he was only nine.*

Arsenal: *That's when, when I used to hang everyone over the bannister, that's what I don't actually realise. Or if I'm playing with XXXXX [Arsenal's current partner has a son aged seven from a previous*

	relationship], he can get upset. He'll go, "Arsenal, Arsenal you're hurting me."
	"Sorry, sorry."
Alan:	So you're a stepdad to a seven-year-old, are you?
Arsenal:	Yeah, yeah. We have good fun, we really do. I'm just a kid, I really am just a kid. Up to about a year ago, Danielle is coming up to seventeen, and I'd go, "Come on. Let's have a fight."
	"Dad, Dad, don't." And I'd be pushing her. Just messing about. And she'd go, "Dad, please don't. Please don't, Dad."
	And I'd be going, "Why?" And she'd be explaining to me then and then she'll start crying and I'd be like, "WHAT?"

Like a lot of grown men, Arsenal simply cannot control or knows his own strength. Even today, his example is of a year ago, but he goes on to explain how he was on a lifeguard course for Autism Wessex recently so he could take the people he was caring for into the water. On this course they did basic lifesaving and one gentleman simulated drowning so that the course attendees could practise saving someone – as much a true to real-life situation as could be created.

The gentleman was lying face down in the water but was quite a big person and most of the attendees couldn't actually turn him over in the pool, the first act of saving his life. So, the course tutor said, "Arsenal, you have a go."

To which the reaction was, "Fucking hell, mate, you're fucking strangling me here." Arsenal openly admits he doesn't know his own strength and it's something he still struggles with today. Whenever he played with his kids, either his boys in Liverpool or his girls in Bournemouth, it always ended in tears. He always hurt them.

I think that's what Simmo may well be referring to as his 'nightmare'. Also being brought up as Arsenal's little brother, plus being hung over the bannister at any and every opportunity. Arsenal has been lucky with this trick as he's never had an accident, yet! He's stopped doing this now as he processes thoughts better than he has ever before but says, "I still need stopping. But to me it's fun."

There are only one or two more points to make on this chapter about the impact of autism on Arsenal's life, but these examples will better help us when we try to understand his infatuation with AFC. More importantly, how autism has impacted his relationships during his life especially with those closest to him.

Arsenal has only ever been out of the country on two occasions. Both of these were for football matches and he doesn't have a passport, nor has ever had a passport. He managed to travel with AFC's supporters' club and could travel on a visa. He knows nothing about other cultures, countries or practices, and due to his autistic behaviours has no interest in pursuing knowledge that might impel him to want to go abroad.

This trait isn't necessarily about 'going abroad' but relates to his inability to pursue information or knowledge. If Arsenal doesn't associate with something he won't follow up and try to gain any greater knowledge applying to that subject. If he is 'introduced' to something that immediately affects him then he will follow this up until he gets obsessed.

An example of this happened on the Starfish Project when he heard that Hayley Westenra practised the methodology ascribed to improve his stammer as preparation for singing. The following extract from his diagnosis says, "Throughout Arsenal's life, he has had a number of special interests which he has pursued with great passion. In particular, Arsenal discussed being interested in Arsenal Football Club, the singer Gary Numan and more recently Hayley Westenra. Arsenal described how his interest in Hayley Westenra, whom he began to listen to while learning how to breathe diaphragmatically, is becoming just as intense [as his other obsessions]."

Without an introduction to some new learning outlet, Arsenal simply wasn't interested. Since his CBT, he has tried to slowly educate himself and is concentrating on the human body at the moment with a GCSE-level handbook, packed with pictures and diagrams, to try and better himself.

Arsenal: *I think that's why I've never been abroad on holiday. It's because I don't have the knowledge. If you said to me, "Why don't you go to Spain?" One: I don't know where it is! And two: why would I go to Spain for, I don't know what's there, do I? My head is so simple that, someone in work was talking about they were going to China. And I said, "What do you want to go to China for?"*

And he said, "I want to see the Great Wall."

And I went, "But there's a wall outside."

And everyone just laughed and said, "That's autism."

Then he said, "It's not a wall like that, mate. It's a big wall that you can see from space."

I didn't get it, though, didn't get it because I didn't have history, didn't have knowledge of it... And I think that's why I haven't been abroad because I don't have that connection to it.

Alan: *If someone said to you, do you want to go to somewhere that's nice and hot, where you're just five minutes from a really nice beach, try new and different foods, relax in pleasant accommodation. If someone described to you what it would be like to go on a holiday to Spain, would you then start thinking, That sounds nice, I wouldn't mind trying that?*

Arsenal: *I think I'd need a connection. Because the only times I've been out of the country was '91/'92 season.*

Alan: *So you went to watch AFC out of the country?*

Arsenal: *Well, I had a connection, didn't I? I went to watch AFC.*

Alan: *What about if you were going somewhere, for example, that Gary Numan had been to? Perhaps in Spain? Would you like to go there because Gary Numan had been there?*

Arsenal: *I'd go there if he was on concert there.*

Alan: *But not just because he'd been there?*

Arsenal: *No. There needs to be something I'm going to watch.*

Alan: *So today, now, talking to me, you still have no desire to go abroad?*

Arsenal: *No, no. If I had the money, next year, Danielle's eighteen. And Samantha graduates. And I remember them, a couple of months ago, two of them were in me lounge, and they were on me settee and I was doing them some tea. They had a duvet over them, and they were having 'sister time'. Talking about – I was doing the dishes, actually – and they were talking about holidays and that. Samantha's been on loads. And both of them said at the same… Well, I think Samantha asked Danielle, "Where would you go, then, if you go on holiday?"*

And both at the same time, two of them said, "New York." And they were going yeah, because they watch Friends and Gossip Girl and Sex in the City and stuff. And all the apartments are there, and you can go. And they were getting really excited and I thought, Wow, what if I could take them there? [Arsenal whispers this to me like we're two naughty children in school and he's sharing a cheeky secret.]

I looked the price up and thought, I wonder if I can just send the two of them.

Somebody in work said to me, "You can't send your girls to New York without you."

And I didn't get it. I was going, "Why?"

And she said, "You can't." But I didn't get it.

Alan: *Why did she say that? I don't get it.*

Arsenal: *She thinks that if I'm paying for them to go on holiday to New York I should go with them because it will be a great bonding thing and they'll remember it for the rest of their lives.*

Alan: *Well, if we can get this book written and get some sales going you'll never know. Like I say, you can have all the money, mate, all I want is fifty per cent of the film rights. Unless by some miracle we sell thousands and then you can have the first £500k and then we'll go fifty-fifty on book sales commission.*

Arsenal: *Film, he says. What!*

Alan: *They're going to make a film of this, I'm telling you.*

[We are both laughing out loud by now.]

Arsenal: *Are they?*

Alan: *You heard it here first.*

Arsenal: OK.

Alan: *So many of the stories you have told me would make great scenes in a movie. Just the 1971 nineteen versus one football story. It's like Billy Casper in Kes! That's the pivotal moment in your life when you became Arsenal.*

Arsenal: *Yeah, yeah. 8ᵗʰ May. And you know what, I remember as well, when we went back home to watch it and I told everyone I wanted AFC to win, I remember me mum going, "You have to support Liverpool. That's where you come from."*

           And I go, "No, no. I want AFC to win." And it was 0-0 at full time. And it went into extra time and I remember, Liverpool scored first, and you know what, at the age of nine, I already had that, it wasn't hatred, but I could feel anger in me. At the age of nine. Yeah, it's amazing. I felt angry when Liverpool scored. And when Charlie George scored [the winner for AFC], I was all round the living room. Mental. Wowww. [In a melancholic voice] Isn't it strange what impacts your whole life?

Alan: *Well, if we get this book knocked out, hopefully you can take your kids to New York. How cool would that be? [I'm talking because Arsenal has stopped talking and seems to be back in '71 somewhere.]*

Arsenal: *Yeah because obviously the two of them have been under CAMHS [Child and Mental Health Services] and stuff.*

The big question for the Big Apple would be, could Arsenal put up with the noise, traffic, sheer chaos that is a New York Street? We hope, through this book, to be able to find out.

Having invested so much time in the diagnosis and the impact of both autism and a stammer on every single facet of Arsenal's life, we are better placed to journey with him through his 'football' years and his relationships both in Liverpool and in Bournemouth. So, let's talk football!

Chapter Ten

Arsenal Football Club

1971 to 2011

> *Some people think football is a matter of life and death. I assure you, it's much more serious than that.*
>
> Bill Shankly

Alan:	Today we're going to talk about your favourite subject.
Arsenal:	Sex?
	[Raucous laughter all round.]
Alan:	Well, you tell me watching AFC is better than sex.
Arsenal:	Well, it lasts longer!

I DID WARN YOU ALL THAT THERE IS NOTHING WRONG WITH Arsenal's sense of humour and with what he's had to endure most of his life, there will have been times when it's all he's had! Seriously, though, the following words are used to describe his love or obsession with football and particularly AFC in his clinical psychology report.

Firstly, the report quotes Mrs Whittick, Arsenal's mum: "Mrs Whittick reported that he had little patience and did not like to share his belongings. She said that he had to win at whatever he did, and if he was losing, he would throw what he was doing down and leave. He was very good at sports and became obsessed with football."

A further extract from the report reads as follows: "Arsenal has followed AFC since the FA Cup final when he was nine years old and changed his name by deed poll at the age of nineteen. [I believe this to have happened later in his life, perhaps twenty-three, rather than aged nineteen.] His mother discussed how he was never without a football when growing up and would play for hours on his own just kicking the ball against a wall. He reported that he attends as many of the games as he can and watches or listens to them if he cannot attend. He described the build-up to a game, during which he runs through the team's itinerary that he finds on the internet prior to the match and imagines where they are and what they are doing from the night before and right up to the game itself.

"During the game, other people refuse to watch with him as he can be very loud, passionate and deliriously happy if they score, and low and angry if they lose. If the team perform poorly, Arsenal punches himself or walls and can spit and use bad language."

We have already read about some of this addiction: the '71 FA Cup final that started events; cutting his fingers almost clean off because he was so excited on match day; as a child, covering half of Liverpool with AFC graffiti; missing his brother's wedding and cheering a goal at his own mother's wake. I believe that it became more important than any other facet of his life and the word I would use is dependence. He couldn't live without his shot of AFC.

I ask Arsenal on several occasions what he believes are the greatest matches that he either went to or saw on television, but he has immense difficulty getting past what he considers to be the best game of his life.

The season was 1988/89, a very sad season for all connected with football and especially all those connected with Liverpool and Liverpool Football Club. On the 15th April 1989, the FA Cup semi-final was scheduled to take place at Hillsborough, the ground of Sheffield Wednesday between Liverpool and Nottingham Forest, but the game never took place as ninety-six Liverpool fans were killed in a crush at the back of one of the goal mouths and a further 766 were injured.

Many words have been written about this disaster, but that is not for here. Liverpool went on to win the Cup, beating Nottingham Forest in the semi-final 3-1 when it was eventually played on the 7th May, and their biggest rivals Everton in the final 3-2 on the 20th May. Emotions were high all through Liverpool as the whole city donned their respective red and blue colours and went down to Wembley in a celebration of football dedicated to those lost but a few weeks earlier.

The season had been specially extended due to the aftermath of the disaster and Liverpool's final couple of games were pushed out on the calendar. The final League game of the season was now scheduled for the 26th May, a Friday night, most unusual for the last game of the season, and the visitors were AFC, Arsenal Football Club. The game had been postponed from a month earlier out of respect for the fallen at Hillsborough.

Going into this final game, Liverpool were top of the league and AFC were second. The unmitigated tragedy of only a few weeks earlier had turned this last match into a one-game shootout. All Liverpool had to do was not get beat by two clear goals and they would win the double of League and FA Cup which had been achieved by AFC in 1970/71. The day that a certain little Flynny became Arsenal. Nevertheless, at this stage of football history, the double had only ever been achieved five times: Preston North End did it first in 1888/89; then Aston Villa in 1896/97; the third team to achieve the illustrious double was Tottenham Hotspur in the 1960/61 season; we know AFC won it in 1970/71 and finally Liverpool themselves in 1985/86.

If Liverpool could stop AFC from winning by two goals, and they were at home, Anfield, they would become the first team in history to achieve the double twice. They would also be winning the title for an unprecedented eighteenth time. The contrary of this of course was that if AFC could win by two goals, they would snatch the League title away from Liverpool in this most difficult of seasons for everyone involved in topflight football.

AFC manager George Graham prepared for the match by giving his squad a minibreak and created a calming atmosphere in their training sessions. He adjusted his usual formation to a defensive one to stop Liverpool's attacking threat; David O'Leary was employed as a sweeper in a back five.

A peak British television audience of over twelve million saw a first half of few chances as AFC successfully nullified Liverpool. AFC striker Alan Smith scored from a header as play resumed in the second half, but as the game drew to a close with the score 1-0, AFC needed a second goal to be crowned champions. In stoppage time, AFC's Michael Thomas made a run through the Liverpool midfield and scored a last-minute goal, in the process denying Liverpool the chance of a second League and Cup double, ending AFC's eighteen-year wait to be crowned champions.

The match is considered to be one of the most dramatic conclusions to a League season in the history of the English game. It is also regarded as the starting point of a renaissance in English football; the ban on English clubs playing in European football was lifted a year later and a new top-flight division –

the Premier League – was formed in 1992. The title decider also formed the centrepiece of Nick Hornby's book *Fever Pitch*.

Arsenal: *I was in the main stand. Row two. Right by the Kop as well. The Kop singing, 'Walk On', because there was only, because there was only thirty seconds left. And I was going, "Oh shit." Because AFC needed to win 2-0.*

Alan: *I know, I remember the game. It was one of the first times they showed a live game on TV. [Not sure about my memory being right here.] Because of Hillsborough.*

Arsenal: *Friday night, yeah. I remember working and them all taking the mickey out of me. I was so up for it. '89 was amazing. I just remember looking up at the Kop and going, "Shit, I've got work on Tuesday." Because it was a bank holiday and then we scored.*

Alan: *And you were still living in Liverpool at the time?*

Arsenal: *Yeah, yeah. The pub I used to go to, The Penny Black, after work I went in The Penny Black and the manager was putting up all these balloons, all in red and white, these balloons. And all the lads are there in red and white all going to the match, and the manager said to me, "Are you going to the match, Arsenal?"*

    "Yeah, yeah." [In a very excited voice.]

    And he said, "We're having an eighteenth celebration later. Why don't you come back after the match?"

    And I said, "Can I?"

    And he said, "Course you can." And the whole pub was laughing.

And I said, "What the fuck are you laughing at?" It was only later on, because everyone thought Liverpool were going to win it for the eighteenth time. And that's what all the balloons were for.

And he'd said, "Yeah come on in. We're having an eighteenth celebration."

And when I got back outside the pub, it was double doors, and on the inside of the double doors they had an orange Perspex in the door so they couldn't see out or in. So, I went [Arsenal now mimes banging on a door like a football chant, bap bap – bap bap bap – bap bap bap bap – bap bap. Say it to yourself, it might make sense?]. Then I ran in and went, "FUCK OFF." [In a triumphant manner rather than insulting, if that's possible.]

Alan: You're lucky you got out alive!

Arsenal: No, everyone knew me in there. But that night, I did, I got really drunk. And the lads had to take us home. And back then, everyone used the back way to get in. And our garden, and there was a door but, we used to bolt it, didn't we? So, it was the early hours of the morning. So, the lads, couldn't get us in the gate so they got an arm and a leg each, and one and two and three and threw me over.

Then it must have been about ten o'clock in the morning, me two boys were let out into the garden. And they were going, "Dad, Dad. Mum, Dad's at the bottom of the garden."

Alan: So you were living with L then?

Arsenal: Yeah, '89, yeah. I just remember the two kids hitting me face: "Dad, Dad, wake up."

And I came round, thinking, Was it a dream? Was it fuck, we won 2-0. Oh, I was so happy. An *amazing time. Amazing. And then over that, one of me brothers, staunch red-nose. Stopped talking to me because of that. Well, it was a bank holiday Monday and I went into his pub, The Daisy, in West Derby village. And he was there with all his boys and I walked in, didn't I, and started shouting, "WE WON THE LEAGUE ON MERSEYSIDE." And you know what, he hated it, absolutely hated it. But I was still hungover, I think, and I was still on a high. And so, the next day, on a Tuesday, I went to pick him up, didn't I? I used to take him to work. And his partner came out and said, "Oh, he's gone. Well, after yesterday."*

So, I went, "What happened yesterday?"

She went, "Oh, he's not talking to you." So, I went to work, and he ignored me. So, after work I done overtime, and he done overtime then he went.

So, I'm going past and he's stood at the bus stop, so I wound the window down: "Come on, are you getting in?" And he blanked me.

So, he done that on Tuesday, done it on Wednesday. I went to his house on Thursday and his missus said, "No, he's gone."

So, I said, "I tell you what, will you tell him if he's not in my car tomorrow, that's it. I'm not coming next week. That's it." The next day I went and he wasn't there so, went to work and he just ignored me. So, he's not spoke to me since 1989!

Alan:	*You're joking?*
Arsenal:	*No, I'm not. I didn't go to his wedding. Didn't get an invite. Not spoke to me since 1989.*
Alan:	*Which brother is that?*

Arsenal:	That's Mark. Just younger than me.
Alan:	Over a game of football?
Arsenal:	Over a game of football. But then, after that, after that, the company was going into liquidation. And I was higher up in the company, and they had a meeting to tell us that we were going into liquidation. My director, Anthony XXXXX, said to me, "You can't tell your Mark. You can't tell him because it will go all round the factory. And we're trying to sort stuff out." So, I didn't tell him, did I? But then he wasn't talking to me anyway before that, so it was definitely the football. He didn't get a lift. He wouldn't talk to me. So, then he was getting a car on finance, but I never put two and two together, did I? So, I didn't tell him, did I?
	So, he's getting this car on finance, and I knew that we could be losing our jobs. But—
Alan:	You never processed that, did you?
Arsenal:	But Anthony XXXXX had told me, "You can't tell him, or it'll go all round the factory and we're trying to save it."
	So, that come out and me mum said to me, "Did you know this was happening?"
	And I can't lie, can I? And I went, "Yeah, but Anthony XXXXX, the owner, said I couldn't say nothing."
	And she said, "But it's your fucking brother!"
	"But I was told not to say nothing." And then it just escalated from then. And then I remember one Christmas, we went round to see me mum. And they were all there, weren't they? Our Mark, his wife, his lad, and all me other brothers and sisters, and I thought, no. I'll just go round

> everyone and say, "Happy Xmas" [in a very cheesy cheery voice].
>
> "Happy Xmas. Merry Xmas. Happy Christmas." And I come to our Mark and I went, "Happy Christmas, Mark." And he didn't put his hand out. And I thought, I've tried. And he still hasn't spoke to me since '89.

Alan: It's nearly thirty years.

Arsenal: Yeah, yeah. And when we were carrying the coffin, there was supposed to be him and me; and you have to put your arms around, and next minute he moved backwards so I thought, Fuck you. So, we haven't spoke since '89. Families, eh. So, there you go.

You can hear the sadness in Arsenal's story and you never know when Mark – if Mark – reads this, he may just have a better understanding of why Arsenal behaved the way he did.

The next game that Arsenal remembers as one of his footballing highlights is in fact a series of five games that still holds the record for the greatest number of professional games played against the same side in such a short space of time. AFC played Sheffield Wednesday five times in replay after replay in the third round of the FA Cup and all over the space of sixteen days. From the first game on the 6th January 1979 at Hillsborough to the fourth replay, the fifth game, played at Leicester. Five games in sixteen days and just to keep fit AFC also had to play a League game at home to Nottingham Forest to make it a nice half dozen games in sixteen days. They complain if they have to play two games in a week today!

The reason for these games, and probably these fixtures went some way to help change the rules, was due to there being no penalty shootouts in the FA Cup at that time. Extra time in the second and subsequent replays if needed, but you just kept coming back until someone could break the deadlock.

The games unfolded as follows:

Sheffield Wednesday 1 AFC 1
6th January – Hillsborough

Terry Neil was the AFC manager in 1979 and when they arrived at the ground and inspected the pitch he said, *"It was the worst he had ever seen"*. Jack Charlton who was the Sheffield Wednesday manager that season replied, *"If you think this pitch is bad you should have seen it earlier in the season."*

The game was not so much remembered for the quality of the football played but the fact that the Wednesday fans spent large parts of the game throwing snowballs at the AFC players. Pat Jennings in particular bore the brunt. The AFC goal scorer was Sunderland with Jeff Johnson equalising for Wednesday.

AFC 1 Sheffield Wednesday 1
9th January – Highbury

Liam Brady, the AFC magician in midfield, did not have his best game for AFC in this replay, but in the eighty-eighth minute he still managed to score after Sheffield had taken an unexpected lead with a goal from Roger Wylde.

Going into the game no one gave Wednesday much of a chance at Highbury as not many visiting teams got favourable results at AFC especially one from the 3rd Division. Nevertheless they packed the midfield and made it difficult for AFC, cramping the style of the home team and setting up the three further games at Filbert Street by hanging on for a tough draw.

Jack Charlton, not wanting to give AFC the opportunity for another home tie refused to toss for home advantage taking the second replay to a neutral Leicester City.

Sheffield Wednesday 2 AFC 2
15th January – AET – Leicester

The third game attracted little media interest as everyone again expected AFC to dismiss the challengers from the lower league with ease but once again Wednesday put up a brave fight. The ground was packed with blue and white as not many AFC fans made the trip, although we know one who did, and Wednesday made it feel like a home game for them.

AFC were in the lead twice in this game, first from Brady with a long raking shot and then again in the 68th minute from Alan Sunderland. But on both occasions, they let Wednesday back into the game.

Sheffield Wednesday 3 AFC 3
17th January – AET – Leicester

The 4th game became Wednesday's proudest moment. Many Wednesday fans who were at the game described the performance as *"heroic"* and a turning point in Jack Charlton's stewardship of the club as they went on from strength to strength. Once again Wednesday were behind twice in the game only to pull back the deficit on both occasions. Frank Stapleton scored twice for AFC but the goals still failed to take them into the 4th round. The players also seemed to be getting sick of the sight of each other as familiarity caused four bookings in a bad-tempered game.

AFC missed a penalty from Brady in this game after Rushbury opened the scoring for Wednesday but Stapleton made it one all. Young then put AFC in front in the 76th minute but back came Wednesday in the 86th through Lowey. In extra time AFC took the lead again with Stapleton's second but a penalty from Wednesday made it three all and another date to meet at Filbert Street was set for the 22nd January.

Sheffield Wednesday 0 AFC 2
22nd January – AET – Leicester

Finally, the tie was decided. Over the five games, which took over eight and a half hours, including injury time, AFC won nine to seven, to take themselves to a home tie with Nottingham County in the 4th round.

AFC scored two first half goals from Stapleton and Gatting and with some resolute defending that was enough to finally settle the tie. It took five games and the defence of a flurry of snowballs in the first one but AFC were through to the next round.

Arsenal, arguably the greatest AFC fan in the land, managed to go to every game.

Arsenal: *1979.*

Alan: *Is that the FA Cup final when you beat us [Manchester Utd] 3-2?*

Arsenal: *That's on there [Arsenal's personal list of greatest games], but I never went to the final. I couldn't get no tickets but what I remember is that in the third round we played Sheffield Wednesday away, but we made history because over sixteen days we played them five times. And I went to every one of them.*

Alan: *All of them?*

Arsenal: *Yeah. But I was lucky because I lived in Liverpool. And the games were at Sheffield, I think Aston Villa—*

Alan: *[In the meantime I am searching the internet.] Here you are, I've got it here.*

      "Sheffield Wednesday versus AFC. This third-round FA Cup tie clash at a snowy Hillsborough. In January 1979, this was the first of five games

	between Division 3 side Sheffield Wednesday and 1st Division side AFC."
Arsenal:	I didn't know they were Division 3, bloody hell. I just knew it was the FA Cup, didn't I?
Alan:	[Back to reading from the website] "At the time, cup ties were played to the death without penalty shootouts. It took four replays, the last three going to extra time, to separate the two teams. The last three fixtures were played at Leicester's Filbert Street. AFC were unhappy with the state of the Hillsborough pitch, with manager Terry Neil declaring it the worst he'd ever seen. Wednesday were managed by 1966 World Cup winner, Jack Charlton."
Arsenal:	Wow, didn't know that.
Alan:	There's pictures here. Do you want a look?
Arsenal:	Bloody hell!
Alan:	"In goal for AFC was legend Pat Jennings." There's even a video here. Do you want to see this video? I don't know what it's going to show.
Arsenal:	Yeah, all right.

At this point I decide to open a short video on the internet that shows the goals and a couple of highlights from the game in 1979. A very fuzzy video, one that you can just differentiate the players on. Arsenal is transfixed and I can see the excitement light up in his eyes. I immediately decide I'm not going to show him any videos of AFC losing, as his level of excitement has increased so quickly that he can hardly contain himself. I can only imagine how he must have reacted when watching a live game.

The video has BBC One commentary over the top as the 1979 AFC team, alongside their opponents, run out of the tunnel onto the pitch, led out by their captain Liam Brady. The team was Jennings, Rice, Nelson, Price, O'Leary, Young, Brady, Sunderland, Stapleton, Gatting and Rix. Arsenal isn't with me anymore. He has been snatched from his own living room and transported in time back to 1979 when he was just seventeen years old. His eyes are shining brightly and his whole body is quivering with the memories of that distant night.

I have never seen Arsenal like this before and it's a little unsettling. I start to better understand what his partners and children have been wrestling to live with all these years. Arsenal is trembling like a child on Christmas morning opening the present they have always wanted. I'm not frightened but I am very aware of the change in the man who, over the weeks of talking, has become my friend. Let us also remember this is the good Arsenal; how would he react if I showed him an old game of AFC being beaten? Again, I better understand why the hospital has asked Arsenal to surround himself with memorabilia from happy memories only and to discard everything else.

Arsenal names every AFC player as they leave the tunnel and run onto the pitch. Sunderland scores for AFC and Arsenal walks away to the other side of his living room, trying to hold himself together. He's clicking his fingers and then hugging himself with delight. I realise this may not be the best decision I've ever made.

Alan:	I'm stopping this, I don't think we want to see them equalise. You don't want to see their goal.
Arsenal:	[Now in a raised voice] Yeah, so that one went to five games and I went them all but then I never went again. I couldn't get any tickets but that's—
Alan:	Did you get to Wembley that year?
Arsenal:	Yeah, that's the 3-2 game [against Manchester Utd].

Alan:	Is it?
Arsenal:	Yeah…
Alan:	*[Incredulously] You played Wednesday five times and went on to win the Cup? Is that a record for the greatest number of games needed to win the Cup?*
Arsenal:	*I think it probably does but another season I think we played Liverpool four or five times in a semi-final, so that might be it?*
	So, in '79 that's what I remember, I went to them five, but I didn't get to the final. [The final is a famous game. AFC went 2-0 up and were cruising to victory when Manchester United scored two goals in the last ten minutes to make it 2-2. Then, virtually from the kick-off, AFC scored the winner in injury time. A very exciting end to what had been quite a drab game.]
Arsenal:	*But when the final was 2-0 and it went to 2-2, I can remember the anger because I was thinking, No, it's all right, but in me head I was thinking of the Sheffield Wednesday game. I was thinking all them fucking games and we've thrown it away.*
	So that's what I can remember… [Arsenal starts laughing to himself.] Oh, dear me.

Arsenal also talks about two other games that are very important to him and these are games that we have already covered earlier. First, the 1971 FA Cup final, the day that someone called him Arsenal for the first time, but really the day when his young mind saw and grasped the opportunity to take on a new identity.

Second, his first-ever live game that he attended at Old Trafford on the 14th May 1977 aged fifteen. This was the day when he got lost and had to be put on a train home by the Manchester police. As these have already been covered in some detail in previous chapters, we shall move on to the Littlewoods Cup of 1986/87 and the last two choices of Arsenal's most influential or important games.

On the 8th February 1987, AFC hosted Tottenham Hotspur in the first leg of the Littlewoods Cup, or the League Cup, semi-final. The semis in 1987 were two leg affairs, with away goals not counting double. If the teams are all square after the second leg, the tie would go to a third game.

Spurs started as favourites having hit a rich vein of form before this match only losing two of their last twelve although their last defeat was against AFC in January. The only goal of the game was Clive Allen's thirty-fourth of the season and Spurs were good enough on the night to go on and score more but couldn't convert their chances. Final score one nil to Spurs.

Spurs' dominance and skill were summed up in a quote from *The Independent* newspaper: 'No attacking side can be more difficult to deal with than Spurs at the moment'.

With the second leg at their own home ground of White Hart Lane, Spurs were optimistic of progressing to their fourth League Cup final at Wembley and strong favourites to do so. Unfortunately for them this proved to be more difficult than anticipated. This match becomes one of Arsenal's all time favourite games.

So, a goal down from the first leg, AFC had to travel to Spurs for the second leg. It was always going to be a tall order for AFC to pull this tie around and over 41,000 fans packed into White Hart Lane for the second leg on the 1st March, and Arsenal Whittick was one of them. Then in the sixteenth minute, disaster struck for AFC and Spurs effectively went 2-0 up in the tie, with Clive Allen scoring again for his thirty-eighth of the season.

There couldn't possibly be any way back; AFC weren't playing well enough to grab two goals away from home when they had hardly threatened the Spurs goal over the length of the tie. It was effectively game over and Spurs were off to Wembley.

But then came the moment which turned the game upside down. AFC looked down and out. Allegedly Spurs half-time tannoy announcements advised their fans how to get hold of their Wembley tickets. This fired up the Gunners who came charging back.

David Pleat, however, the then-Spurs manager, disputes that version of events. "I suspect it is a myth that AFC were fired up by hearing that in their dressing room."

Whatever AFC heard at half-time, they were inspired by it, and Viv Anderson and Niall Quinn scored second-half goals to earn a 2-1 victory, making it 2-2 on aggregate. The referee Alan Gunn tossed a coin to see who would have home advantage for the deciding leg. Spurs won the coin toss and the replay was again to be at White Hart Lane.

History shows that AFC, with two goals in the last ten minutes from Allinson and Rocastle responding to yet another from Allen went onto an appointment with Liverpool at Wembley. AFC with the deciding goal seconds before the final whistle had taken the lead for the first time over the three games.

It was the second game that Arsenal managed to get a ticket for and that's the one he remembers most fondly. He especially likes the fact that Spurs started celebrating too soon and announced how to get their tickets for the final with a half of football still to play. Sport in any form has a great propensity for coming back and biting you in the arse! Or should that be in the Arsenal?

Arsenal: *In '87 we were in the Littlewoods semi-final, so it was a two-legged game and the first game was AFC 0 Tottenham 1. And we went to White Hart*

Lane and I went there. And at half-time it was Tottenham 1 AFC 0. So, over the two legs it was 2-0.

And then at half-time, I remember it because I was there, but I've heard some AFC players talk about it. At half-time, in the second game, they announced that anyone with a ticket stub can, after the match, can go to somewhere and pick up their Wembley Cup final tickets. And allegedly the AFC team heard it, and that's what spurred them on then [no pun intended].

The final match in Arsenal's collection of favourite memories was the Littlewoods final from the same year on the 5th April at Wembley Stadium. Another game that he managed to get a ticket for, and who was it against? I think if Arsenal ever played James Bond then his Blofeld would be personified by Liverpool Football Club. As he was raised in Liverpool supporting AFC, he sees Liverpool as his archenemy and many of his greatest and happiest times were getting one over on Liverpool FC.

On the 5th April 1987, AFC and LFC lined up to run onto the hallowed Wembley turf to do battle once again. The line-ups were as follows:

- AFC – Lukic, Anderson, Sansom (c), Williams, O'Leary, Adams, Rocastle, Davis, Quinn, Nicholas and Hayes. Substitutes – Groves and Thomas.
- Liverpool – Grobbelaar, Gillespie, Venison, Spackman, Whelan, Hansen (c), Walsh, Johnston, Rush, Molby and McMahon. Substitutes – Dalglish and Wark.

The teams were managed by two Scottish men, Graham and Dalglish respectively.

I have read several match reports of the final itself and below is my take on the game. I do remember watching the final live as I was in hospital at the time and on this particular Sunday afternoon had two visitors who were fanatical Everton supporters. Hence, they were AFC fans for the day and we were the only three people sat in the hospital television room.

We know how AFC reached the final but Liverpool had an easier time of it beating Southampton 3-0 on aggregate over the two legs.

Liverpool managed by Kenny Dalglish had the better of the first exchanges and it was no surprise when Ian Rush – joining the Italians' Juventus at the season's end – put them a goal to the good after twenty-one minutes.

This 202nd goal of his Liverpool career meant that they simply could not lose. If Rush the Welshman scored, Liverpool didn't get beat. That was a hard fact over the 144 games that Rush had played for the club and it surely wouldn't change today in the glorious Spring sunshine beating down on Wembley Stadium. For a seven year stretch, Liverpool never lost when Rush scored.

AFC didn't subscribe to the same rule of law as the thousands of travelling Liverpool fans and they steadily started to build themselves back into the game. After thirty minutes Charlie Nicholas grabbed an equaliser from within the box after Viv Anderson had hit the post. Then luck turned further against the Reds of Merseyside and in favour of AFC with only seven minutes remaining.

Perry Groves had come off the bench to replace Quinn in the second half and positioned himself on the left wing. Beating Gillespie for pace he thrashed a cross into the penalty area where from twelve yards out Nicholas's shot was off target. The football Gods were wearing red with white sleeves on this day as the shot hit Ronnie Whelan and deflected into the net leaving Bruce Grobbelaar stranded. It was AFC's first trophy for eight seasons.

Liverpool then went on to lose a nine point lead at the top of the table to their Merseyside rivals Everton who took the title.

Ian Rush looking back at the game said, *"After seven years and all those games and goals we'd never been beaten when I scored, but the following week we went to Norwich and lost 2-1 and I scored then too."*

Arsenal: *What's good about that final is I went; I was living in Liverpool and I went up on Barnes Travel. So, I got to the Jolly Miller, that was the pub in West Derby and there must have been about twenty coaches there. All lined up. I was the only one there with an AFC top on. They were all knocking on the windows, shouting, "You're fucking dead."*

Alan: *I'm surprised you're here today, mate.*

Arsenal: *But the reason I remember that one is Liverpool had never been beaten when Ian Rush scored and in that final he scores first. And I was in the Liverpool end [the only way he could get a ticket], and they were all jumping on me and everything. They were jumping on me in celebration. Ian Rush had just scored, and everyone was saying, "Rushy scored. We can't get beat."*

It's at this point that we watch a couple of videos and Arsenal gets so high he's shaking like a leaf. "That's the problem," he says, "I get so high but if they score, I get so low." These are videos of games that took place more than thirty years ago, Arsenal knows the result, who scores, when they score, but his emotions run at such extremes that he still cannot watch them.

These are Arsenal's favourite, best, most memorable, choose whichever word you wish, from his days of going and watching football, but as we know, he's had lows as well. What are the 'bad' memories? Which games took him to places where he didn't want to go? I have to be very careful and ensure he's comfortable talking about these moments from the past.

Arsenal: *Every Monday, it was just awful. People who weren't even into football would say to me, "Argh, AFC got beat again, I see." Fucking hell, every Monday I used to dread it. Back then Liverpool were just amazing, weren't they, in the '70s?*

Alan: *Under Shankly, Paisley, Moran, Dalglish, they won everything.*

Arsenal: *They were just amazing. But every Monday, I used to dread it, here we go again. I'd get loads of stick. Someone's going to say something, get angry. We'll have a bit of a tussle. You know.*

Alan: *But AFC were pretty good in the '70s as well.*

Arsenal: *They won the FA Cup in '71 but they never won it again until '79 and I'd left school then. Ipswich beat us in the final in 1978. I think we got beat in 1980. That was one of the worst years because we got... [Arsenal and I then spend ten minutes debating FA Cup final results and who scored before researching the results.]*

   Oh yeah, it was West Ham, Trevor Brooking got the winner. It's coming back to me now. In eight days, AFC got beat on the Saturday against West Ham. Then we lost in the European Cup Winners' Cup on the Wednesday against Valencia on penalties. Graham Rix hit the post with his penalty. And then on the Monday night we had one League game left, we went up to Middlesbrough, away. It was the old Ayresome Park, and we went up to Middlesbrough, thousands of us went, don't know why?

> *AFC needed a draw to get into Europe and we got stuffed 5-0. So, in a matter of eight days the whole season was gone.*

Alan: *And was you going to games in 1980?*

Arsenal: *Yeah, yeah.*

Alan: *So did you go to the FA Cup final?*

Arsenal: *Against West Ham I didn't. I went the Ipswich one. Didn't go the Man U one in '79. Alan Sunderland got the winner. Wow! Football's amazing, isn't it?*

Alan: *How soon did your addiction to football and all things AFC start?*

Arsenal: *1971. From that day forward I was addicted. It was just amazing. It was just Match of the Day, I used to watch Grandstand, and back then on Grandstand it was really old, and I remember it was a teleprinter. And it would go like, A… R… And you'd be going shit, watching the name spell out. [The tension for someone with autism would be extreme.]*

I remember once, it went AFC 2 and I thought, Oh yeah. And I think it was Coventry… 3. And I remember there was something on the table and I just like… [Sweeping motion with his arm and hand.] Knocked everything off the table. And I'm like, wow…

Alan: *Did your dad give you a crack for that?*

Arsenal: *Errr, most times, most times. [Arsenal smiles fondly and not with any recrimination.] I was always getting hit, though, back then. Doing things and that, I was always getting hit. It was just a normal thing for me, to get hit and that. [Arsenal isn't just referring to his dad here but his whole life. As we know, lads at school used to hit Arsenal for the fun of it.]*

Yeah, it just builds up and that. And I just used to get really angry if they never won. But, again, no one ever sat me down to explain that, "You know, they can't actually win every game, don't you?" No one ever sat me down to say, "Listen. Do you know your anger, you can't be doing that, you can't be doing this?" But everyone just let me get on with it. And that's what our Simmo said. He said, "You were a nightmare." And I made his life a nightmare as well.

But me mum would always have a go: "This is my house. Stop kicking them doors. You're under my roof, right. You can't be doing that." And I'd just be keep on doing it because I'm getting angrier and angrier because they're telling me. But I've always been angry ever since I can remember over football and that. Even when the violence at the football was really bad [mid-'70s onwards], I never got involved in the violence. Sort of never ran at no one, I never aimed at anyone, I used to watch it. When they used to run at you, for some reason, my brain never told me to run, did it?

I'd be standing there and next minute you're getting battered and that. At the end of the day, AFC might have won the game, so what was more important? AFC winning the game and that. It sounds stupid now, though, but back then [pauses], it was more important to me. I could give you; I could give you... I could speak to me dad, he'll be all right, but and me brothers and they'll say to you that, I'll give them your number, or they'll give you theirs... If you want to talk to them about how bad I was and that...

I used to, if AFC got beat on a Saturday as a kid, I'd take me ball out and I'd be so angry that I'd be hitting it against anything. A car. The glass in the school. Every Saturday you'd probably hear, smash! And it would be me smashing a window at the school because I'd just be so angry, I wanted to get it out.

I wasn't doing it back then because I wanted to get the anger out because I never knew that. [Even now Arsenal doesn't realise that's what he was doing. He thinks because he didn't know that he was releasing anger back then that he couldn't have been. Autism in action again.]

But I'd always do something on a Saturday. Break loads of glass in St Albert's and that. Why, I don't know? Wow!

Alan: *And did your mum and dad have to pay for that?*

Arsenal: *No. I used to run. I just used to run. But I would always be breaking glass or booting it against a car. A lot of it, I've never gone, "I'm going to break that." I'd just get the ball and I'd kick it. Because in the playground, you had the playground here and all the classes alongside it. And they all had the windows but… There used to be an alcove where the two classes joined up and that would be my goal. But on either side was all the glass, wasn't it? So, if it didn't go in the goal, I'd smash a window.*

And that's the way it was, every Saturday. I never went out to get the anger out but that's what I did.

Alan: *It couldn't have been every Saturday because you might have won. AFC were not a bad side, were they? You won more than you lost, that's for sure.*

Arsenal: *Yeah, yeah.*

Alan:	*And what would you do if AFC drew a game?*
Arsenal:	*I'd get angry because they haven't won, have they?*
Alan:	*They had to win?*
Arsenal:	*Yeah, yeah. They had to win. I mean…*

Arsenal paused here and smiled sadly to himself before lifting his head and looking directly at me – not something that he always does – and it was at this point that he came out with the following bombshell. I nearly dropped my pen.

| Arsenal: | *The last time I tried to commit suicide was March 23rd 2011.* |
| Alan: | *WHAT?!* |

I couldn't believe what I was hearing. We had been having chats for several months by now and had gotten to know each other pretty well. For a person with autism, you have to ask the correct question. I had never asked this question, so I never found out until Arsenal felt that it fitted into our conversation. I wasn't ready for this.

Arsenal:	*We were playing Barcelona in the second leg and we went out 4-3 on aggregate, but in our game [at home] we won them 3-0. And I remember watching it at The Brunswick in Charminster. And I was getting angry, and I tell you what, when the whistle went all the AFC fans were going, "Hooray, we won 3-0."*
	And I'm going, "We got beat 4-3."
	"But we won 3-0 tonight."
	And I'm going, "But we got knocked out." And that's all I could think. And walking home, woohoo, I went, didn't I? I went. Wow!

I'm now wondering how to handle this news. Arsenal is talking on, so matter-of-fact, and to use Arsenal's words, I'm trying to process what I've just been told. I'm an accountant who's written a couple of books, should I have started this? Do I carry on or call a halt? He doesn't seem fazed by the news he's just shared with me so I push on, but listening back I can hardly hear myself on the recording. I am whispering, sounding too frightened to use the words. Like a child, scared of saying the bogeyman's name in case he appears.

> Alan: *So what do you mean by trying to commit suicide?*
> Arsenal: *I've done it about five times. [If I didn't know better, I'd say Arsenal almost exclaims this statement with an element of pride.]*
> *And I can't do it, can I?*

Chapter Eleven

A Matter of Life and Death

1971 to 2019

It's like everything in football and life. You need to look,
you need to think, you need to move, you need to find
space, you need to help others. It's very simple in the end.

Johan Cruyff

So, from starting a conversation about Arsenal's favourite sport and team, we very quickly moved onto something far more serious. My only consolation is that he's sat here in front of me so I do know we have something of a happy ending, but it's yet another lightning bolt out of the blue, or red with white sleeves, that no one could ever have anticipated.

The other point I need to process is the date. Arsenal has tried to take his own life at least once since he had started to be diagnosed and I check the date of his clinical psychology report: 26th May 2011. Almost exactly two months after his last suicide attempt. I ask him if he's OK to talk about this and he believes it will be good for him. I don't know at this point that he's never told his family. They have regularly seen him self-harm, sometimes quite violently, but no one knew he had tried unsuccessfully to kill himself.

Alan: You've never ever mentioned that to me.

Arsenal: Haven't I?

Alan: We have now sat down and talked several times and you've never told me?

Arsenal: Haven't I told you about—

Alan: You've tried to commit suicide? [My voice on the recording is incredulous.]

Arsenal: Yeah! About five times. [Arsenal is now openly laughing because I'm astounded.] But you know what, I know I'm laughing because when I tell you the answer—

Alan: It's not really funny, though, is it?

Arsenal: No, but do you know what executive functioning is?

Alan: No, not really.

Arsenal: OK, then, it's your processing skills.

So, what exactly does executive functioning mean? "Executive functions" are a set of cognitive processes that are necessary for the cognitive control of behaviour. The brain chooses and monitors behaviour to meet the chosen goal of the individual.

These include the following but not exclusive list of functions.

Emotional Control – the capability to control your feelings through rational thought.

Initiation – the capability to start a task and to apply problem solving techniques to that task in order to *get the job done."*

Inhibition – the capability to stop yourself from acting inappropriately or recklessly at the correct time. Arsenal has had numerous examples of this sort of behaviour discussed previously causing him to be impulsive and not think situations through.

Organisation of materials – the capability to control and manage tools and individual elements when undertaking tasks either at work or leisure activities. This is a function that Arsenal is actually excellent at performing if we remember his storeroom escapade at the Co-op.

Planning/Organisation – the capability to think around a complex task, complex to someone with autism, and to break it down into a future timeline of individual parts to complete the whole.

Self-monitoring – the capability to look at your own behaviour and to compare it to accepted standards.

Shift – the capability to mentally shift from one concept to another while maintaining control over both thought processes.

Working memory – the capability to hold the right information in your head to be able to complete a task successfully.

But what do these functions mean for a person with autism? Executive Functioning is very difficult for someone on the spectrum and most people with autism show the following positives and negatives:

- They are more than capable at seeing details clearly, but have a difficult time seeing a big picture.
- They are great at following schedules and routines, but are so inflexible when asked to move away from the same schedules or routines.
- They can understand and follow rules but get upset when rules are broken or quite simply are not rigidly adhered to.
- They have problems with sustaining focus and motivation when engaged in something that isn't

interesting to them or as Arsenal says, *"He doesn't have a connection to."* They will not seek out information.

- They have a hard time in switching tasks.
- They have a difficult time effectively communicating their own needs and desires to other people.
- They will not use their peripheral understanding of a situation to self-inform. If I got up to leave Arsenal would not necessarily do the same until I prompted him.
- They can work better with physical items more readily than with conceptual ideas.
- They have great difficulty with "theory of mind", which is comprehending that others' cannot necessarily understand your own thoughts or feelings. Remember the Sally-Anne test.

We have seen many of these conditions all the way through Arsenal's life. He was explaining to me why he was laughing because he hadn't told me about his attempted suicides.

Arsenal: *So, to me I don't have that [executive functioning], I'm learning it. I'm getting there. So, to me, on that actual night. I got home and I went in and I think Nicola just happened to say to me, "Happy, aren't you? 3-0?" And I just went, flipped. Woah. I remember giving myself a real good hiding. And there was blood up the walls and everything. So, Nicola started screaming and that. So, I came downstairs and come out the house... Nicola never knew, I don't think and rang the police to say I was harming myself. But I'd come out the house and I'd gone for a walk [he's still smiling at his recollection].*

And I was on the bridge. Ready to jump off onto the Wessex Way. And there were wagons coming towards me. And you know what, I didn't know what to do? And that's me… I don't have the processing. Because I was thinking, when do I jump? Are those wagons ten feet away? Or a hundred feet away? Because if I jump too early, the wagons are going to swerve round me. And if I jump too late, I might just hit the top of the wagon. And I couldn't work out until later on until people told me, "You don't have executive functioning."

Alan: *So your autism saved your life!*

Arsenal: *Yeah, it saved me, yeah, yeah.*

Alan: *[Aghast] Why did you want to kill yourself over AFC losing? Just because AFC lost.*

Arsenal: *Yeah. And then, do you know the Royal Bath Hotel in Bournemouth?*

Alan: *Yes, I think so.*

Arsenal: *As you come down from the roundabout as if you're going into the city centre it's on your left-hand side.*

Alan: *Yes, I know where it is.*

Arsenal: *I'm not too bad now, but I still get images of it. I'm not a hundred per cent, but back in the day I used to go down there. And every time I was walking down there, I always wanted to walk into the water and kill myself. I'd be walking to the water and I'd get to the beach and I'd be thinking, I'll go to the waves. And I'd be thinking, So what do I do?*

    And I wouldn't know what to do? And later on, they'd [Alderney Hospital] be saying to me, "What did you used to think?"

    And I'd be thinking, Swim out. And then I'll get tired and go underneath. Or, what do I do, do I walk in? So, what do I do? And I didn't know

	what to do. So, even now if I go down there, it's the first thing I think of!
Alan:	*Do you start putting slides in?*
Arsenal:	*Yeah, yeah. It's amazing. But I don't know why it's there because I can go down Boscombe and it doesn't enter me head. But if I go down to Bournemouth [Arsenal only gets this impulse as he walks towards and past the Royal Bath Hotel], the first thing I want to do is walk in the water. And I go, "Shit!" Woah, Michael Thomas 1989. [Arsenal uses one of his coping mechanisms that we'll come on to later.] Yeah, I've done some mad things, mate.*
Alan:	*So that's two occasions, what about the other three?*
Arsenal:	*I went to... We were playing Watford in the quarter-final of the FA Cup. And back in the day they used to announce where the semi-finals were going to be. And it was at Villa Park. So, I booked the hotel for Villa Park. I thought, Watford, quarter-finals at Highbury, bang on cert. We got fucked, didn't we, 3-1. I remember being at Finsbury Park and they announce, "The next train will be in three minutes." I remember going down to the tunnel end... Have you been on the Underground?*
Alan:	*Yes, lots of times.*
Arsenal:	*Yes, sorry, it's obvious now, isn't it?*
Alan:	*Don't be sorry for anything.*
Arsenal:	*The tunnel that the train comes out on the platform. And I thought, I'll go down the tunnel where it's dark. It's not dark at all. The tunnel's dark but the platform's not. I thought no one would*

*see me. Fucking too right they won't! [Arsenal gets
very animated telling this part of the tale.] Sorry,
sorry.*

What Arsenal was suggesting was that he was going to walk
right down to the end of the platform to the tunnel edge, where
he thought it was dark and he wouldn't be seen. From there he
was going to pitch himself in front of the next Underground
train that emerged from the tunnel. Once more his executive
functioning let him down, or as I like to see it, saved his life
again.

Alan: *God. What stopped you this time?*

Arsenal: *[He's laughing again at himself] Because, I didn't
know how low, the, the, the… [Arsenal's stammer
is far more prominent as his memories kick in and
his emotions are heightened.]*

*I didn't know how low the train was to the lines.
For some reason, all I could think of at the time,
and it sounds stupid now, was the locomotives.
But they're not, are they? Locomotives? But and
then I'm thinking, what happens if it goes over
me? And then it was too late, and the train was
in the station. But then the train, as it went past
me, wow!*

*I got like, this like, I don't know what it was? It
was probably the draft of the train there. It was a
suction. It was like a buzz for me that. So, I started
doing that for a bit [he's laughing again now] just
to get that buzz of it coming in. Not so near to
the train but there was something there that I was
getting sensory issues. But, but you see at the time
I never knew what it was and that.*

When it first comes out of that tunnel at that speed, wow, it does something to me. [I have found out that this game was a sunny 14th March 1987.] Don't know what it does, but it does something to me. But then there'll be days were I'm going, "Should I jump, should I jump?" [I can hardly hear him as he's almost speaking to himself now and not me.] Look at those big wheels, what happens if, yeah… [Arsenal is moved to silence.]

During this intense discussion about his suicide attempts – and this was meant to be a happy session about football – Arsenal is less fluent. His sentences run into each other and don't always make sense as his mind is jumping about. It feels as though he's telling me a story he's read in the paper or he's relating a tale of someone else, a friend or a relative. He never refers to himself in the third person, but I know he believes that he's a very different person from the one in 1987 who seriously considered stepping off a platform and into the path of an Underground train.

I think it's right to use his words as much as I possibly can to try and capture what he's reliving in telling me his story. Also, to try and capture what he thought the state of his own mind was when he had these suicidal tendencies. In 1987, Arsenal was twenty-five and living in Liverpool with L, who had given him his first son, X. He wasn't working, in between jobs after getting made redundant in 1986 after the horrible injury to his hand.

I refer back to his Psychology Report: "There are a number of factors associated with Autistic Spectrum Disorder which may predispose Arsenal to the **depression** and distress he is currently experiencing."

As well as being on the spectrum, having a stammer and not being able to communicate properly, his form of autism also leads him to have bouts of depression. His comments about keeping busy; getting so high one moment and so low the next, especially around football; his obvious identity issues as a child and young man and now this confession – because that's what it feels like – about his suicide attempts. I will use this word several times in this book, but I'm sat in front of a true hero in Arsenal Whittick.

How he has turned his life around is nothing short of a miracle and as he himself admits, he's still on the journey, trying to make every day better than the last.

We continue.

Arsenal:	*Wow, yeah, so that was Watford in the cup.*
Alan:	*You've told me of three attempts… Let me get you a drink.*
Arsenal:	*Just water, please.*
Alan:	*[I've had a chance to gather my thoughts.] You know, Arsenal, you've never even mentioned this to me before?*
Arsenal:	*Sorry, mate.*
Alan:	*It's quite a thing to try and take your own life… It's another example of how a person with autism's mind works differently to someone who isn't on the spectrum. Because I have never specifically asked you that question, it's never come up.*
Arsenal:	*Yeah, yeah.*
Alan:	*But it's because it's linked to Arsenal Football Club. So, you said there's five games that have caused you to try and kill yourself. The Watford and Barcelona games. What are the others?*
Arsenal:	*I've give you three.*
Alan:	*Sorry, yes, the third was the Royal Bath Hotel; the hotel is the trigger, not a game?*
Arsenal:	*Yeah, I don't know why the hotel.*

It's then that Arsenal has a lightbulb moment. He realises why the Bath Hotel causes him to want to commit suicide. Even to this day he wants to 'walk into the water' whenever he walks past the hotel. He's never known why. Sat in my front room, talking about his past, I see the dawning, the realisation, what causes him to want to kill himself whenever he's associated with that particular hotel. But that's for another chapter.

> Arsenal: *Let me write that down. Wow! That's the first time that's ever popped into me head.*
> Alan: *Is it linked to football?*
> Arsenal: *No! The Royal Bath isn't. But this the only bit that you can't put in the book, about the Royal Bath.*
> Alan: *OK.*
> Arsenal: *It's connected to me…*

As I wrote a moment ago, that's for another chapter, as Arsenal, a few months later, changed his mind. Back to the football and, more importantly, the triggers that caused Arsenal to try to kill himself.

> Alan: *Tonight was supposed to be the fun night when we talked about football.*
> Arsenal: *[Laughing out loud] I can tell you about Watford, Barcelona, Nayim from the halfway [10th May 1995].*
> Alan: *So, let's go back to you. What were the last two occasions?*
> Arsenal: *Nayim, from the halfway line. I don't know if you ever ever remember?*
> Alan: *Was that when David Seaman let it go over his head or through his hands?*

Arsenal: *Well, sort of. It was David Seaman in goal for AFC. And he was on the penalty spot, we were playing in the Cup Winners' Cup final and it was the last minute of the game [in fact the 120th minute at the end of extra time and was heading for a penalty shootout], this guy called Nayim, and it was on the halfway line, and he used to play for Spurs, didn't he?*

Alan: *Was this at the Emirates?*

Arsenal: *No, this was abroad, it was the final. It was from the halfway line, but he was on the touch line. And whether he meant it or not, but from the corner, from the halfway line, it went over David Seaman and into the net.*

Alan: *I do remember the goal. It was an incredible goal.*

Arsenal: *Yeah [quite obviously not thinking it was an incredible goal].*

Alan: *Whether he meant it or not, and purely from a neutral's perspective, I remember being gobsmacked when it happened. So what year was that then?*

Arsenal: *Not sure. [I looked this game up, it was the 10th May 1995 in Paris versus Zaragoza of Spain.]*

Alan: *And this caused you to try and kill yourself?*

Arsenal: *Yeah. I watched it in a pub in, used to be The Malt and Hops, in Southbourne. I watched it there. And then, coming home, I always walk the bus route. So, I walked past the Bell and I thought, and right opposite there's a train station. Pokesdown for Boscombe.*

    So, I walked onto the platform and I'm waiting for a train. And there's no fucking trains. [Laughing] Just my luck. Just no trains. Just no trains.

Alan:	You've had some terrible things happen to you, but you've had some good luck when it's come to these incidents.
Arsenal:	Yeah. Just no trains. *[Arsenal exhales deeply. I think that he thinks he had bad luck as there were no trains, but no trains meant he couldn't throw himself in front of one which was absolutely his intention.]*
Alan:	What's the last one and then we'll call it a night?
Arsenal:	Robbie Fowler when he scored that hat-trick against AFC in about, in about three minutes, wasn't it? *[August 28th 1994 – still the fastest hat-trick in the Premier League at four minutes and thirty-three seconds. Final score 3-0 to Liverpool.]* When he scored it, I remember him, he was just, by the AFC section, and I just hated him. And it just sent me down. I think because it was against Liverpool as well, and it was Robbie Fowler. And they were good goals, well some of them were.

I just, I couldn't handle it. I think we got beat 4-1 *[it was 3-0]*, and I just couldn't handle it. So, on the way home, I walked from Anfield and that, and I was just walking home through every dangerous area. Just hoping to get fucked or something. Or get battered, die, whatever? And I walked through Croxteth, walked through Tuebrook—

Alan:	With an Arsenal top on?
Arsenal:	Yeah. Just hoping someone would just give me a hiding. I was just walking and walking, just fucking trying to bump into people. I don't mean literally, but hoping there would be gangs about, and they'd go, "Look at him, with that top on. Let's go and fuck him."

Alan:	*Do you suffer from clinical depression?*
Arsenal:	*You know what? I wouldn't have knew, but in the notes from the hospital it says that I had some type of depression which no one had ever told me so I wouldn't know! But I was under Kings Park Community Hospital in Boscombe, then I was under Alderney Hospital, then I had a, had a, let's see what it actually was? I had a social worker under mental health, and they used five times…*

Arsenal then spends several minutes going through his personal files looking for any reference to depression. He finds a reference for how he deals with feeling down.

> *In the hospital book I have a strategy for when I'm feeling shit. I say to myself, "Yeah, but look how far I've come."*

Alan:	*Trust me, mate, you're an inspiration.*

We now have the knowledge that Arsenal has tried to kill himself at least five times. We are starting to understand what his mind will allow and not allow him to do. So, we can now look back with an informed view of why he behaved in certain ways and his lack of ability to strike up meaningful relationships. Taking all this into consideration, we zoom back in time to 1984 to examine Arsenal's first proper relationship and his two sons, X and Y. For the sake of propriety, we shall call her 'L'.

Chapter Twelve

Fatherhood

1984 to 2013

Please, be tolerant of those who describe a sporting moment as their best ever. We do not lack imagination, nor have we had sad and barren lives; it is just that real life is paler, duller, and contains less potential for unexpected delirium.

Nick Hornby, AFC fan, *Fever Pitch*

WE GO BACK TO 1984 WHEN ARSENAL MET L FOR THE FIRST time. He was twenty-two years old, working at Gostins of Halewood and yet to master his stammer and over twenty-five years away from being told he was on the spectrum. To quote Arsenal himself, "He was just different."

Dressing as Gary Numan's many alter-egos when he went out in Liverpool at night and proudly wearing the only AFC shirt seen in Liverpool during the day, he was cast as an outsider wherever and whenever he set foot over the doorstep. He hadn't been that bothered about sexual relationships with anyone, thinking that 'if it happened, it happened'. His psychology report confirms: "Arsenal reported that he did not become interested in women until his twenties. He reported not being able to tell when girls showed their interest. His first girlfriend, with whom he had a chaste relationship, turned out to be sixteen – something which he only became aware of when confronted by her father. He went on to have a nine-year relationship with another woman [L], who bore him two sons. However, Arsenal discussed how he wanted the relationship to end after two months but felt unable to say, "No."

Here is Arsenal's autism kicking in again and preventing him from making the break that he expresses he so clearly wanted. Instead he embarked on what from the outside can only be described as an unpredictable relationship.

Arsenal:	*In 1984, I met a girl. Off our estate, and that was me first girlfriend. About 1984?*
Alan:	*What was her name?*
Arsenal:	*L. I'll show you some information when you come round on Friday about that relationship. But I was with her from 1984 'til 1992.*
Alan:	*So, you must have been in love then?*
Arsenal:	*I had two boys; I've got two boys. [I did notice that Arsenal had answered a different question to the one I asked. He can't lie but he can avoid telling you the truth.]*
Alan:	*Did you get married?*
Arsenal:	*No, no.*
Alan:	*You must have lived together, I guess?*
Arsenal:	*Errr, briefly. I've got a file at home and it's the history, well not the history but... This might sound stupid to you, but I'd been with her about a couple of weeks and I knew that I didn't want to be with her.*

Alan:	*I've read this. You've said this to somebody else.*
Arsenal:	*It's in a letter from Alderney Hospital.*
Alan:	*But, you never told her?*
Arsenal:	*Not that I didn't tell her, I couldn't get that message down from me brain to tell her.*
Alan:	*So, when you say you didn't want to be with her, did you know at the time you didn't? Or did you only know afterwards when you looked back, and you realised you didn't want to be with her?*
Arsenal:	*I knew there and then in the pub.*
Alan:	*You knew there and then, and you couldn't say anything?*
Arsenal:	*I couldn't get that message coming down.*
Alan:	*What do you mean by that? You obviously felt it, so you were thinking it, so you knew it. Could you not bring yourself to say it?*
Arsenal:	*I don't know what it was? I just couldn't, I don't know what it was?*
Alan:	*So, in answer to my question I asked you: "Did you love her?" You didn't?*
Arsenal:	*[He takes a very long time to answer.] No, but you know what—*
Alan:	*Did she love you?*
Arsenal:	*Yeah. We had two boys. And then I watched Dead Poets Society. I've got a picture frame on my wall of four movies. And when I watched that for some reason, that just went right in there. [Points to his own temple.]*
Alan:	*Carpe diem?*
Arsenal:	*So, I watched that to about two o'clock in the morning. And when I got up the next day, I said to L, "I need to talk to you." I said, "I'm going. I'm leaving."*

> *And she went, "What?"*
>
> *Just by watching that film, I don't know what it done but it done something to me.*

Alan: Seize the day. That's what it was. Obviously, it went into your thought process and you knew you had to do something about it.

Arsenal: It's near the end, isn't it? And the lad shoots himself.

Alan: That's right.

Arsenal: And the dad has realised then, but it's too late, isn't it?

Alan: Exactly.

Arsenal: And the next day I went, "I'm leaving."

As Arsenal has told me many times, either he sees something that resonates with him or alternatively someone has to tell him specifically to undertake an action. For example, his dad telling him he could now have a drink every weekend because he had turned eighteen. It was over twenty years later before Arsenal realised he didn't have to have a drink if he didn't want to.

Such is the case here. He was unhappy. We know he had tried to kill himself once or at the very least had had suicidal tendencies. He was stuck in a life that he had never wanted but had stumbled his way into. He loved his two sons but for whatever reason, he says he and L had never been in love. Certainly, from his side. He watched Robin Williams and decided, subconsciously at first, to seize his own day. He hadn't thought this through and had nowhere to go, he just knew he needed to go.

The relationship had not been easy for them both from the outset, having to live with L's mother in her house. I can only imagine how difficult that would be for both parties. We know how Arsenal can behave and I'm sure it was a difficult set-up for all concerned.

In order to try and get a balanced view of these years of
Arsenal's life I also rang L, to seek her permission to include
the following elements of their relationship, which she gave me
but only if I included her version of the story. L and Arsenal
have very different memories of what happened during these
years and I think it's only fair that we hear both sides of the
story.

Alan: *Do you think L behaved the way she did because
after you watched Dead Poets Society and you
spoke to her the next morning it was just a
complete bolt out of the blue and she couldn't
understand it?*

Arsenal: *No. Because the first time we lived together was in
her mum's actually. And her sisters and that so…
And then I got asked to leave at three o'clock in the
morning. Her mum knocked on the door. On the
bedroom door and she come in and she said, "Can
I talk to you? I want you to leave."
And I said, "OK."
And then she said, "Now."
And I said, "OK." I just left at three o'clock
in the morning. I just walked round and that. I
didn't have that processing, did I? So, I just done
it. Left and then—*

Alan: *What did L say?*

Arsenal: *She didn't say nothing. She never said nothing. So,
I got a flat and after about six months L started to
visit each weekend.*

Alan: *And did you have children at this time?*

Arsenal: *Yeah, yeah, X. We had one. Every weekend I used
to see them and then they stayed every weekend
and then go home.*

Alan:	*And was L living with her mum and dad or just her mum?*
Arsenal:	*Her mum and her three sisters.*
Alan:	*Oh, OK.*
Arsenal:	*And then one weekend I got a knock on me door and I thought I'd better answer it as nobody knocked on me door. So, I went to answer it and it was her mum and her sisters. They all come in. And they said, "Oh, we've got some good news. We've got a letter from the council saying you've got a house."*
	And L was happy and that and then she said, "Where is it?"
	And they said, "It's opposite us."
	And I went, "Shit!" So, it was right opposite. It was her mum there, then it was ours. And then it was me L and X in the house and then in '89 we had Y. And then I watched Dead Poets Society in '92 and I told her.
	And then… I told her in June of '92 and for some reason, I don't know why, I stayed in the same house with… Well, I slept in the boys' room for seven or eight months.

L doesn't remember anything about Dead Poets Society, I asked her specifically and she says that she was told by people in the local pub, The Penny Black, that Arsenal had been seen with Nicola and he was still living with her. We need to remember here the black and white thinking of an autistic person. Arsenal believes he had told L that it was over between them. He then moves into the bedroom where his sons slept. To him the relationship is finished. If he wants to talk to somebody else in the local pub, he will do so.

He believes he is doing no wrong but to L he is still living under the same roof as her and his two sons, something that he openly admits to and tells Nicola's mother when he meets her. In Arsenal's mind he has done no wrong. L says, 'I had a terrible time for three years with him. I was in and out of court for three years because Arsenal was trying to get custody of the kids'.

Alan: *So between '86 and '93 when you were either living with her mum or in a flat or the house and you had your two young sons with you, how was you earning a living in those days?*

Arsenal: *I was working in a company called Nouveaux Security. They used to make timber and aluminium doors and windows. They were security doors and that. I've always worked [very proudly said].*

Alan: *I know that, I'm just trying to work out where you'd got to at this point.*

Arsenal: *I worked for Nouveaux and they went into liquidation. And when they went into liquidation that's when L's mum said to me you've got to go.*

Alan: *OK. Where did you go from there?*

Arsenal: *A company made up of parts of the Nouveaux company. They brought certain sections over like the aluminium section. They took the welder and me. So, I went to TGS Doors of Aintree.*

Alan: *So when you walked out of this house that was opposite L's mum's house. What did you do?*

Arsenal: *I was homeless. Only for a matter of days. Because I stayed there, and I got together a deposit for a flat and stuff. And when I had everything that's when I was going to move. And I was supposed to*

Arsenal cooking his first ever meal at the age of fifty-one in his new flat.

Arsenal managing to get his hands on an Olympic Torch in 2012.

Sam looking for affection, 2005.

Danni looking for affection, 2008.

Arsenal picked these photos as he believed they best embodied his reluctance to hug his kids. On both photos he is shying away from bodily contact when his daughters are just looking for some sign of affection.

A heavily pregnant Nicola carrying Sam needing some chocolate – HELP.

A beautiful photo of the young Arsenal, Nicola and Sam.

Married in Gretna Green in 2001.

Arsenal and his much younger sister Jeni.

Arsenal and Sam, circa 2000.

Sam realising the Valentine's card was from Arsenal.
(He can only write in block capitals and never thought Sam would notice!)

Sam and Danni with their pet rats, named after AFC players, 2006.

Samantha's eighteenth at Arsenal's new flat after he and Nicola separated.

Autism in action.
Arsenal thinking no one will know him if he has a bucket on his head?

Like father like daughter?

Arsenal with his mum at his 2001 wedding.

The only photo Nicola has of her, Arsenal, Sam and Danni together.
Taken about 11/12 years ago at a family wedding.

pick the keys up on a Friday. So, I left on a Friday and I went to pick up the keys and he said, "Oh, can you pick them up Monday?"

I never even thought, did I? I just went, "Yeah, OK." And I didn't have nowhere to go.

Alan: *Could you not go back to your mum and dad's?*

Arsenal: *Well, I didn't think of that one, did I? I never thought of it, I never processed it. That was the problem I had back then. Never used to process stuff. It's amazing. If you told me something, I'd be, "Yeah, OK." And I'd do it. I didn't have that ability to process stuff. It's amazing. The amount of mistakes I've made by not processing stuff, by not either going away... But now I have strategies for that.*

Alan: *You say you made mistakes, but making a mistake is when you know you should be doing something, but you do something else instead. You weren't making a mistake because you didn't have the capacity to behave any other way. Don't beat yourself up for that [in hindsight this was probably the wrong choice of words].*

Arsenal: *So I had the weekend just having a little walk. I slept in St Nicholas's Church. Well, in the doorway.*

Alan: *What about all your clothes and all your belongings?*

Arsenal: *I'd borrowed me brother's car so I'd only took clothes I had left that hadn't been destroyed. I had the bare minimum of stuff. I had a duvet, a kettle and some clothes. That was about it.*

Alan: *And during all these hard times you carried on watching AFC?*

Arsenal: *Yeah [as if I had just asked the most stupid question on God's green earth]. I was addicted, wasn't I? That was the most important thing for me, wasn't it?*

I think we need to make some facts absolutely clear here. Arsenal loved his two boys. In his black-and-white mind, he can clearly differentiate between loving L and loving his sons. As can most of us, but not so granular as Arsenal. What he didn't understand due to his executive functioning shortfall was the problems that telling someone that 'I don't love you' may cause when he was trying to be a good father, even though he didn't live with L anymore.

Society in 2019 is full of marital breakdown and custody arrangements for children. Sadly, it's a common fact of life. According to the Office of National Statistics in 2016, "The estimated percentage of marriages ending in divorce (assuming 2010 divorce and mortality rates throughout the duration of marriage) is forty-two per cent. Around half of these divorces are expected to occur in the first ten years of marriage."

These figures don't include breakdowns in relationships when people haven't got married but children are still involved. In 2012, over 130,000 divorces occurred in the UK.

When Arsenal 'seized the day', he couldn't think through the consequences of his actions. His brain simply didn't work that way.

Arsenal was having terrible issues in gaining quality time with his sons and eventually went to the law to help him. L has told me that the lads did not want to see him and it was not her stopping them. She was carrying out their wishes. This came up in a different conversation with Arsenal when we were actually talking about his favourite movies.

Arsenal: When I left the boys and that, I went to a solicitor
            to gain better access to them. I went to a solicitor
            called XXXX in Anfield and he asked me a
            question: "How much do you want to see your two
            boys?"

            And I went to him, "All the time." So, he writ a
            letter, which either I never really understood it...
            He writ a letter to L which I didn't know about.
            And it just asked something along the lines, "My
            client is going for full custody of the boys." And it
            just, boom. [Impersonates a big explosion.] World
            War III.

Alan: And was that what you wanted to say?

Arsenal: No, I wanted to see me boys, but I didn't want full
            custody.

Alan: Did L just fight then?

Arsenal: It was more than fight, mate. I got... Every time
            I went to court to get better access, about a week
            earlier, and I've got it all in black and white.
            I've got all the forms and papers. About a week
            later [earlier] you can guarantee I got arrested.
            [Arsenal laughs ruefully.] Oh dear, I got arrested.
            You know, just by allegations. All the allegations
            I was cleared of, it was L making the allegations
            against me.

            And but, I've kept all me paperwork. I've got
            all the court papers [and Arsenal has because
            I've seen them all]. I've been arrested for assault,
            and then a week later I'd go to court. The family
            court to get access to me two boys. And their
            solicitor would say, "Mr Whittick is out on bail
            for assaulting Ms L XXXXX."

            And the judge would go, "Is that true?"

And I'd go, "No."

And their solicitor would say, "Here's the paper, your honour."

And he would say, "No, it's true."

And I would say, "I haven't touched her."

So, to me it wasn't true, was it? So, then I couldn't see the boys until that court case was over. I won that court case and then one of the bail conditions was I couldn't go to the house to pick me lads up. So, I had one court order saying I could see them on these days at these times and I had another piece of paper saying I couldn't go the house to get them, could I? For weeks.

I'd go again, a new court date and I'd be so happy. [Arsenal claps his hands as he remembers the joy of getting another chance to see his sons.] Right, I'm going to me boys again. But, the week before that court date, there'd be an allegation, arrested for kidnapping me boys, that was horrendous.

I was at the bus stop with me two boys, and this Escort just pulled up at the bus stop. And these two guys got out, jeans and that. They went to me, "Are you Arsenal?"

And I went, "Yeah." And I thought, Shit, I'm going to get beat up again.

One of them just showed me this badge. It was a round copper thing, it was only about that big [holds his fingers about two inches apart]. I think I'd watched too much telly as I thought police badges were much bigger. And he went, "CID [Criminal Investigation Department]."

And the other one said to me boys, "Are you X?"

> *And he went, "Yeah." [Arsenal impersonates a little boy speaking.]*
>
> *"And are you Y?"*
>
> *And he went, "Yeah."*
>
> *Next minute, and I don't know where he came from, but he came from somewhere, he come behind me and he put these plastic pulls on me hands behind me back and he put me head on the bonnet. This police car was unmarked, and they said, "Right, we're arresting you for the kidnapping of these two boys."*
>
> *And I'm going, "What?" I got arrested for kidnapping me two boys. I got cleared. They were just all allegations. And I thought, wow, amazing. I got it. I got all the paperwork here.*

Alan: *Do you want this going in the book?*

Arsenal: *Yeah, you can put it in the book because it's there, it's in black and white; it's true. Me and me boys were all right. I've got pictures of them from that high [Arsenal holds his hand two feet from the floor], until they were in their twenties.*

I spoke at length to L about these two specific allegations. She says that Arsenal assaulted her late one night after knocking on her door. He had been drinking and words were exchanged before he assaulted her. Arsenal denies this ever happened and the CPS, (Crown Prosecution Service), discontinued the proceedings as it was not in the public interest to proceed. The decision was made on the evidence and information provided.

As to the allegation of Arsenal kidnapping his two sons L knows nothing about it and knows nothing about Arsenal being arrested for the said allegation.

At a later date I asked Arsenal why he had left Liverpool and moved down to Bournemouth. There were several reasons, but basically Arsenal had met the lady who was his next big relationship, a relationship that would last, ironically, until he found out he had autism. He met Nicola and then by the time he moved to Bournemouth, Sunday 5th February 1996, Samantha was seven months old.

To quote Arsenal when speaking of this time in his life: "Every week was mayhem when I was trying to pick me boys up."

Arsenal was being pulled every which way he could and because of his autism and poor executive functioning, he found himself not capable of thinking around the problem. Eventually he had to deal with the whole situation and moved away. Arsenal needed piece of mind that his new partner and baby daughter were going to be happy.

Alan: *So why did you eventually leave Liverpool after fighting for so long and so hard to see your lads?*

Arsenal: *A mixture of reasons. The biggest thing was, 'the blue file'. I was just getting beat up all the time because of the lies getting told about me and that. [Arsenal keeps all his records of this time in his life in a bright blue ring binder.] So, Nicola was on a bus and she was about six months pregnant. And as Nicola was at the back of the bus when she was getting off the bus, she was coming down, she tripped up. And then, wow [Arsenal still can't believe it. Was it all becoming too much for Nicola as well]. She was like that [he holds his hands out in front of himself indicating how big Nicola was carrying Samantha].*

It was just all... It was getting... [Arsenal runs out of words.]

Alan: Was she OK?

Arsenal: Yeah, yeah. She was all right. It was just every week was mayhem for me to just go and pick me two boys up.

And one week I went, and I knocked on the door, L come to the door, and stuck a V up to me and just shut the door. I knocked again, and knocked and knocked, and I was getting no answer. She screamed that I wasn't seeing the boys. So, I went back home, and I spoke to me solicitor on the Monday, back then. And I said, "I never seen me boys."

And he went, "OK. Speak to your court welfare officer."

I think, Mr M. So, I spoke to him and told him I'd turned up and I didn't see the boys and he said, "OK. Let me talk to L." About two hours later he come back to me and he said, "I spoke to L and she said you didn't turn up?"

And I went, "No, I did."

And I remember him just saying to me, "Arsenal, if you want to see your boys, mate, it's imperative that you keep to this order." And I was so pissed off because he wasn't supporting me.

So, I went back to me solicitor and I went, "This is what I've been told."

And he went, "What! There's only one other way. When you go next week, you go and if… Don't cause no trouble or nothing, and you have to take your court order with you."

So, I knock on the door. L comes and she goes, "You're wasting your time. You're not going to see them."

	And I thought, Fuck— Sorry.
Alan:	*Don't be sorry. I've swore all the way through my notes and I'm going to quote you verbatim for many sections. So, say it as it was. If you say 'fuck off', it's in the book.*
Arsenal:	*OK. So, I done what I was advised to do. I walked away, I rang the police at Prescott and I said, "I've got a court order under the Children's Act of 1989 and it's not being carried out. I've been advised by me solicitor, XXXX of Anfield, to call the police."*

And he said, "OK."

He got the address and he come down and he knocked on the door [Arsenal starts laughing as he remembers], L came to the door and went to the police, "You're fucking wasting your time," gave a V sign and shut the door.

Alan:	*She gave the police the V as well?*
Arsenal:	*So, the police actually knocked again, so she opened it. And then they gave her this spiel about the court injunction, and she said, "I don't fucking care." And she slammed the door again.*

And the police said, "Listen, you're not going to see your boys today. But we can write a number down for you to say we've been out and witnessed this court order being broken."

And so, Monday morning I ring me solicitor and tell him I've got this number. He said, "All right. We're going to take it back to court because we've got proof, she's broken the order." So, I thought, OK. And then on the same day, Mr M rang me up and he was fuming at me. And I goes... I couldn't understand it?

Alan:	*Remind me who Mr M is please?*
Arsenal:	*The court welfare officer. He said to me, "Can you explain to me what happened over the weekend, Arsenal?"*
	And I said, "Yeah. I went to the house. I never got the boys, so I rang the police." And he bollocked me. He ripped into me for getting the police. And he said to me, "You know you have made a big mistake. Those boys are never going to want to see you. The stress you've caused them by bringing the police to the door."
	I was going, "But last week you wouldn't believe me." Oh, mate, it was just loads of things.
Alan:	*So what was the outcome of that? How did it end up? You went back to court?*
Arsenal:	*Mr M said to L that he would turn up with me and if I didn't see the kids at least he could witness it. But then I think he turned up once for the first time the next week and I think that warned her off then.*
Alan:	*So you started to see your lads from that point?*
Arsenal:	*Yeah.*
Alan:	*Approximately what year was this? How old were your lads then?*
Arsenal:	*Seven and four. Because I left when they were six and three. Then on the seventh birthday, X was seven in the February, and I had a party for them. And in the May Y was four, and when I went to get them L said to me, "You're not giving him a party, you know, today." So, I wouldn't answer back. I wouldn't answer back because I can't lie, so I couldn't say I'm not. So, I never seen him that day on his birthday. So, the next year I never*

mentioned no parties at all. And I picked X up on his eighth birthday, never had a party or anything. But then it must have been about April time, so halfway between X's birthday and Y's birthday I gave them a party because no one expected it. So, I got the two boys...

And I've got a picture in a frame in the house of two cakes, one with five candles and one with eight. And when they went home, they obviously said, "Oh, we've had a party..." And it was like World War III!

I've got loads of photos of me and the boys, but when you read the report it says that, "The boys don't have a memory of any good times with their dad."

L has a very different version of these events. The boys did not want to go with Arsenal and she was protecting her children. She remembers Arsenal bringing the police to the door but she never screamed at them or slammed the door in their faces. The police actually entered the house and spoke to the boys and then concluded that Arsenal would not be seeing his lads.

L told me, 'They didn't want to go with him. I never didn't let them go. It was down to them. They didn't want to go.' I agreed in my conversation with L that I would include her responses as she told me.

The report Arsenal refers to is a 'Report of the Family Court Welfare Officer', dated 21st May 1997 for a custody hearing on the 4th June 1997 at Merseyside Family Court Welfare Services, Barrow Street, St Helens. The following is my summary of the report:

THE CHILDREN

The boys, X and Y, were seen on two occasions and presented to the welfare officers as unhappy and uncomfortable. They really didn't want to be there and on the whole were largely non-committal.

They seemed to have close relationships with their mum and her partner of whom they spoke positively. Contrarily they didn't want to speak about Arsenal but when they did speak said that, 'They had no good memories of time spent with him.'

They felt that these Court proceedings were upsetting for their mum and were therefore angry towards Arsenal for instigating them. Both children expressed the view that they, 'Never wanted to see him', and they could not be persuaded otherwise. They believed that meeting their dad would only cause them both more worry for their mum.

They didn't want any more gifts or letters and were not going to change their minds any time soon. They didn't know how Arsenal felt about them and didn't want to know. The majority of these views had to be dragged out of the boys as they were unwilling to talk. One of Arsenal's sons expressed the view that Arsenal had told him that he preferred his brother to him which caused obvious anger and a sense of injustice.

If only all interested parties had known at the time of Arsenal's autism, many of these statements could have been explained. The boys didn't know how Arsenal felt because of his social interactions and if he wasn't specifically asked something, he wouldn't have said it. Did he love his lads deeply: YES. Did he tell them on a regular basis, if at all, undoubtedly: NO.

Had he at some point expressed a preference for one son over the other: probably. But what the circumstances were we will never know. Why did the boys say they had no good memories with their father when we have many photos suggesting the opposite? We can only speculate. It just seems all so sad when all Arsenal wanted to be was a good father.

The report goes on to discuss the applicant, Arsenal, and the respondent, L, before offering an opinion and recommendation. Again, the following is my summary, not to weigh one side more heavily than the other but simply for brevity's sake plus the document cannot be produced in its entirety due to legal restrictions.

The report as written is in the favour of L more than Arsenal. This is based simply on the answers given to the family court officers in their pursuit of the best outcome for the boys. Secondly, it represents Arsenal's inability to actually understand some of the nuances of the questions and his inability to give anything other than what to him is a hundred per cent truthful answer.

When asked in court if he was on bail for whatever the latest accusation was, Arsenal always answered honestly and truthfully: yes, he was on bail. He was also on bail for an accusation for which he would eventually be cleared – I know as I've read the letters either cancelling the court hearing, dropping the accusation or actually acquitting him in court. But when asked the simple black or white, yes or no, question Arsenal's answer would never be in the grey. Which is where most custody hearings do sit.

ARSENAL

Arsenal presented evidence of his monthly letters to X and Y which L had agreed he could write in 1995 at a Court hearing. He also had copies of all his telephone bills proving he had made calls in order to speak to his boys.

The tribunal stated that his sons are influenced by their mother and her extended family, (but the majority of children are influenced by their parents and family). It quoted Arsenal as saying that,

"When they are on their own, they will talk to me but when their mum is there, they look for eye contact from her."

It was Arsenal's belief that the boys thought that any contact with him was deemed as wrong, but he had no idea what his sons would say to the welfare officers and in his own interview he told them this fact.

L, in her responses, made several points but most were to the fact that the lads themselves did not want to see their dad and she was merely acceding to their wishes. She acknowledged that Arsenal did write to their sons, but they didn't want the letters. Arsenal did turn up at their school to try and see the teachers as he never got the letters telling him when the parents' evenings were, and as these were unannounced, this seemed to work against him.

L did not believe she influenced the lads and said that if they wanted to see their dad then she would facilitate the meeting. Everything in the report from L is right and proper and as it should be.

The opinion of the officers in the report then all but killed Arsenal's chances of seeing his sons.

OPINION

X and Y's loyalty to their mum made it impossible for them to move forward or feel free. L stated she bore no animosity towards Arsenal but that hadn't always been the case.

X and Y had witnessed so much stress and antagonism that they had locked into a negative perception of their dad. They felt that they needed to protect their mum and felt guilty about any positive view they held about Arsenal.

As a consequence, the Courts did not want to put the two boys under any added pressure as it would be too emotionally damaging for them.

The officers were also concerned that L couldn't present a more positive attitude of Arsenal to their sons as the boys would miss out on a vital part of their development. They also suggested that X and Y may eventually hold this against their mum when they realised the opportunities they had missed.

This last statement proved to be totally incorrect as the two grown-up men today have little or no contact with their father. The final part of the report was the recommendation to the court which was carried.

Arsenal lost and the indirect contact remained as it was in the 1995 Order and there was no Order passed for direct contact between Arsenal and his sons. The 1995 Order allowed postal contact at Christmas, Easter and their birthdays plus one additional postcard in the month of September. All correspondence had to be via the court welfare officer.

Prior to this, in an order raised on the 14th December 1994, Arsenal was allowed for: "Contact to take place at Whiston Family Centre every Wednesday between 4pm and 6pm. The applicant, L XXXXX, shall use her best endeavours to facilitate contact."

> Arsenal: *I had one interview with the court social workers type people, and I was living in Bournemouth and I went down to Prescot to meet them. And they were forty minutes late and I think I got about twenty minutes with them. I was talking about the boys [in a very enthusiastic voice], "Yeah, we have a good time. Look at all of these photos."*
>
> *I remember them saying to me, "We'll have a look at them next time," but I never ever got a next time. They spoke to me for about twenty minutes*

and they visited L about four or five times. So, when you read that, how can they do that for twenty minutes, meet me and they never seen any of the proof that I had, that I had good times with the boys. I've got all the photos at home, so I know it happened, so, so, that's what I go by.

Yeah, so that was the biggest reason for coming to Bournemouth. To get away from all that shite.

Arsenal, over the course of three years, had had his custody rights moved from a visit with the lads once every two weeks to four postcards a year. I leave you to make your own mind up.

Arsenal has kept copies of every single letter he wrote to his sons during these years. He continued to write to them once a month until the 20th November 2007. There are 155 letters in the file, all numbered and dated; he never missed a month. As a father myself, my heart broke reading the simple messages of love sent out from Arsenal, starting on the 24th April 1995. He started them as weekly letters that then became monthly. He also keeps copies of all the replies he got back from his sons. Unfortunately, that file remains empty.

MONDAY 24 APRIL 95

DEAR X AND Y

I WAS WITH YOUR MUM ON THURSDAY MORNING. HOW GLAD I WAS TO HEARD THE BOTH OF YOU ARE DOING REALLY WELL AT HOME AND SCHOOL. YOUR MUM AGREED IT WOULD BE BETTER IF I WROTE TO YOU BOTH EACH WEEK NOW, SO I AM VERY HAPPY. DID YOU GET MY POST CARD OK. DID YOU WATCH THE ARSENAL MATCH ON THURSDAY. (PARIS HERE I COME)! SHARE THE £5.00 BETWEEN YOU BOTH EACH WEEK (NOT £4.00 TO YOU Y) LOOKING FORWARD TO WRITING MY NEXT LETTER ALREADY. TAKE CARE, MISSING YOU BOTH

LOTS OF LOVE
FROM YOUR
DAD XX

MONDAY 5 JUNE 95

DEAR X AND Y
    LOVE ISOLATION
    THESE ARE WORDS JUST FOR YOU, ONLY
WORDS BUT IT'S ALL I CAN DO. REASONS FADE AS
REASONS CAN DO, ALL I WANT IS TO TALK WITH
YOU, YOU CRIED WITH ME, LAUGHED AT ME,
TALKED TO ME, SHELTERED ME, (YOU) FOUGHT
BY ME, LIED FOR ME, YOU LIVED FOR ME. (SO) CAL
ME, AND I'LL RUN TO YOU, ASK ME, AND I'D DIE
FOR YOU, YOU WERE THERE, YOU WERE ALWAYS
THERE, LIKE A FRIEND, LIKE A LIFELONG FRIEND,
AND I LOVE YOU. I BROKE YOUR HEART, AND YOU
STOLE MINE, MEMORYS LIE, BUT THEY'RE ALL I
CAN FIND. CALL MY NAME, SING MY SONG, CALL
FOR MR, I'VE BEEN WAITING SO LONG, (JUST)
CALL ME, AND I'LL RUN TO YOU, ASK ME, AND
I'D DIE FOR YOU. YOU WERE THERE, YOU WERE
ALWAYS THERE, LIKW A FRIEND, LIKE A LIFELONG
FRIEND.
    AND I MISS YOU.
                      LOVE FROM DAD XX

Printed with kind permission from Gary Numan.

WEDNESDAY, 14 FEB 96

DEAR X AND Y.

HOPE BOTH OF YOU ARE KEEPING WELL, HAVE YOU GOT THE £40 BIRTHDAY MONEY STILL I GAVE YOU BOTH OR DID YOU BUY A HELICOPTER? FOR EASTER WHAT WOULD YOU LIKE! LET ME NO AND I WILL TRY MY BEST, OR MAYBE ME AND YOUR MUM CAN GO HALF EACH. MY NEW HOUSE IS REALLY NICE & 10 MINUTES FROM THE BEACH AND 20 MINUTES FROM GUERNSEY. MAYBE YOU WOULD LET ME TAKE YOU BOTH DURNING YOUR SCHOOL SUMMER HOLIDAYS, I WOULD LIKE TO PHONE YOU EACH MONTH & WRITE IF YOU BOTH DON'T MIND. PLEASE WRITE BACK AND LET ME KNOW ABOUT THIS.

MISSING YOU BOTH LOADS

LOVE FROM
DAD XX

MONDAY, 1ˢᵗ JULY, 96

DEAR X AND Y,

HOPE YOU BOTH ARE KEEPING WELL AND LOOKING FORWARD TO YOUR SUMMER HOLIDAYS, HOPE THE WEATHER IS GOOD FOR YOU BOTH. ARE FLAT IS REALLY GOOD AND FINISHED NOW, I HAVE YOUR MONEY TO FINISH YOUR BEDROOM OFF, LET ME NO HOW TO GET IT TO YOU. DID YOU BOTH WATCH EURO 96? SAMANTHA IS WALKING AND HAS TWO TEETH NOW AND WHEN I ASK HER WHERE X AND Y ARE SHE POINTS TO YOUR PICTURE I HAVE IN OUR LIVING ROOM. LOKKING FORWARD TO MY NEXT VISIT TO LIVERPOOL SO HOPE TO SEE YOU BOTH THEN,

MISSING YOU BOTH LOADS

LOVE ALWAYS FROM YOUR
DAD XX

SUNDAY 1st DECEMBER

DEAR X AND Y,

ONCE AGAIN YOUR SCHOOL REPORT I GOT FROM YOUR TEACHERS ON PARENTS NIGTH LAST WEEK WAS BRILLIANT (WELL DONE). PLEASE NOTE MY NEW ADDRESS ON TOP OF LETTER. OUR PLACE HAS 2 BEDROOMS SO SAMANTHA HAS HER OWN ROOM IN WHICH YOUR PICTURE HAS PRIDE OF PLACE HOPE YOU CAN CASH THE CHEQUE O.K. (£25 EACH) FOR CHRISTMAS, IF NOT LET ME NO BEFORE WEDNESDAY 11 DECEMBER AND I COULD PUT IT INTO YOUR CHRISTMAS CARDS IF YOU REALLY WANT, WHAT ARE YOU GETTING YOUR MUM FOR CHRISTMAS, LET ME NO AND I WILL PAY.

MISSING YOU BOTH LOADS, KEEP IN TOUCH

LOVE DAD XX

(LETTER 32)
FRIDAY, 1ˢᵗ AUGUST, 97

DEAR X AND Y,

HOPE YOUR BOTH ENJOYING YOUR SUMMER HOLIDAYS, I HAVE JUST GOT YOUR SCHOOL REPORTS, (WELL DONE BOTH OF YOU). HOPE YOU ARE LOOKING FORWARD TO YOUR NEW CLASS (Y) & SCHOOL (X). I WILL BE VISITING BOTH WHILE IN LIVERPOOL, BUT HAVE NO DATE YET? ARE YOU LOOKING FORWARD TO THE FOOTBALL SEASON, IF YOU WOULD LIKE THE NEW LIVERPOOL KIT LET ME NO YOUR SIZES, I WILL GET YOU ONE EACH. A CHEQUE FOR £10 IS £5 EACH FOR A GOOD SCHOOL REPORT, PLEASE KEEP IN TOUCH, YOUR MUM WILL NOT LOVE YOU ANY LESS AND IT WILL NOT BE WRONG IF YOU WRITE TO YOUR DAD. IF YOU CAN WRITE TO THE JUDGE YOU CAN WRITE TO YOUR OWN DAD.

MISS YOU BOTH AS ALWAYS LOVE

FROM YOUR DAD XX

(LETTER 34)
WED 1ˢᵗ OCT. 1997

DEAR X & Y,
THANK YOU SO MUCH FOR TUESDAY NIGHT, I
AM LOOKING FORAWRD TO DECEMBER ALREADY,
I WAS HAPPY SPENING TIME WITH YOU BOTH
AND MEANT WHAT I SAID ABOUT NOT GOING
BACK TO COURT EVER AGAIN, I HAVE STARTED
LOOKING FOR YOUR PLAYSTATION & GAMES. (X)
DID YOU BUY A CASEBALL & Y HOW OLD IS YOUR
CHICKEN? PLEASE WRITE AND LET ME NO, ALSO
SAY THANK YOU TO YOUR MUM FOR TUESDAY
NIGHT ALSO

LOVE FROM
YOUR DAD XX

(LETTER 43)
WEDNESDAY
1st JULY, 1998

DEAR X AND Y,
    PLEASE RING ME AT WORK, I JUST NEED TO
TALK TO YOU BOTH!
LOVE FROM YOUR
DAD XX

(LETTER – 49)
FRIDAY 1st JAN, 99

DEAR X AND Y,
  THANK YOU BOTH FOR GIVING ME THE BEST
CHRISTMAS TIME I HAVE EVER HAD, HOPE YOU
BOTH ENJOYED YOUR TIME, ALSO MY JOB AT
WORK HAS CHANGED I AM NOW WORKING IN
THE KITCHEN DOING FOOD FOR 280 PEOPLE ALL
DAY. (VERY HARD WORK INDEED) HOPE YOUR
MUM AND XXXX ENJOYED XMAS ALSO CAN I
HAVE YOUR TELEPHONE No SO I CAN TALK TO
YOU ON YOUR BIRTHDAYS

LOVE ALWAYS
FROM YOUR DAD
XX

(LETTER 72)
FRI – 1ˢᵗ DEC – 2000

DEAR X AND Y,
CONFIRMED DATES FOR MY CHRISTMAS VISIT ARE FRIDAY 8 DEC, 3 15PM UNTIL SUNDAY EVENING, MY RETURN TRAIN IS 3.10PM MONDAY AFTERNOON ALSO CONFIRMED JUST SIGNED TO A BSM FRANCHISED APPROVED DRIVING INSTRUCTOR, LOOKING FORWARD TO SEEING YOU BOTH ON WEDNESDAY

LOVE FROM
YOUR DAD XX

It's probably worth reminding us all at this juncture that X would have been fifteen years old in 2001 and Y would have been twelve. Arsenal has never missed a month writing these letters that you are reading a selection from since the first one in April 1995. There are many referencing birthdays; asking for phone numbers; requesting letters or meeting times; asking what his sons would like for Easter or birthdays or Christmas; planning trips to Liverpool or football matches; always expressing love simply and dearly. I can almost read the heartfelt prayers for some form of reciprocation between the simple lines of everyday life.

Arsenal shares everything that happened to him every month, from Samantha's first tooth to a change of job or home just hoping for something coming back. Nevertheless, he always says that when he got the chance to meet up with his sons, they always had a great time, and this can be read in the letters, plus Arsenal has an array of photos from when he did get the opportunity to spend time with them.

Let's continue Arsenal's personal history lesson from the early twenty-first century.

(LETTER 77)
TUE, 1ˢᵗ MAY, 2001

DEAR X AND Y,
    GOT BACK HOME TO BOURNEMOUTH O.K, JUST LIKE TO SAY A BIG THANK YOU FOR THE 3 DAYS WE HAD & FOR PLAYING WITH SAMANTHA ON MONDAY, LOOKING FORWARD TO MY TEST DAY AND MOVING HOUSE & HAVING OTHER BABY IN THE COMING MONTHS. ALSO ANY NEWS ON A BOURNEMOUTH HOLIDAY?
                        MISS YOU BOTH
                        LOVE FROM
                        DAD XX

(LETTER 80)
WED, 1st AUGUST, 01

DEAR X AND Y,
HOPE YOUR HOLIDAYS ARE GOING WELL, JUST HAD OUR SECOND DAUGHTER BORN AT 12.04PM TUESDAY 24 JULY. NAMED DANIELLE, WEIGHT 3lb 14oz, BABY OUT OF INTENSIVE CARE BUT STILL IN HOSPITAL AFTER 8 DAYS BEEN TOLD WILL LEAVE HOSPITAL IN 5-6 DAYS? DUE TO BEEN 5 WEEKS EARLY, ANYWAY HOPE EVERYTHING AND EVERYONE AT HOME IS O.K.
MISSING YOU BOTH
LOTS OF LOVE
DAD XX

(LETTER 84)
SATURDAY 1st
DECEMBER, 2001

DEAR X AND Y,
  HOPE ALL IS WELL AND LOKING FORWARD
TO CHRISTMAS. I HAVE SOME DATES FOR YOUR
CALENDAR.
  MONDAY 10 DECEMBER, 2001.
  START DATE FOR MY BUSINESS
  SATURDAY 15 DECEMBER, 2001
  MARRIAGE IN SCOTLAND
  SATURDAY 22 DECEMBER, 2001
  VISITING LIVERPOOL. (2 DAYS)
                              LOOKING FORWARD
                                 TO SEEING YOU
                                         BOTH,
                                LOVE FROM YOUR
                                       DAD XX

(LETTER 86)
FRIDAY, 1ˢᵗ FEB. 02

DEAR X & Y,

MY 40TH BIRTHDAY IS FAST APPROACHING, HALL AND DISCO BOTH BOOKED, BOTH OF YOU ARE INVITED OF COURSE, ASK YOUR MUM IS THIS OK, PLEASE LET ME NO ON WEDNESDAY HOW MANY DAYS YOU CAN STAY FOR, SO I CAN BOOK YOUR HOTEL & TRAVEL

LOTS OF LOVE
DAD XX

(LETTER 89)
WED 1ˢᵗ MAY. 02

DEAR X & Y,
LOST MY CASE AGAINST BSM, BUT GOING BACK TO A DIFFERENT COURT, HAD GOOD PRESS REPORTS & DONE 14 RADIO INTERVIEWS, GOING ON THE STARFISH PROJECT IN EAST SUSSEX FOR A WEEK ALSO. MY PARTY WAS REALLY GOOD (I HAVE A LETTER FROM ARSENE WENGER & A SIGNED SHIRT. ALL PLAYERS) LET ME NO THE BEST TIME/DAYS TO RING YOU BOTH AS I KEEP RINGING WHEN YOUR OUT. HOPE BOTH OF YOU ARE KEEPING WELL.

MISSING YOU BOTH
LOVE DAD XX

(LETTER 107)
SATURDAY, 1ˢᵗ NOV 03

DEAR X AND Y,
HOPE ALL IS O.K, Y TELLS ME MY LETTERS ARE
ALL THE SAME SO FROM NOW ON I WILL CHANGE
THEM. OUR FLAT IS NOW SOLD AGAIN FOR THE
THIRD TIME (SUBJECT TO CONTACT) £69,950, OUR
MOVING DATE IS THURSDAY 1ˢᵗ JANUARY 2004
(NEW YEARS DAY) WE ARE LOKING TO RENT A
2 BED FLAT FOR ABOUT £575 – £625 PER MONTH,
BUYING A FLAT IS ABOUT £125,000 SO THAT'S OUT.
SAMANTHA & DANIELLE LOOKING FORWARD TO
CHRISTMAS AND VISITING LIVERPOOL.

LOTS OF LOVE
DAD AND NICOLA
XX

(LETTER 116)
SUNDAY 1ˢᵗ AUG 04

DEAR X AND Y,
    DUE TO THE COST OF MOVING 4 TIMES THIS YEAR, I CAN NOT VISIT LIVERPOOL UNTIL OCTOBER. IF YOU WANT (& SPEAK TO YOUR MUM) WOULD YOU LIKE TO VISIT BOURNEMOUTH FOR A LONG WEEKEND AT THE END OF AUGUST I WILL PAY FOR EVERYTHING

HOPE TO SEE YOU
BOTH SOON LOVE
DAD XX

(LETTER – 120)
WED 1ˢᵗ DEC 04

DEAR X AND Y,
    HOPE ALL IS WELL AND LOOKING FORAWRD
TO MY VISIT JUST BEEN INVITED ON TO THE
BOARD OF SCHOOL GOVERNORS AT KINGS PARK
PRIMARY SCHOOL WHICH I AM VERY PLEASED
                      LOTS OF LOVE
                      FROM YOUR
                      DAD XX

(LETTER 125)
SUNDAY 1ˢᵗ MAY 05

DEAR X AND Y,
MY BIRTHDAY (43ᴿᴰ) WHEN WELL I GOT A BOOK, ELECTRIC PIONEER (GARY NUMAN) FROM SAMANTHA & DANIELLE AND FROM NICOLA I GOT A F.A. CUP SEMI-FINAL TICKET AND N.T.L. I HOPE Y HAS A GOOD BIRTHDAY AS WELL AND X IS ALLOWED BACK INTO THE PUBS/CLUB SOON. THIS IS LETTER 125 WHICH MEANS I HAVE BEEN WRITING TO YOU BOTH FOR OVER 10 YEARS NOW WHICH I AM VERY PLEASED ABOUT, DON'T FORGET YOUR MUMS BIRTHDAY THIS MONTH AS WELL WILL VISIT SOON BOTH TAKE CARE

LOVE FROM
YOUR DAD XX

(LETTER 128)
MON 1ˢᵗ AUG 2005

DEAR X AND Y,
HOPE ALL IS WELL AT HOME, I NOW HAVE
DATES FOR OUR VISIT TO LIVERPOOL
THURSDAY 25 AUGUST TRAVELLING
FRIDAY 26 AUGUST BLACKPOOL
SATURDAY 27 AUGUST NIGHT OUT
SUNDAY 28 AUGUST X & Y
MONDAY 29 AUGUST TRAVELLING
BOTH OF YOU ARE MOST WELCOME TO
COME TO BLACKPOOL AND ARE NIGHT OUT IN
LIVERPOOL LOOKING FORWARD TO OUR VISIT
LOVE FROM
DAD XX

(LETTER 129)
THURSDAY 1st SEPT

DEAR X & Y,
    SORRY YOU COULD NOT COME TO BLACKPOOL AND TOWN, AND X MISSED SUNDAY, BUT Y DRANK X'S SHARE ANYWAY ON SUNDAY AND WHAT A SUNDAY IT WAS, (MANY THANKS Y) TRYING TO SORT OUT SOME DATES IN OCTOBER (HALF TERM TIME)

MISS YOU BOTH
LOVE FROM YOUR
DAD XX

(LETTER 139)
SATURDAY 1ˢᵗ JULY 06

DEAR X AND Y,
   I HAD A VERY GOOD FATHERS DAY LAST MONTH. SAMANTHA WAS 11 YEARS OLD AND WHEN TO WEMBLEY TO WATCH THE PUSSY CAT DOLLS & THE BLACK EYE PEAS, THIS MONTH DANIELLE IS 5, AND I AM IN HOSPITAL ON THE 19. WE HAVE MY MUMS CARAVAN AT THE END OF THE MONTH AND ALSO GOING TO BLACKPOOL OUR AIM IS TO GO ON EVERY RIDE BOTH OF YOU ARE MOST WELCOME, IT WOULD BE GREAT TO SEE YOU BOTH, Y I HAVE A WEEKS WORK FOR YOU IF YOU WANT IT.
                          MISSING YOU BOTH
                    LOTS OF LOVE, DAD XX

(LETTER 145)
MONDAY 1ˢᵗ JAN 2007

DEAR X & Y,
    HOPE YOU BOTH ENJOYED LAST NIGHT AND WISH YOU ALL THE BEST FOR 2007. Y THANK YOU FOR 2 GREAT NIGHTS OUT (AGAIN) AND FOR YOUR HONESTY. X LET ME NO WHY YOU ARE NOT SPEAKING TO ME AT THE MOMENT AS OUR ALST NIGHT OUT TOGETHER WAS GREAT, IF IT WAS SOMETHING SAID BACK AT THE HOTEL IT IS NO DIFFERENT TO NOBODY TELLING ME I HAVE A GRANDSON, ANYWAY I WILL NOT ARGUE OR FALL OUT WITH YOU AS WE HAVE JUST BURIED MY 46 YEAR OLD BROTHER IN LAW AND LIFE IS TO SHORT.

                                  LOVE YOU BOTH
                                  ALWAYS, DAD XX

(LETTER 148)
SUN 1ˢᵗ APRIL, 2007

DEAR X AND Y,
    *HOPE YOU ARE ENJOYING YOUR EASTER
HALF TERM. MIXED NEWS, OUR JENNY HAS LOST
HER BABY AND EDDIE IS GETTING MARRIED
WORSE STILL ARSENAL GOT BEAT YESTERDAY BY
LIVERPOOL*

SEE YOU BOTH
VERY SOON
LOVE DAD XX

(LETTER 150)
FRIDAY 1 JUNE, 2007

DEAR X & Y,
*   HOPE ALL IS WELL IN LIVERPOOL, EVERYTHING GOING WELL IN BOURNEMOUTH LOOKING FORWARD TO THE SUMMER, BOTH OF YOU AND FRIENDS ARE MORE THAN WELCOME TO STAY DURING THE SUMMER OR ANY WEEKENDS. HOPE ??? IS OK AND LOOKING FORWARD TO HOLDING HIM WHEN I VISIT THIS MONTH. I HAVE TO MENTION WHEN MY DRIVING SCHOOL WAS CLOSED DOWN BY THE D.S.A. I HAD DEBTS OF £18,880.08 THE EASY WAY TO NOT PAY THIS WAS TO DECLARE MYSELF BANKRUPT, AT THE TIME NOT ONE PERSON ASKED HOW I WAS AND HOW I WAS GOING TO COPE. BUT THIS WAS MY DEBT AND I WAS GOING TO PAY IT BACK. WHEN I RECEIVED £9,317.85 AFTER LEGAL FEES FROM THE COUNCIL I AGREEDED WITH THE BANKS TO PAY OFF SOME OF MY DEBTS IN WHICH I DID. Y, WE AGREED TO HAVING DIFFERENT VIEWS ON THIS BUT WE MOVE ON AND TALK. X AS YOU STUDY BUSINESS AND FINANCEL I HOPE YOU CAN DO THE SAME. AS BOTH OF YOU ARE NOW 18+ AND YOUNG MEN. SADLY THIS WILL BE MY LAST LETTER I HAVE ENJOYED WRITING ALL 150 LETTERS SINCE JANUARY 1994. (12 YEARS AND 6 MONTHS.) ALL COPIES ARE NOW SAFE AND PUT AWAY WITH ALL THE COURT PAPERS.*

LOTS OF LOVE
FROM YOUR
DAD XX

(LETTER 151)
TUESDAY 20 NOV 07

DEAR X & Y,

SORRY YOU BOTH FEEL AS YOU DO, X YOU HAVE TO STOP HIDING AND STAND UP FOR YOUR SELF YOU WALKED OUT OF THE HOTEL BECAUSE I CAUGHT YOU GOING IN MY WALLET "YOUR REASON WAS Y SAID I HAD LOADS OF FIFTY POUND NOTES" IS THAT A REASON? Y ONCE AGAIN WE HAD A GOOD NIGHT AND YOU HAD GOOD IDEA'S ABOUT MY BUISSNESS WHICH ONE OR TWO WILL BE USED. BUT YOUR DRINKING GIVES YOU NO RIGHT TO TRY AND HEAD BUTT YOUR DAD. I NOW WILL CARRY OUT YOUR WISHES AND NOT MAKE ANY CONTACT WITH YOU BOTH, BUT MY DOOR WILL ALWAYS BE OPEN.

LOTS OF LOVE
DAD XX

And that was the end of the letters! Arsenal writes in block capitals and the letters have been reproduced here exactly as they were written, mistakes and all. They're honest words, letters and sentiments so let's keep them as they were meant to be. For twelve and a half years Arsenal diligently produced these letters, addressed them in an envelope and went off to the post office to send them on their way. He never missed and never got one reply and yet there is very little animosity in the substance. Occasionally he will remind his sons that Father's Day is coming soon or his birthday. His sons never sent Arsenal a reply.

When I quiz him about this, in his normal, phlegmatic way he tells me that's how it is; or the equally non-political answer: "That's life." Not until the very last two letters when he tells them that he won't go against their wishes do you perceive any anger in the words. I think after so long even Arsenal's patience was wearing thin. Yet, I feel that all it would take is a phone call from either of his lads and every bridge ever broken would be fixed anew. The love is still there, simmering away; Arsenal just needs the all-clear to release it once more to the world.

X was twenty-one and Y eighteen when the letters stopped for good.

> Arsenal: *Me and me boys were all right. I've got pictures of them from that high until they were in their twenties and we went out for a drink. I took X out one night and Y out the other night because they both like different things. So, and then I was in a hotel in Liverpool, because I used to travel down from Bournemouth to see them. We'd had a good night actually and then we got back the hotel and X said to me, "I want to talk to you."*
>
> *And I went, "Yeah, OK."*
>
> *"About you and me mum."*

"OK."

He said, "So, when you left, how come you left loads of bills?"

And I went, "What?" I said, "Tell you what, you're drunk, and I am so wait 'til tomorrow, we'll have some breakfast, we'll come back, and you can ask me anything you want, and I'll tell you."

And he said, "No. I want to talk to you now."

So, I said, "Tell you what, as long as one condition. I'll show you paperwork and you have to read it."

"OK then."

"OK."

So, everything he asked me… He asked me about child support agency. He said, "You're not giving any money."

So, I went, "There you are. Just have a look at that paper. Can you see there, child support?"

And he's going, "Fucking hell. Mum said you don't pay."

And I went [mimes holding up a piece of paper], "I pay."

And, he said about the electric and the gas getting paid. [Arsenal pretends to look through a pile of papers and holds one up, in his mind's eye once again showing X evidence of the bill he paid all those years ago.]

"There you are." British Gas and Manweb. That's what it was back then in Liverpool. "All paid up, look at that." And, he was getting more angry for some reason?

And, he said, "And you don't come to the

school no more."

And I went, "Read that, read that paper." And it says something along the lines that I'm barred from the school. And he was reading it, but he was getting so angry with me. My God. At one stage I thought he was going to lamp me. But I'm just going, have a read of that, have a read of that.

Alan: And how old is X today?

Arsenal: He's thirty-two.

Alan: And how old was he when you had this conversation?

Arsenal: It must have been...

Alan: They must have been still at school?

Arsenal: No. He'd left school. The two of them were over eighteen because that's why I took them out.

Alan: And how old is Y today?

Arsenal: He's twenty-nine.

Alan: So he was eighteen, nineteen, twenty, something of that ilk?

Arsenal: Possibly.

Alan: But he was a grown man?

Arsenal: Yes. Everything he asked me, I asked him to read it and then he said, "I don't keep in contact." But I wrote to them every month and I've photocopied every letter and labelled it. And when I showed them there's 150 letters I've got. And when he seen them, he was like, "I haven't seen none of them."

I went, "What?!" Because in the early days I had to send me letters through the court welfare officer, Mr M. And, he'd read them and vet them and if they were OK, he would take them, and he would read them to the boys. I thought, You know what, I actually haven't done nothing wrong. I

just want to see me boys.
So, X wasn't happy.

I spoke to L about Arsenal leaving unpaid bills when he left her and their two sons and she told me she has, 'Never said anything to her lads about Arsenal not paying any bills.'

Alan: *So what's your relationship with them like today?*
Arsenal: *Zero.*
Alan: *So, even though you explained everything to them, and you told them you had the paperwork to show them, why is it zero?*
Arsenal: *When me mum died, 2013, they went the funeral. And, I actually went up with me two girls, and we were in the wake afterwards. And, me two boys wouldn't acknowledge at all me two girls. And, I went, "Are you going to say hello?" And they just actually blanked them. And I said, "Listen, see these two girls, done nothing to yous at all, so can you acknowledge them please?" And, the two of them just stood there in silence. So, I went to me girls, "Come on, let's go."*

          Y will text me now and again after he's had a couple. He'll go, "How are you, Dad? I love you," and stuff like that. But that's only when he's pissed. And Y has actually been up to Bournemouth, he stayed for about six weeks. And he stayed in the house and everything and it was all right but when he goes back in that environment, I don't know what happens but...

Sam confirms that X wouldn't speak to either Sam or Danni at their nan's funeral, but Y actually spoke to them both. Arsenal was trying to get X to engage with Sam by asking him to offer her some advice about her impending move to university, but X answered Arsenal as though Sam wasn't even in the room. She said, "As if he wanted him to relay the messages to me rather than speak to me himself."

> Alan: *Do you think L behaves the way she did because after you watched Dead Poets Society, and you spoke to her the next morning, it was just a complete bolt out of the blue and she couldn't understand it?*
>
> Arsenal: *No because… The first time we lived together was in her mum's, actually. And her sisters and that. So, I got asked to leave at three o'clock in the morning. And L said nothing. She didn't say nothing.*

Arsenal's relationship with his two sons simply doesn't exist anymore. We know that he's a grandad two times over but spends no time with his grandchildren either. I just have a small hope that should X and Y ever get the chance to read this, they may just understand a little more about their deeply caring father and give him a chance to be part of all their lives. Time will tell.

Chapter Thirteen

Nicola

Ongoing

My greatest challenge is not what's happening at the moment, my greatest challenge was knocking Liverpool right off their fucking perch. And you can print that.

Sir Alex Ferguson

AS WELL AS HIS RELATIONSHIP WITH HIS FIRST PARTNER, L, and his two sons, X and Y, being on the spectrum has impacted on every other social encounter that Arsenal has made in his soon-to-be fifty-seven years. The most important following immediately on from L was Nicola, the mother to Samantha and Danielle. Arsenal was still sleeping in the boys' bedroom when he met Nicola and therefore the relationship didn't have the space to grow. Another consideration was that Nicola was just leaving school at the age of sixteen and Arsenal was a twenty-nine-year-old man with two sons.

The relationship worked, as they were together for twenty-one years before Arsenal's diagnosis of autism – plus several other factors we will discuss – led to them getting a divorce in 2012. They remain very good friends, still meeting socially and sharing time with the girls with no animosities that I have recognised at all. In fact, in interviewing Nicola for this book I held the discussion at Arsenal's flat while he sat in another room with his new partner. It's all very civilised.

Arsenal: *I met a girl in a pub, and I didn't know how old she was. It was a Sunday night. I was in the pub, The Penny Black, Whiston. Because at the time I was still sleeping in me boys' room. And I met a girl and she said to me, "Do you mind leaving the pub early?"*

And I said, "No."

And she said, "Because I've got school tomorrow."

And I went, "What?"

So, we never done nothing like, and the next day I went round to her mum's, and I went to her mum, "You know your daughter; I didn't know she was still at school and I really like her, and I was going to ask her out."

And her mum said to me, "You know what, everyone in the pub says you're a gentleman, so I don't have a problem with you."

And I said, "But I live round the corner with me two boys in the same house as the boys' mum."

And she said, "I know."

And then we were together for twenty years.

Alan: *Twenty years? Oh, my goodness me.*

Arsenal: *My two girls, that's their mum.*

This was one of the very early times Arsenal and I had met to start the writing process and I had no idea of his full story. It was then that I realised I had already met Nicola at the fiftieth birthday fete of the charity where both Arsenal and I worked, Autism Wessex. She was a small, blonde lady with spiky hair and almost bird-like mannerisms who seemed a little shy when we were introduced. I got to know her better once I had the opportunity to speak to her about the book.

Nicola: *The first time I saw him across the pub it was Christmas Eve, and I was sat with my mum and my auntie and I wasn't supposed to be in the pub. I did look eighteen, I've got to say. It was different back then, people did go in the pub at sixteen. It was The Penny Black in Whiston. And me auntie said, "Look, there's a man there and he's just staring at you." That's how I noticed, because I could feel his eyes on me.*

                    And then somewhere along the night he said, "Hello. Are you not dancing tonight, then?" And from that I knew he'd been there before.

Alan: *And how did he say that? Because I know he had a bad stammer at the time. Did he stammer?*

Nicola: *No, not at all. I never noticed it. He was a bit slow, almost as if he'd thought it out before.*

Alan: *He'd probably been stood there thinking what to say for thirty minutes.*

Nicola: *And then process it in his mind and yeah! But no, I didn't notice anything like that.*

Alan: *How did you reply? Did you realise at the time he was a lot older than you?*

Nicola: *No, I knew he was older; I could see he was older, but I don't think he's ever looked his age?*

Alan:	*No, he doesn't actually.*
Nicola:	*No, and he could have been about twenty-two, maybe. But he was twenty-nine.*
Alan:	*And how did it go after that?*
Nicola:	*I'm not sure, not a lot. I don't think we spoke that night. Maybe it was New Year's Eve…*
Alan:	*And what was the name of the pub?*
Nicola:	*The Penny Black. In Liverpool. I think it's closed now [it closed down on the 2nd June 2015]. It's where I went every Thursday, I think it was a Thursday night with my auntie and me mum for karaoke night. With Colin's disco, I think it was Colin.*
Alan:	*Was this Cantrell Farm?*
Nicola:	*No, it was Whiston. This is where Arsenal lived when I met him. He lived in Whiston, literally over the road from The Penny Black. He lived there with L and the boys. They'd moved there because they got a council place there. I'd seen him walking the boys to school and stuff.*
Alan:	*So you knew he had a family then?*
Nicola:	*Somewhere, I can't really remember how it came about at the moment, when I thought, Oh, he's living with someone. Can't really remember anything like that. I do remember him telling me it's not what it was, it wasn't a relationship, he was there but she knew already that he wanted to leave because he'd already told her. And he was literally looking for somewhere to live.*
	And I thought, Oh, yeah. Here we go. Likely story. It turned out it was true because he doesn't lie!
Alan:	*No, he doesn't. He may not remember everything, but he isn't lying.*

Nicola:	*Exactly. That's exactly it. I thought the, likely story. If I'd have known then what I know now. I knew it was true, but it didn't take me very long to go, "This fella means what he says. He turns up on time. He's this… He's very…"*
Alan:	*So did he ask you out?*
Nicola:	*I think he asked me if I was going to be there the week after, probably. And I remember going away for that week, thinking, waiting for that day, for that day so I could see him.*
Alan:	*So you really liked him?*
Nicola:	*I really liked him straightaway. I didn't know it was love or anything, I was young at the time. I just knew I wanted to see this guy all the time and it was quite a time seeing each other in the pub, speaking little because everyone knew everyone. I think we went to the bar and we sat down, and he got me a drink and he was like, "So, do you know what me name is?"*
	And I was like, "Yeah, I think it's XXXXX."
	And he went, "No, it's not, it's Arsenal."
	And I thought, Hmmm, that's a bit weird.
	And he said, "Does that bother you at all?"
	And I'm like, "Well, should it bother me?"
	"Do you know it's a football team?"
	I said, "Yeah, I know what it is."
	"Does it bother you?"
	"It doesn't bother me. There could be a million names and different reasons why you're called that. It doesn't bother me. It's not going to give me an opinion of you." But I was thinking at the back of my mind, Bit weird.
Alan:	*If you'd sat down next to someone and they'd said their name was Liverpool you'd have been surprised.*

Nicola:	*I'd have been, behave! I thought nothing else of it when I got talking to him. A name is just another name. It's been a problem over the years, an embarrassing one, if I'm honest. Arsenal, what, what? To this day I find myself explaining to people why his name is Arsenal.*
Alan:	*I must admit, I never thought about it. When I heard his name was Arsenal I thought, Oh, here's a bloke who's into Arsenal Football Club. I was more surprised to find he's a Scouser called Arsenal.*
	So, after these first encounters in the pub, when did you start going out?
Nicola:	*I'm not sure. As I said he was literally looking for somewhere to live and he was. It was sometime later.*
Alan:	*And what about the age gap?*
Nicola:	*All I know is that if my daughter brought a twenty-nine-year-old bloke home I'd tell her to get rid of him.*

We know that Nicola's mum didn't do that, and once Arsenal got his own flat, Nicola eventually moved in with him. We know that Arsenal and Nicola didn't have an easy life, as she says, "Everyone knew everyone." They were living in a working-class, close-knit community, and Arsenal had an ex-partner and two sons living within hailing distance. They moved to Bournemouth after Samantha was born prematurely on the 14th June 1995. Nicola was seventeen years and seven months old when Sam was born.

They had no relationship until Arsenal had Nicola's mum's blessing and Nicola turned sixteen. They then lived together for a short time in Liverpool before Nicola fell pregnant and then on the 5th February 1996, with a seven-and-a-half-month-old baby, they left Liverpool behind them, plus Arsenal was leaving his two sons there as well.

Arsenal: *Nicola's mum had moved down there, so we knew someone. And when Samantha was born, she was, she was always cold, permanently cold. And she had this valve, I know nothing about the human body but, she had this valve going into her heart or something, that should close over a couple of hours after being born. But, hers was just open, so you know what, she was just blue all the time. Not blue, but her fingers and her lips were blue.*

She was born in June and even in the July and August we had to wrap her up, she was just blue. So, we were talking to the doctors and they said they were going to give her six months and if it hadn't closed over, they were going to have to operate on her. And that's the joke. I think the doctor said something like, 'a warmer climate' could help her and I said as a joke, "The nearest we can go is Bournemouth."

And Nicola went, "Should we go to Bournemouth?"

So, I said, "Yeah. If you want to go to Bournemouth, we'll get up and go to Bournemouth. Get away from all that shite and that." We come down to Bournemouth and I used to push her in her pram from pier to pier every day, for some reason. And then she went to, I think it was Southampton Hospital, and then it closed over [the valve], so we stayed. So, yeah, that was…

So, we come down here, as I said, Sunday 5th February '96, Samantha was seven-month-old. So, yeah, so we come down to get away from all that but for Samantha's health reasons as well. That tipped it over, if you like, but you know what, come on...

Alan: And when you came down, did you have a job?

Arsenal: We stayed in Nicola's mum's. Didn't have a job. But then I got a job in a matter of two weeks, I went down to Harry Ramsden's. It wasn't open but the doors upstairs to the restaurant were open and they were having a morning meeting with the managers and luckily enough for me Alan Simpson, the owner, was there.

We know from here that Arsenal went on to work for Alan Simpson for four to five years. Arsenal doesn't say much about the time in Liverpool, with Nicola pregnant and Samantha being born. He just remembered it as a tough time. Nicola remembers more of the details that caused her and Arsenal to move south.

Nicola: We just loved being together and talking. I was living with me nan and I just packed me bag and got the bus to Anfield where Arsenal's flat was, and I remember going sitting on the steps with me bag. I'm ringing the bell and he wasn't in. He was at the job club, trying to get a job. He walked down the street and he seen me sitting on the stairs and he was like, "Are you OK?"

And I said, "I'm going to have to live with you. I'm going to have to move in."

And he said, "OK, pick your bag up, let's go in. Let's talk." And I think he spoke to me mum, *before he said I could move in or whatever and they had an understanding. My mum just loved him, right from the day when he said to her, "I love your daughter. I've got nothing but good intentions." And from that day she loved him.*

Alan: *At that time, all these conversations that he was involved in, what was his speech like? Did he have a bad stammer?*

Nicola: *It was bad, yeah, it was bad. He stammered a lot. Every conversation he stammered, yeah.*

Alan: *OK. Because he's really in control of it now, isn't he?*

Nicola: *He's really in control now, he really is. When he came back from Starfish his mum was like, I preferred you the way you were. It really got to him, I think. He couldn't understand why his mum wasn't happy for him. But I could see both sides, I could see what his mum meant. She never meant those words that she said. What she meant was, you were OK before, I loved you before. That's what she meant but she didn't say it like that. She meant, it's fantastic that your speech is better, but you were fine before.*

And the way she put it wasn't meant to be the way it came across. But Arsenal is literal. The words are the words. But I know Pat and I know, even the way she said it, is not how it was meant.

Alan: *Do you want to tell me about the relationship with L and how it impacted you and your relationship with Arsenal?*

Nicola: *I used to see her walking to school with her and X would be like [Nicola imitates putting her head down to avoid eye contact]. And she'd be shouting her mouth off. She shouted once, and I just couldn't believe what I was hearing. She shouted across the street. And the two little kids were like… And Y who was four, I just remember him giggling. White, white hair, and giggling and looking. And X was like, they were opposites and he was seven, but he was petrified. I'd be petrified if I was seven and my mum was screaming at the top of her voice over the road in front of all me mates as I'm walking to school, which is right there.*

Alan: *And she was like this because Arsenal had walked out on her?*

Nicola: *Yeah. People had been talking about us. And I think you want an excuse, don't you? You want someone to blame, and although I was there, the stuff she was saying happened hadn't.*

Alan: *And there was no crossover?*

Nicola: *There was no crossover. And it was months later, but obviously if you've got a reason and you're hurting, you grab that reason, don't you?*

L admits to shouting at Nicola but she was obviously hurting. When I asked her was she really upset when Arsenal and Nicola got together? She replied, 'Yeah. Wouldn't you be very upset.' The answer to which is obviously, yes. As in the previous chapter Arsenal's autism had drawn a line under one relationship and started a new one with far more ease than anyone not on the spectrum could understand.

L admits that it was a very hard time for her as well. She says that she will never forget when it all started in 1993. Nicola has much darker memories than Arsenal does about what drove them away from Liverpool. It could be that Arsenal has blocked these out or simply doesn't want the past dredging up again; he's very much about tomorrow and being a better person tomorrow and next week and starting afresh each day. Perhaps he just doesn't want to relive these difficult times.

Arsenal's dad is very complimentary about L in the email he recently sent to Arsenal and it's clear from this email that Anthony Whittick thought L was a good mother to X and Y:

> *"Your two sons were only young when you split with L, but they have been well brought up and then you met your next lover [Nicky] and she gave birth too two lovely Girls Samantha and her sister."*

Plus, we have to remember this all happened such a long time ago that memories vary in what one individual remembers in comparison to another. This book just tells it as it was told to me.

Several years later, newly diagnosed, Arsenal remembers his ability to understand and to process the fact that Nicola wanted a divorce. We will hear two slightly different stories about how and why this happened, but I believe there are many divorces whereby the two sides of the same story sound as different as war and peace! This was also on the back of Samantha's attempted suicide and we will hear Sam's side of the story later.

Arsenal: *When Samantha tried to take her life, Nicola went the doctors and went, "My husband who is forty-nine has just been told he's got autism and he hits himself and he does this, he does that…"*

And Nicola told me the doctor looked it up on her keyboard and went, "Forty-nine, he's not going to change, is he?" And that was the signal, wasn't it?

And on the same day, Samantha said to Nicola, "It's either Dad or me." And so, the next day Nicola just gave me a letter.

And I went, "What's this?" *[Arsenal's voice is getting quieter and quieter and he's now almost whispering.]*

And she said, "I want a divorce."

And I said, "OK." And I never processed it, did I?

I know it sounds so stupid, but two of us actually done all our paperwork together; went down to the court to give it in together; and the guy at the court got her paperwork and my paperwork together and went to Nicola, "That's really neat." Because I can only write in block capitals, I write like that all the time.

And the court officer said, "That's neat writing."

And Nicola went, "Oh, Arsenal done it."

And he went, "Is that the guy you're divorcing?"

And she said, "Yeah, this is Arsenal here."

And he was, "I've just seen yous having a laugh over there for half an hour, while you're waiting. And you've come down to get a divorce? And you're giving your papers in together?"

And I went, "Yeah!"

And he said, "In all my thirty-three years I've never got a couple coming together giving their divorce papers."

But you know what? I never twigged it was me getting a divorce. I never... *[Arsenal starts clicking his fingers.]* I never twigged and on Tuesday April 17th 2012 I went down to the courts. And I went to the usher, "I've come down to get divorced."

And he went, and he had a bit of a giggle, and he went, "You don't come down to get divorced, mate." He said, "You get it in the post."

And I went, "Oh no, I have to see myself getting divorced."

And he went, "No, you can't." I told him I had autism and that and he said he'd have to go and see the judge. He come back and he said, "The judge said you can go in." [Arsenal starts laughing at this point.]

So, I went in and this old guy's looking over at me [Arsenal mimics looking over the top of a pair of spectacles sat low on somebody's nose]. And he said, "So, you've come to get divorced?"

And I went, "Yeah."

"Are you getting divorced for mental health issues?"

"Yeah."

And then he gave me the paper, and I got in the car and then I went, "What?" Boom, I twigged it. It was me. And I went home, and we still lived together, we still lived under the same roof.

Alan: *Sorry, do you still live together today?*

Arsenal: *No, no. But when I got divorced, I went home and I went to Nicola, "I've got these pieces of paper I'd like you to read."*

And she went, "OK." And you know what, she bawled and bawled her eyes out.

And I'm going, "Why you crying?" Because I never understood.

And she said, "We're divorced."

And I'm going, "I know. I only found out half an hour ago!" And she was just bawling her eyes out and I went, "But why are you actually crying, though?" And she was getting really upset so I went, "Do you want me to make you a cup of tea?" [Arsenal is smiling and laughing all the way through this story because he finds it comical, his behaviour, even though how serious the topic is, and ultimately how sad.] So, I made a cup of tea, come back down to her and said [in an incredulous voice], "Are you still crying?"

And she said, "Yeah. Aren't you upset?"

And I said, "You asked me for a divorce, and I said yeah."

And she said, "But you said yes, so I thought you wanted a divorce."

"You asked me for one! That's what I thought..." Oh, it was mental, mate. It was, it was mental. And then what... And then in the June, the 11th June, me Nicola and the two girls went to Liverpool to see me parents. Next day, we went on to Blackpool for a day out, all of us. Because, I said to the kids, this will be our last family outing together. So, we're going to go out, and we went out. And I come back, and, in the July, I went back to Liverpool on me own.

And I went to see me mum and dad and I said, "I've got something to tell you. Me and Nicola are divorced."

And me mum went, "You and Nicola are getting divorced?"

I went, "No. We are divorced."

And she went, "Will you stop fucking messin'?"

And I went, "No, I'm divorced. Look."

"We've all just been out last month, a family—"

And I said, "Look, that's what I wanted. I didn't want you to think, here we go again, like with me boys."

And she said, "I can't believe it, why?" And then I told her about me mental health and that.

And me dad said, "Is that why you slept on the couch that night?" Because there was boxing on at two in the morning, so I'd said I was going to watch the boxing. Did I not? I just wanted to sleep, didn't I? But... And that's how I told me parents.

Arsenal believes that it was one or two incidents that sparked the divorce, but I think his family was getting worn down as his autism escalated and his behaviour got worse and worse, culminating in the attempted suicide by Samantha. He narrates an episode about Nicola walking down the stairs in the townhouse, the decree nisi in her hand having changed her mind about getting a divorce. Right up to that point, she wasn't sure about seeing it through. As she's walking into the room, the dog barks and Arsenal flips, shouting and swearing and hitting himself, just because the dog barked. He was still learning about his triggers and how to deal with them.

He says that Nicola simply said, "That's why I'm getting a divorce," turned around and walked back up the stairs. In Arsenal's simple black-and-white mind, that was still a big turning point, but it was the months and years that went before of dealing with these situations that I believe were the real reason. Nicola tells it slightly differently, and let's face it, it is her perception, not mine, that is the most important.

Nicola: When I first met him, I thought, this is great. Here is a bloke who doesn't lie, he doesn't do this, he doesn't do that... Little did I know then how much of a major problem that would be. He was angry for years and years and years.

Alan: Talk to me about that. What was it like living with him when he was an AFC football addict?

Nicola: I don't know where to start off? Where do I start from? There's twenty years of—

Alan: OK, well, start from when you first thought it was becoming a problem?

Nicola: I can't answer a question like that. I can't.

Alan: Just talk to me.

Nicola: Getting up in a morning was a massive problem. Three girls in a bathroom, trying to get ready and get out of the house for 8.30, NOT 8.31 I'll have you know because all hell would break loose. Three girls sharing a bathroom and trying to get ready is not real life and trying to get that across to him, he could not understand why we couldn't be ready for that time.

And he'd make us all get up fifteen minutes earlier or thirty minutes earlier and he'd have that contingency time, if you like, to get ready. And he'd be like, "Bad hair day? What do you mean? Just get up earlier." And he didn't ever understand, the things that happen in a normal everyday life.

And in the end Sam would say to me, "Mum, why's my dad like this? I can't cope with it." And she used to say this to me for months and months. They would be arguing every day, every morning, they'd be arguing. And I'd be getting myself up a little earlier. And I'd be running upstairs and make sure Sam had got that ready, and that ready, and that ready, so that wouldn't be a thing.

And then I was always in the middle, trying to... But it didn't matter how many things I got ready, something would happen in the morning would happen... [Nicola is talking faster and faster as she's offloading what are clearly still issues to her.]

Alan: So, it was getting worse, then?

Nicola: Yeah.

Alan: Because you didn't recognise that kind of behaviour at first, did you?

Nicola: I just thought he was being awkward. An awkward dad.

Alan: Was it having the girls that made him worse? Living with other people? Where he couldn't live by his own rules.

Nicola: No. I think, moving, when... Even when we got back to Liverpool. Arsenal's a different person in Liverpool. He won't admit it, ever, but he is. He changes completely, I can see it. I can feel it.

Alan: In what way?

Nicola: He relaxes more and he stammers much less when we went back to Liverpool [Nicola is talking here in the years prior to the diagnosis and presumably prior to the Starfish Project], although it's his main problem in life, but when he goes back there and he's with his brothers, I think he just relaxes and forgets things. And it's a different situation.

During his first ten years living on the south coast something happened in Arsenal's life that made him angry. That made him, according to Nicola, fifty per cent more angry all the time. This is something that I haven't heard from Arsenal; he hasn't processed the incident and come out the other side. Still, considering this incident has caused him to be even angrier. I will explore this with him in the penultimate chapter of his life so far, as this trigger altered his behaviour to such an extent that it prompted both his divorce and potentially Sam attempting to take her own life.

Nicola:	*Over the twenty years [they were together], he just got angrier and angrier and angrier. And angrier. All my problems seem to start when we got that house. He seemed to change. Things seemed to change. It was only a couple of months before all that had finished with me daughter and I think that made him angry.*
Alan:	*But do you think it's also having been a person with autism for the best part of fifty years and nobody has ever known? And living with it, and living with it, and getting no help, and not being able to cope with it. Do you not think that, with the build-up over his whole life of how he is, and then all of a sudden, he knows what's wrong? Do you not think you more than anybody else will see the difference in him? You must do!*
Nicola:	*Yes, I do. He's everything I wanted him to be.*
Alan:	*I know Sam has said that Danielle is the lucky one because she's getting the best of her dad.*
Nicola:	*Danielle has no idea the extent of the difference. Sam will look now at situations and be a little bit... Because Danielle will sometimes talk to her dad a little bit rude. If that was Sam... And it's shocking the difference.*

Alan:	*So, if Sam spoke back to Arsenal and was rude to him—*
Nicola:	*Well, they were every morning and afternoon when she came home.*
Alan:	*But he would self-harm, wouldn't he? Hit himself?*
Nicola:	*When the football was on, he would do that mainly. But when he did that, he took himself off, he took himself away. Most of his life he self-harmed, which he didn't tell anyone about.*
Alan:	*So, you didn't know?*
Nicola:	*No. We didn't know. You know what? He told me that there's something that nobody knows in his life. I don't know if I'll ever tell you. And I said, "You must do. We're married." But he would say he couldn't and then get a little bit upset about it. And it was after he was diagnosed that he told me what it was, what this thing was. And it was because he didn't understand it. To cope with what was going on and he felt like this and he knew it was different from the way other people felt. To cope with it, he'd just go in a room, shut the door and hit himself. But he thought it was OK because he wasn't cutting himself.*
Alan:	*But you must have seen the… When he walked out of the room, because he's told me he came out once and the blood was dripping down off his head into the tea he was making? Was this after he'd been diagnosed?*
Nicola:	*This was before he was diagnosed not after. I think the first time the girls saw him hit himself was a Saturday afternoon after AFC had lost. And he was… [Nicola mimes thumping herself in the face several times.] I was so shocked.*

And he was like, "Just leave me alone." And then he'd go downstairs, and he'd take himself downstairs and say, "Just leave me alone." Now if he used to say that – "Leave me alone" – you used to do it. He'd said to me, "Look, if I ever don't understand something and I say, 'Leave me alone,' just do that. I need time to think it through." Because he didn't know how to express things.

But then I'd hear [Nicola punches her fist into her other hand, making a punching noise]. You'd hear him hitting himself and I'd go down and I'd be like, "God, you are hitting yourself. Why are you doing that?"

"LEAVE ME ALONE!"

Alan: So you'd been together eleven years and you didn't know Arsenal self-harmed? You must have seen the marks on his face? You must have had doubts?

Nicola: Yeah, I would say to him, I would say, and sometimes he would come back upstairs, it would be raised up. When we first met and I asked, how did you get that scar there, what's that mark? Where did you get those lumps on your head? Because he always seemed to have lumps on his head. If he got angry or upset, they would flare up, they would come out in his skin. And I thought they were just coming out because he was stressed, not because he'd been belting himself.

Alan: So, what did he say to you?

Nicola: He said they just come out on his skin when he was angry and stressed.

Alan: So he lied to you, then, because we all believe he can't lie?

Nicola:	*Arsenal doesn't lie, does he? He puts things in another way, and he's learned to do that because he's had to. He needs other words. You see, when he used to stammer… So, if something begins with 'S', he'll try to come up with another word that doesn't begin with 'S'. So, although he would never lie, he would never say how it was.*
Alan:	*OK.*
Nicola:	*But that's not lying.*
Alan:	*Well—*
Nicola:	*No, to him, to him, that's not lying.*
Alan:	*To him it's not, because he's black-and-white, but to you and I—*
Nicola:	*It's insinuation, but he doesn't understand that.*
Alan:	*But if I asked you a question and you avoid telling me the truth—*
Nicola:	*That's lying to you and me, but to him? To him it's, "Did I say those words?"*
Alan:	*No, I get it. I understand.*
Nicola:	*And that's been hard to live with itself over the years.*
Alan:	*So, he told you he was self-harming, and you were in the middle of him and Sam over the years, and Arsenal was getting worse and worse and worse.*
Nicola:	*All I know is that over the twenty years we were together it steadily got worse and worse. I just remember him on a day-to-day basis being angrier, when he come home from work, for example, and then the Sam incident.*
Alan:	*And that's probably why you found out about Arsenal's self-harming. He was angrier, he was hurting himself more, you noticed more, and you probably found out?*

Nicola: *Yeah.*

Alan: *It was likely the chain of events. Do you agree with that?*

Nicola: *Yeah. Definitely, yeah. More likely, but I can't pinpoint anything to anything.*

Nicola remembers these years of living with Arsenal's undiagnosed autism in much bleaker and harsher terms than Arsenal does. She talks about the day-to-day impact on trying to live a normal life, whereas Arsenal's memory tells him he believed that this was a normal way of living and therefore more acceptable to him. Was Nicola bearing the brunt for the family? Then, finding out that Arsenal was autistic and could 'never change', did that tip her over the edge, the edge being divorce?

Plus, she was in the middle of her husband and daughter, and forever refereeing. Not only refereeing but doing her utmost to keep them from engaging in an argument in the first place and thus stretching the relationship between them even thinner. Can one even imagine the daily stress she must have been under?

Nicola: *Basically every single day was a nightmare between Sam and Arsenal. They argued, for a couple of years they were arguing for. I even thought about divorce or contemplated it. And obviously over the time I had a thought that I can't be in this relationship anymore. I can't be here watching you hit yourself, football is your life, it doesn't really make any sense to me. I don't know why you don't love me no more.*

Alan: *And is that what you felt? That, Arsenal didn't love you anymore?*

Nicola: *No, I thought that he did, but for me, he never told me he did. HE's only ever told me he loves me four* or five times. Twice when we had the kids, once when we got married and once on that drunken night out that I remember when he was sliding down the walls. And he said, "I lubya!" And that's the one and only time I ever saw him drunk because he didn't get drunk. And he doesn't drink now because it made him angry in the end. But it only brought on the anger that he already had.

But Sam would literally be crying, and I'd go in and say to him, "Why did you say that to Sam? You've made her feel like this."

And he'd go, "As long as I'm not hitting you, what's the problem?"

And I'd go, "You can't hit yourself in front of the girls like that, it's upsetting the girls."

And he didn't understand why they were getting upset because they weren't getting hit. And I tried to explain that to him and he was like, "Leave me alone."

And I'd go in and see Sam and she was crying on the bed and she'd be like, "Why's me dad like this?" And I'd say, and I'd try and excuse some of the things he's done or said and anything to try and make Sam feel better. And she'd say, "Why does me dad hate me?"

And I'd be, "But he doesn't hate you, love." And I'd sit and cry of a night and wonder why my daughter and my husband hate each other. It must be my fault. It's got to be my fault because I'm their mum. And then you've got Danielle, who's ever so quiet, which is worrying anyway. It's always been a worry to me, Danielle not being very... Because when she was a baby, she would look at people and she would never giggle and stuff like that.

I remember I was thinking about divorce and Sam would say to me, "I mean it, Mum." And every morning before she went to school and every night when she came home the first thing, she would say to me was, "I'm going. I can't do this no more. I cannot live with him anymore." And I would sit and think about it and I'd obviously try and talk her out of it and talk to Arsenal: "It really upsets me why you and Sam don't get on." And he didn't want to know, and I was like, do I lose my husband, or do I lose my daughter? And for me it was a no-brainer.

So, I said to him, "I think I want a divorce." And do you know what his answer was? And I'd played this through me mind. If he says this and I say this… That's my excuse to Sam that I can't divorce Dad because I don't really want to. It wasn't really my decision, well, it was my decision obviously, but I didn't want Sam to take the blame for all that because she now says, "I'm sorry I made you and Dad divorce."

And I say, "It's not like that." It was a factor because I didn't want to lose me daughter or me husband. But he didn't want to know, and she didn't want to know, and there was no other way to get around it. No way at all.

And his answer to me was, "You're wrong." When I say I want a divorce, he went, "OK, but you're wrong."

Those were his actual words and he walked out the room and I thought, He doesn't love me.

> *Why doesn't he say, "Don't be silly. I love you. I don't want a divorce," like normal people would. But he went, "You're wrong."*

Alan: And what do you think he meant by that?

Nicola: That I was wrong in that decision.

Alan: Isn't that the same thing? Isn't that what he was trying to say to you? In his logical way?

Nicola: But in my logical way he should have been saying to me, that would have been the moment, if any, to go, "But I love you." But now I know that he couldn't do that, as a person, because—

Alan: Had he been diagnosed at that point?

Nicola: He was… It was a couple of weeks before, after, during, it was right on the… He was right in the throes when this was going on.

Alan: When Arsenal told me this story, he said he didn't really understand.

Nicola: After we had been divorced and we'd split up and it was so hard, and he was getting all his counselling, he would come to me and he would say, "Let's get back together." [Nicola says this with real emotion in her voice, whispering the words, almost too frightened to hear them herself.] When he came to drop off Danielle or whatever. And he would say, "Why didn't I tell you more? Why didn't I tell you that I loved you? We can't divorce. I don't know why I didn't say that."

And I said to him, "That's exactly what I was hoping for. Why didn't you say that?"

And he's like, "Looking back now… What is wrong with me?"

The problem was one that we all now know the answer to: "What was wrong with me?" Arsenal simply could not process what Nicola was conveying to him. She was trying to save the relationship between father and daughter at the cost to herself, but Arsenal didn't grasp the seriousness of the situation. Add to this the fact that for years he had had difficulty uttering those most important of words: "I love you." These words can be difficult to use properly at the best of times, but when you cannot communicate your feelings very well because of autism they became almost impossible for Arsenal to say.

> Nicola: *If we'd had known he had autism we could have talked about stuff. But I didn't know what was happening to him. He didn't know what was happening to me because I was sleeping all the time. But I was ill. My body would wake up in the morning and I'd already be stressed, but I couldn't tell anyone how my body was feeling because it didn't make sense to me, never mind anyone else.*
>
> *So, I'd go and sit and cry by myself, in the bathroom usually. Because that's where I could get away with it.*
>
> Alan: *You were making yourself ill because of what you were having to live through.*
>
> Nicola: *It was the stress. My nervous system couldn't take that, and it comes out in different ways. In pain, in me shoulders and legs and stuff. I know now if I get stressed and I was stressed earlier on. It was starting to flare up when I was at home and I was… [Nicola stops talking and I can see that she's getting stressed all over again, so I change the subject.]*

Nicola thinks back to six years ago when her and Arsenal got divorced. Arsenal continually asked her to get back together, but she said no for Sam's sake. Now before Arsenal enters into a new relationship, he still checks with Nicola that there is no hope for him and her before embarking on something new. Sam says that Nicola saved her and Arsenal by doing what she did. But then Nicola decided she couldn't divorce Arsenal after all and decided to call the divorce off.

Nicola: *Looking back, I would never have divorced him, but looking back, I don't think we can ever get back to that place. If it was me and him living together in a house, we could have sat down, and our differences would have been different. But the fact that he couldn't live a normal life…*

I was walking down the stairs one time; I'd been upstairs doing the washing, and this was when we were getting divorced. Arsenal wouldn't move out until we were divorced. So, we lived together with all the letters coming through… [Nicola let's out a very heavy sigh; this is not a good reminiscence.] And I was upstairs, and I was putting the washing away and I was like, "What are you doing? What am I doing? I don't want a divorce or to break up this family. What am I doing?" Literally, I was on my way down the stairs and they were in the living room and Arsenal was watching TV and the girls was on the table and they'd be colouring, and they'd be chatting. And they started laughing about something.

And as I'm halfway down the stairs I hear Arsenal go, "For fuck's sake," like he used to whenever he got angry. [Nicola says this very aggressively, spitting the words out.]

It stopped me in me tracks on the stairs and I went, "How can you be angry at the girls laughing?" Because when I heard them laughing, automatically I thought, Aww, and then I heard him go, "Fuck," and shout at them. For laughing! But it wasn't even a loud laugh or anything and I thought, I cannot compete with that ever. And I turned back around and went back up the stairs.

Alan: Arsenal has told me that story, but he said it was the dog barking that set him off.

Nicola: It wasn't the dog barking, that was a different time. The dog barking was a major thing, but the girls, it was Samantha and Danielle laughing at the table. More Samantha's laugh than Danielle's, because hers was a bit more. But a million percent it wasn't the dog barking.

Alan: It was definitely the girls.

Nicola: It was the girls laughing because I couldn't compete with that! I could teach the dog not to do that, I could get him one of those dog collar things or anything.

Alan: He's told me exactly the same story, but it was the dog barking that he started swearing at. Effing and blinding. And he said you realised he wasn't going to change.

Nicola: No, that wasn't the time. He's blocked that out because he now understands that wasn't right. I would not have made that decision at that point… I say made that decision, but it was already going on. But the fact that I made that decision I wouldn't have made it over the dog.

There is a real difference of opinion here as to why Nicola turned on her heels and marched back up the stairs. For her it was undoubtedly the fact that Arsenal was snarling and angry just because his two daughters were playing together and laughing.

Arsenal firmly believes that it wasn't the girls that triggered the response but the dog, and it wasn't just what caused the reaction that was the problem for Nicola so much as she knew he would never change. They both firmly believe what they say. At a later date I do challenge Arsenal on this point and he admits he may be wrong, but that is genuinely what he remembers: the dog barking. I believe that he believes it, but I also think Nicola believes her memory is the correct one.

Nicola goes on to tell me she loves Arsenal, always has and always will. There is that 'one' in your life that you always love and for her it is still Arsenal.

"You can love someone without being in love. Is that how I feel? I don't know; haven't a clue." All she ever wanted was for Sam and Arsenal to have a relationship and they have that today. She could have managed Arsenal and 'put up' with his behaviour had they been on their own, but the girls were being badly impacted. She always thought that Arsenal was in the wrong but now knows he wasn't. Not only does Arsenal now understand himself so much better than he did, but so does Nicola as well.

Unfortunately, it took them being apart to come to this realisation.

Chapter Fourteen

Coping

2011 to 2019

At my lowest point as a gambler, the night before an away game for Aston Villa, I sat on the edge of my bed in a Bolton hotel room and thought about breaking my fingers.

Paul Merson

I HAVE SEEN ARSENAL SPEAK. I DON'T MEAN SAT ACROSS A table from me. I mean standing up in front of a room full of new employees at Autism Wessex and keep them enthralled for over an hour as he explains what it's like to be diagnosed as autistic at the age of forty-nine. To hear him talk lucidly and more than candidly about how he came to be diagnosed so late in life; sat in a hospital trying to understand why his eldest daughter had felt so unloved she decided to kill herself.

I have also seen him perform – because that's what Arsenal is doing, he's performing and trust me, it's not easy for him – at a Christmas carol concert in front of a priory packed to the rafters, literally, with happy children and parents starting their

286

Christmas celebrations. They are hanging on to his every word. I watch him using his abdominals to get his breathing right so he can start. My breath has stopped waiting for him to utter those words, that I now know he will start with, "My name is Arsenal Whittick." He's away. His storytelling ability kicks in. The vicar has already told us there will be no applause until the very end and everyone has finished performing. Try and stop the congregation as they uproariously clap, with even the odd cheer. Arsenal, startled, runs off, down from the pulpit and exits stage left. The sudden rush of noise and air is still too much for him, eight years after he's told he's on the spectrum.

His current partner, Sophie, runs after him and a minute later – a long time when you're waiting for someone to reappear – he's back at the front and persuaded to sit back at his own pew. He's got through another day. He's coping, and to cope he has strategies. This chapter is about how Arsenal now copes; how he uses his autism to help others struggling with the same condition as he has and how in a short space of time, he has turned his life upside down. In a good way. He now lives as 'normal' a life as you or me but the stigma of mental health issues, for both him and his family, is never far away.

When he was initially diagnosed, he was asked to keep a diary of every time he self-harmed and what caused him to react in such a way. Arsenal thought that it was predominately football – or AFC, to be exact – but he soon came to realise that there were many more trigger points than he was recognising when he undertook the simple task of logging these occasions. After several months of logging the abuse, which had escalated to virtually a daily occurrence, Arsenal and Alderney Hospital arrived at the following list that would 'trigger' Arsenal into self-harm. There was a minimum of ten triggers:

1. Sleeping,
2. Mistakes,
3. Laziness (in others),
4. Lateness,
5. Sudden noises,
6. Aeroplanes,
7. Time,
8. Social interaction,
9. Directions (information overload),
10. Football.

Let's explore these triggers one by one.

> Arsenal: *A trigger for me, originally, was sleeping. I used to sleep for two hours. So, when I come down, imagine I go into the kitchen and that was still there and that was still there, that would be a trigger for me. Because I couldn't understand why the dishes hadn't been sided. Or washed or rinsed. And I'd be thinking, Why've they left that there?*
>
> Alan: *Just a simple cup on a table would trigger it?*
>
> Arsenal: *Yeah, and I'd go, why've they left it there? And then I'd be thinking, Why have they done that? And I couldn't. And then I'm getting angrier and angrier and then I've either taken it over there myself or I've smashed it. [I can tell by Arsenal's demeanour that this tale saddens him. He now knows this could have been avoided had he been aware of his condition and received the therapies earlier in life, and his shoulders slump as he recollects.]*
>
> *I would just launch it against the wall because I'm angry by that time. And what they were saying [the hospital], how they explained it to me,*

simple. *Throughout the course of the day when everyone wakes up their anxiety and stress and everything else is right down there [Arsenal holds his hand down near the floor]. And throughout the day it rises. So, say by the time they're home from work or something, say their partner could just say something and it would just… [Arsenal clicks his fingers several times, indicating that the fictitious couple are now arguing.]*

The hospital said, when I wake up, I'm like up there already. [Arsenal now holds his hand high above his own head.] So, when I come in and I see something out of place, that's it, I've gone already. Gone straightaway.

Alan: *You said you only slept for two hours?*

Arsenal: *Two hours.*

Alan: *Every single day you only slept for two hours?*

Arsenal: *Yeah.*

Alan: *And was you not getting so tired you couldn't function?*

Arsenal: *[Arsenal has difficulty answering this question.] That's the way it was. And me strategy was, I had to put an alarm on for two hours and ten minutes. And I wasn't allowed to get out of bed until the alarm actually went off. Then it took about a couple of months and then I started to sleep for two hours and ten minutes. And then I kept an alarm on for, must have been a couple of months again. And once that was routine, I had to put the alarm on for two hours and twenty minutes. And that's how I done it.*

Alan: *To get to seven hours?*

Arsenal: *Mmm. Yeah.*

Alan: *But you must have been, during the time when you were only sleeping for two hours, you must have been unbelievably shattered. [I hear in my voice on the recording incredulity.] Were you working at the time?*

Arsenal: *Yeah, yeah.*

Alan: *How did you function with two hours' sleep?*

Arsenal: *I dunno! And that might have been why I was always angry. So now I get seven hours and me strategies are nine o'clock of the night, I watch a drama nine 'til ten. And then from ten until, say, twenty past, do all the kitchen. Do in here and then sit on the couch. I get me mobile; I delete all me texts from the day.*

Alan: *Yeah, including my address.*

Arsenal: *[Laughing] I forgot to write it down. Then I get all me negatives out of this bowl here [Arsenal points at a pretend bowl that he's holding under the crook of one arm] and I turn them into positives.*

Alan: *What do you mean by that?*

Arsenal: *Say I go into work and I know who the lazy boys are in work and it annoys me. So, when I come home tonight, all the things that have annoyed me, made me get a bit angry or anxious, I take it out me bowl and think about it.*

Alan: *Do you physically do this, write them out?*

Arsenal: *No, it's all in me head. Can you see this bowl here? [I am unceremoniously having the piss taken out of me.] So, I'll take one out and think, You pissed me off today, so I'll drop that and turn it into a positive. The only note I'll ever do is if it's a negative were, I need to speak to someone about it. So, I'll think you know what, I need to talk to*

*them about that, so I make a note in me pad and
have it out with them.*

Arsenal then relates several tales whereby someone has done
something wrong, invariably at work, and he takes them into the
conservatory for a 'talk'. It's an efficient way of dealing with his
anxieties; he is externalising what the rest of us would probably
lose sleep over. I have a lot to learn from Arsenal. Then if it's
something that the two of them cannot agree on Arsenal seeks a
manager to mediate straightaway or to 'play Solomon'.

Returning to the trigger – which was one of sleep, I think –
we can say this has been safely 'put to bed'. I can only be amazed
at how Arsenal managed to function for years and years, holding
down several jobs and steering his way through life on two
hours sleep a night. Theory around why this may occur explains
how 'for those on the autism spectrum, sleeping well may be
particularly difficult'.

Reasons for this could include:

- not having a natural body clock due to irregular
  melatonin secretions, the hormone for sleep.
- not knowing when to sleep. As we read earlier just
  because everyone else is going to bed doesn't mean
  an autistic person will be aware. They won't make that
  social connection.
- waking several times during the night and not being
  able to go back to sleep.
- an inability to wind down.
- increased sensitivity to stimulants such as caffeine.
- anxiety decreases the ability to relax and then sleep.
- heightened sensory problems, blue light, white noise,
  etc.

For someone on the spectrum, diagnosed or not, overcoming sleep disorders can be a life-long quest, yet once again Arsenal has shown the resilience and sheer persistence to overcome one of his triggers. I'm sure that as his sleep increased to the seven hours he now gets every night, it made the world seem easier to traverse than when dealing with all the anxieties of autism on two hours' sleep.

The next trigger he identified was dealing with other people's **mistakes**. Arsenal tells me again the story of when he worked at the Co-op and someone had put a box on the shelf upside down. His manager locked himself in his own office he was so scared of Arsenal, who was proceeding to punch himself out on a metal cage, breaking two knuckles.

Arsenal: *The box was upside down. And in my head, I couldn't understand why someone had seen the box with an arrow saying this way up. And to me it's black-and-white, isn't it? It's telling you how to do it.*

Alan: *And is there not a set of circumstances, never, where you, YOU, could put that box the wrong way up?*

Arsenal: *[He answers me as if I've asked the most stupid question on God's own earth.] No? No, no, no.*

Alan: *I think it's a fair question. What happens if the building's on fire and you had to get out, would you still make sure the box was the right way up?*

Arsenal: *Yeah, because if you watch the video of me and Samantha talking, she says something very similar to what you just said. She'll say, "Dad's reaction to everything that's not actually right, to him, is as if I've burned the house down." And that's how I've been reacting to everything.*

Alan: *How do you deal with this, because people are making mistakes every day in every part of life?*

Arsenal: *The strategy, you know what, it's so simple, but I wouldn't have thought of it. What I have is, I have a pad on me now, at all times. I've got it there now. And what I do is if anything's wrong or there's anything I can't do, I write it straightaway in the pad.*

So, the anger, instead of going from me hand to me head, it goes in the pad. And it's amazing! Just by writing it down. But I mention this in me talks when I go, like there's a guy, I was in town and he walked past me, and bumped into me. And you know what, I just turned and went, "You fucking knobhead, what are you doing?" And there was a bit of a scuffle, but I told Alderney Hospital and they said, right, here's the strategy. "Just write it down." In me pad, people might have said things or done things, and you know what, I just put it down in the pad and I use bad language in the pad, but it gets it out.

Alan: *But let's say I just came in here now and bumped into you by mistake: "Oh, sorry, Arsenal, didn't see you." Would you still be getting angry?*

Arsenal: *I have to tell myself to step back. I have to TELL myself.*

Alan: *Even though you know we're mates, and I just slipped, you still have to deal with it?*

Arsenal: *Yeah. It's like, you know when I still go to bed every night, I have to TELL myself to go to sleep. I have pressure spots [indicates back of his neck] and I have to squeeze them and tell myself to go to sleep. I go to bed at five to eleven and by five past eleven, I've gone, I'm asleep.*

> *And then I get up the same time every day,*
> *five past six, I know what my plan is for the day*
> *and it's just brilliant, brilliant. [You can see the*
> *genuine pleasure Arsenal gets from starting each*
> *day anew and trying to make himself better every*
> *single day. It's a humbling experience.] I get me*
> *seven hours and it's brilliant for me.*
>
> *I get up and I know that I can come in here*
> *and it's all nice and tidy. I have plans for me day*
> *because I've done them the night before, I have a*
> *Plan A and a Plan B.*

Alan: *And you're refreshed after a good night's sleep.*

I think it was during this conversation when I started to see Arsenal as a modern-day hero. He has had to overcome so many obstacles in his life to just live a straightforward, hardworking, normal life and still he battles every day to improve himself and make things better for him and his family. As I said above, it's a humbling experience and one that has made me think about my everyday grumbles and complaints in a new light.

Arsenal virtually has to plan, think and execute every mundane task of modern living to ensure he can get through the day. He does it with a smile on his face and he does it with the wellbeing of others as his first consideration rather than himself. I can't think of a better word: hero!

The third trigger that he and Alderney recognised was people being **lazy** and he has already touched on this above. The truly great thing about Arsenal is that if he sees a misjustice, even someone at work not pulling their weight, he confronts it and deals with it. He describes one of these situations at work when others are dealing with a service user who we will call ABC.

Arsenal: *I know when I go in today, I'm going to have ABC. [What Arsenal means by 'have', is that he will be working and caring one to one all day with one of the Autism Wessex service users in one of the residential homes.] Now today he will stay ninety per cent of the time, in bed until I get there. And so, the people who are supporting him have to stay outside his bedroom all day. In case he comes out and anyone else is coming upstairs and then, if they touch, or get into an argument or... Then that's a safeguarding issue so they have to stay on the landing and there's a chair there.*

So, on a Friday he goes out to get some bacon or goes to Boscombe Pier so at eight o'clock he's asleep. Everyone knows he's asleep. So, they knock on the door, take a look, see he's asleep and they can go down as long as someone's on the landing. And then, you'd go down, you'd do the risk assessment, you'd get the money out for the bacon, you'd write and date his paperwork for the day, check the daily log, date his food diary; so you've got about half an hour to do all the paperwork.

Then you'd have to take the scales up with you because he gets weighed before he goes home every Friday and pick up all his washing. Then I get there, and I'll go, "How's he been?"

"Oh, he's in his room still. He hasn't come out yet."

"Have you done all the daily living skills?" So, every ten minutes they're supposed to go in and say, "Clean the window." And he'll clean the window. And then clean his cabinet and his wardrobe so he's doing all his cleaning and that

stops him from falling asleep again. And that's his strategy as well. And I'll get in today and I'll think OK. So, I'll go up to the landing and I'll get his file and I'll say, "What's he done?"

"We haven't had time to do that yet?"

"OK. As he been weighed yet?"

"Oh no, no. I'll go get the scales now."

"Has his homework been done?"

"I haven't done that yet."

I'll go, "So, what have you been doing from eight until two?"

So that for me is people being lazy.

Alan: OK. And that in the past would cause you to self-harm?

Arsenal: Yeah, yeah.

Alan: So, how do you deal with it now?

Arsenal: *I go in. I do a routine every morning before I start. Everyone knows not to talk to me why I do my routine. Walk upstairs. And I'm looking at everything, aren't I? Taking it all in. Then I go back downstairs, I go in the staff room. I get every pad out and I go [Arsenal mimes scribbling intently and deeply into a pad].*

And then I'll go, OK, I'm on two to ten, and can do all them jobs myself, and then I know they're done. And then, next team meeting as a group, I bring it up. That, can whoever is with him on a Friday, can they make sure all this is done? And then everyone's heard it, and people have to sign off on it.

Alan: And does it get better?

Arsenal: *Yeah, because in the team meeting, everyone has to sign that they've read the minutes. Then the next month if certain people haven't done it then I have no problem calling them on it. [Arsenal points his finger.] "It was him. It was him." And then if someone claims they didn't know, I pull out the minutes. So, last time you signed it. And everyone knows how it works.*

I do think to myself that we should all adopt the Arsenal Whittick view of working. Wouldn't it be good if we could call out lazy people or people who weren't doing their role to their best, sit down as a group and agree a way forward that we all sign up to and can then be held accountable to? I know it's pretty basic and a simplistic view to work life, but it seems to work for Arsenal.

We then move on to trigger number four: **lateness**. This is a real problem for Arsenal, even today, and I've been close to late for our meetings a couple of times due to roadwork traffic. As we know, Arsenal never misses a kick-off of a game or the start of a concert, as he gets to the venue early enough to open up most times. We discuss.

Arsenal: *The next trigger is lateness.*
Alan: *Hey, I was early this morning.*
Arsenal: *I know, yeah, I thought it was the bailiffs.*
Alan: *I did try and warn you because the traffic at the minute is awful and I thought, I'll just make sure Arsenal knows I might be late. And I'll do my best not to be but… And I gave myself over an hour to get here [should be about thirty minutes] just to make sure I got here on time because I know that's important to you. And then I got here early.*
Arsenal: *Thank you. When I got the text I thought, wow. Lateness, when Nicola says tea will be ready at six*

o'clock, and then it went to a minute past six and I'd go, I'd go in the kitchen and go, "Where's tea?"

"Just doing it now, be about ten minutes."

And I'd go [whispers], "But you told me six o'clock."

"I know, but it's going to be another ten minutes."

And I'd go, "But you told me six."

And she'd go, "Arsenal, it'll be ten minutes." But by then, in my head, if you tell me six then that's what time it is: six. Not when it goes past a minute, six o'clock.

And I'd go in the kitchen and I'd cause an argument and I'd say, "I tell you what, I'll do some myself."

And she'd go, "What?"

And there'd be an argument and I'd either… The dinner would probably end up on the wall or it'd be in the bin or maybe, I don't know, something would happen.

In school, when I used to take the two girls to school, I'd get there ten minutes early so we would leave at twenty past eight. So, once it gets to twenty-one minutes past eight, I've gone [Arsenal clicks his fingers, indicating that the second it gets to twenty-one minutes past his reaction is instantaneous]. Because I've told them twenty past and then they'll be going, "Dad, I'm not ready yet."

And I'll be going, "But you know every day it's twenty past eight. You get up the same time…"

And they'd say, "I know, but I'm having a bad hair day."

"Then get up ten minutes earlier then."

And they'd say, "But I don't know I'm going to have a bad hair day until I get up." But it's too late then. I'll be downstairs in the hall and I'll be hitting myself and the kids can hear the thumps and I'll be kicking the walls and everything. So then, it's got to the stage where they're scared to come down because I'm harming.

Then Samantha would come down to me and say, "But Dad, there's another nine minutes." But I wouldn't see the nine, I could only see the minute gone.

Alan: How did you used to deal with public transport? Because public transport is never on time. You go for a train, say the nine o'clock train and the electronic sign tells you it's going to be five minutes late, and then that goes out to ten, and this must be even worse for you because it moves in increments. Five minutes late, six, no, now it's seven.

How did you deal with that?

Arsenal: If I'm going to a match and AFC are playing at three o'clock, I'd get the half six coach in the morning. So, even if the coach could overrun, I'm still thinking I can't be late for the match. And so, my focus is on the match and not the coach, really. So, even when I go to concerts, I'm going a concert on the 19th. So, I've said it's at half seven, but we're getting there at eleven o'clock in the morning. I know I'm going to be there a hundred per cent, so even if that train is delayed or something, I've got eight hours.

But, my strategies for being late, if Danielle is running late, because she has that understanding now that she can come in and say, "Dad, I'm

> *going to be twenty minutes late." So, what I do is I sit over here [Arsenal moves to the middle of the big couch in the lounge area], I get this book [a book he's using to learn about the body called See Inside Your Body], I don't understand anything about my own body so I'm learning, all this stuff, it's amazing, my God, it is. It's a kid's book for, I don't know what age, but you know what, I don't have no knowledge, because I told you about school, didn't I?*

Alan: *Yes, you did.*

Arsenal: *So, that's what I do and then all my focus is on the book and when she comes back in, she'll stand over there and say, "I'm ready now, Dad."*

        And I'll just say, "Let's go."

Alan: *Brilliant.*

Arsenal: *So, that's my strategy for people being late.*

And it truly is brilliant. We can see already that while Arsenal has to prepare himself for every little incident that can occur in 'a day in the life of', the solutions are very very simple. Another strategy he uses for lateness is to say he will arrive between two times, say ten and eleven, and as long as he is in that timescale, he no longer gets upset, self-harms or makes the lives of those he loves a waking nightmare. Now he knows he can do something about it. Plus, when someone offers him a solution to a problem, he is a great listener, always ready to try anything that he thinks may or can improve his quality of life.

A **sudden noise** is the next trigger, and, on several occasions, I've seen Arsenal use his strategies when there is a sudden noise, for example the round of applause I saw him receive at Christchurch Priory.

Arsenal:	Another trigger is sudden noise. Do you know the scooters or the trial bikes that the teenagers ride? Those really loud noise type ones? Are they mopeds or something?
Alan:	Yes, I know what you mean. When they rev them up?
Arsenal:	Well, that's a trigger for me.
Alan:	That must be difficult because there are many of them on the road around here.
Arsenal:	So, what I have to do is I, I get… That's a negative for me, a negative noise so I have to turn that noise into a positive. And what I do, I've got the noise up here [points to his temple], and I try and connect it to a positive. And the positive is for the trial bikes or the scooters or whatever they're called, so my strategy is… 1975, I was thirteen, and Evil Kinevil was at Wembley Stadium.
Alan:	Jumping all those buses?
Arsenal:	Yeah, seventeen buses. But for me as a kid that'd be exciting. Because he was revving it before he went. And I watched it on the telly and for me that was a happy time. So, if I'm out there now and I see or hear a scooter… Have I told you about my projector?
Alan:	Yes, I know you put slides into the projector at the front of your mind.
Arsenal:	If I see a teenager come down on a bike, I get my Evil Kinevil slide and I can see Evil Kinevil on Wednesdays, Fridays and right now.
Alan:	You have a projector and I have a house in my head with a cinema and I see myself for example performing presentations I have to do before I do them and its similar stuff to what you do. It's

called Mindstore and I went on a course years ago.

> *So how do you deal with football crowds? There are always loud and sudden noises at football matches.*

Arsenal: *It's not a sudden noise, is it? It's a build-up. When I go into the ground, I get there really early, and I might get in the ground an hour before. [Reminder to the reader here that Arsenal has not been to a live football game for over five years.] So, the levels are lower then and builds up.*

> *When I get the coach, ninety-nine per cent of the time I'm always first one on the coach. Get there early, I'm lining up, so I get on the coach, and as the rest of the passengers is getting on, the noise is slowly building.*

Alan: *It's a gradient rather than a sudden noise. When a goal goes in though there's always a roar. Does that not bother you?*

Arsenal: *No.*

Alan: *It's because it's bloody football!*

Arsenal: *Plus I'm roaring myself, aren't I?*

Alan: *Not as often as you'd like.*

Arsenal: *Another sudden noise is dogs when they bark. We lived in a townhouse and Nicola tells this story on the talks. She said, in the divorce, that took a year, I stayed there throughout the divorce, I think the last eight weeks you get the decree nisi, I think it's called. And that gives you eight weeks to call it off, the divorce. So, we're all in the house, lived in the townhouse, so, our lounge is on the first level, and the two girls are in there and Nicola's upstairs and the dog's there, Alfie.*

Alan: So you had a dog?

Arsenal: Yeah. [We both start laughing as he's telling me that
           a trigger for self-harming is sudden barking from
           dogs and low and behold, he has a dog.] I know.
           Anyway, Nicola was coming down the stairs to call
           off the divorce. And the dog in the lounge, sees the
           postman going past, with the jacket on, and barks.
               And I flip. "Fucking hell!" Like that.
               And Nicola goes, "That's why I'm getting a
           divorce." And goes back upstairs. True story. So,
           my strategy for dogs, I took Danielle to Crufts.

Alan: I've worked at Crufts when I worked for Spillers
           Petfoods.

Arsenal: Have you? I took her to Crufts because she loves
           dogs. And you know what, I've got a slide of
           when she was in Crufts. She was so happy. I
           just drop it in and wow, wow. [Arsenal puts his
           slide of his daughter in his imaginary projector
           in his head and he immediately becomes very
           emotional. It works for him instantaneously
           and I see him remember the joy experienced
           by Danielle emanating out of him as raw
           emotion. The power of the mind is quite simply
           incredible.]

Alan: How fantastic is that!

Arsenal: Phew. [Arsenal now has tears coming down his
           cheeks and is gasping to control himself.] That's
           emotional that for me. Wow! [He really struggles
           to compose himself.] So, that's me slide for dogs
           barking, Danielle hugging the dogs at Crufts.

Once again, I marvel at Arsenal's coping mechanisms and the
power of his own mind that he can invoke in himself such strong

emotions from within his own memories. On such occasions he clicks his fingers many times, but you can watch him holding a slide in his hand as he slots it into his projector just in front of his forehead. It's the physical movements linked to the cerebral that together brings forth such a powerful sensation in him. Instead of swearing and thumping himself in the face, he remembers his love for his daughter and that love effectively pulls him through.

His next trigger is **aeroplanes**.

> Arsenal: *Next is aeroplanes. When I give talks at the school at work in the pool room upstairs the planes are always... I'd be giving a talk and then a plane and I'd go, "FUCK!" Like that. [Ironies of ironies, the school that Arsenal gives his talks on autism at is situated right next door to Bournemouth Airport. You couldn't make it up!]*
>
> *And everyone would go, "Shit!" And I'd go, yeah, I can't deal with sudden noise. But I have a strategy. I went over to the Aviation Museum opposite the airport. So, I went there and the guys, they were really good there, and they were telling me all about the planes and how they make the noise and all that. And I was fascinated. And then what I had to do, if the noise of the plane turned into a positive, and the positive is...*
>
> *There's a picture up there of Gary Numan. He was the captain of the British Formation Team. [This wasn't quite correct, and the following is what Gary Numan actually did.]*

Gary Numan met a gentleman called Norman Lees who had the same love of flying as he did and they joined forces to form the two-man Radial Pair team. Lees had a military background and as we know Numan was a singer and songwriter. Together they shared a passion, flying. In 1992 Gary and Norman got together and flew two 1943 Harvard 2B aircraft in a routine of formation aerobatics. The difference in their show was the synchronised opposition manoeuvres whereby they *"acted out"* routines in which they took opposite sides in an aerial dogfight.

Arsenal: *And he had a Harvard and he had it painted in Japanese colours and when he used to do the events and all the air displays, he was the one getting shot down. But for me that was exciting because there was someone I liked in the plane so, so when I'm in the meeting on Tuesdays, I'll hear a plane and I'll go, "Oh, here's Gary Numan in his Harvard." And everyone will laugh and then I'll explain it.*

  So, all the negatives I have to get a connection and turn them into positives.

Alan: *By the way, where was your strategy in dealing with dogs barking and buying your own dog?*

Arsenal: *We got the dog—*

Alan: *It's asking for trouble, isn't it?*

Arsenal: *Well, I didn't know, did I? I think Alfie's seven so, or he's eight, actually, next month so, must have been—*

Alan: *Do you still have a dog?*

Arsenal: *Yeah, yeah. Not here, but I'm off every other weekend and I go to Nicola's, pick the dog up and I take him to Hengistbury Head. And that's a strategy, see. I have strategies for everything. But other strategies for sudden noise is when I go into a room, I view it. So, when I go into the pool rooms for meetings, I know up above there's* fourteen windows, and I'll see how many are open, on their sills. With the wind they can bang, so I'm already aware of them, ready.

And in there I know there's three doors and the middle door to the toilet squeaks so, if anyone gets up to go to that toilet, I know it's going to squeak. [We both laugh.]

Alan: It's incredible!

Arsenal: I'm aware there's a phone by the door so I know someone can ring up and I normally I sit in the corner of a room so I can watch everything, and I can scan everything. And I'm watching what can make a noise and I'm processing it. So, that can make a noise; the windows could; I'm getting all this information. Yeah, I like to know what's going on.

Another trigger is **time**!

I time everything. When I iron it takes four minutes. So, for work stuff that's twenty-four minutes. And if for some reason it goes over it triggers me. It just triggers me.

Alan: But different items take different times, a shirt takes longer than, say, a T-shirt? Collar and cuffs take longer than a rugby top.

Arsenal: [Laughing] I'm a Scouser, I don't wear shirts! Unless I'm going to court. The accused! It normally takes me four minutes an item and if I go over... Wow! I've hit myself with the iron; I've pulled the plug from the iron; smashed the iron against the wall; I've hit myself, oh man. But, but, what I do, I still time everything, but what I do now, me strategy is, I just add on fifteen minutes.

	And that's how I do something. Sounds so simple but—
Alan:	*As long as it's within that time—*
Arsenal:	*[His stammer is getting quite bad now, which is normally a sign he's talking about a stressful series of incidents, but what hasn't been stressful for him?] So, I'll either add on fifteen, or half an hour or forty-five and I go, wow, why couldn't I think of that? And Alderney'd go that's your theory of mind skills and your executive functioning.*
Alan:	*You did think of that, but it became a new target for you. As you said earlier, you wanted the kids to get in the car ten minutes before they needed to. You had already done that. But, then, for you, that moved the goalposts, literally, and that became your new target time. You had allowed yourself ten minutes leeway but then ignored that allowance and moved it, so it became the new target. So, you did think that yourself.*
Arsenal:	*Yeah, yeah. Plus, if I come in from work, I have to get changed first. No matter what! If the kids were laying there on the floor with a broken leg I'd be going, "Let me get changed first." Because that's a new thing for me because work has finished so, I just get changed.*
Alan:	*And would you do that now or are you now perceptive enough to know the broken leg needs seeing to before you get changed?*
Arsenal:	*[Laughing] Process it, don't I?*
Alan:	*You have to be quick, though, if someone is lying there with a broken leg.*
Arsenal:	*I have to actually stand back. Sometimes you can see me step back. I take a step backwards.*

Alan: I have seen you do it.

Arsenal: OK.

Alan: When I first met you and I walked into the big conference room in Parley 3, we were in a meeting and I came across to introduce myself to you. I put my hand out and you shook it and then you stepped back from me and I thought OK.

Arsenal: Did you wonder what was wrong with him?

Alan: I knew you were a Scouser, so I understood. [Both laughing now at the memory. I had obviously been told beforehand that Arsenal was on the spectrum, so my approach had been cautious, but I was ready if he didn't want to take my hand or engage.]

           So, shaving takes me twenty-two minutes, for some reason?

Alan: You've told me that before. It takes me twenty-two minutes to shower, shave and anything else. I can do all that in twenty-two minutes, so what are you doing?

Arsenal: God, that takes me an hour!

Alan: What are you doing for twenty-two minutes? [Listening back to this I had no sympathy here for the fact that Arsenal was a person with autism.]

Arsenal: In my talks I say it takes me twenty-two minutes to have a shave and then I say, "And that's just me face!" [He really tickles himself here and laughs for quite a while; then I join in and after a moment we can't get our breaths.] Then if the audience are receptive, I always throw in another one. And I'll say, "Sex is ninety-six minutes." But then I'll say, "Oh, I've got the wrong way round, it's sixty-nine minutes." I do try to get humour in the talks as well. They are hard and I get so emotional though doing my talks.

Alan: *It's good, though, people like to see emotion.*

Arsenal: *My next trigger is **social interaction**. I never like, I never danced at me wedding; I'd never been for a meal; I'd never hugged the kids; or if anyone used to ring our doorbell, I used to flip, because I was, "Why they coming to the house?" So, I'd be walking down the stairs, and I'd be so angry I'd be screaming, "Who the fuck's coming to the house?" And obviously they can hear me, can't they, coming down the stairs, and they must have thought, Who the fuck's that? By the time I get to the door, there's no one there. I'm going, "Where've they gone?"*

Alan: *When I was here last time, so you do cope with this now, because when I was here last time and the front doorbell went, there was an Amazon bloke asking you to take a package in for someone else. And you just said, "Yeah, OK, no problem, mate." So, you're dealing with that now.*

Arsenal: *Because, in the morning times I am processing the day ahead. So, when I go into work, that's something that could happen, lazy boys going to have ABC or that doorbell could go? When I go into a room, I'm processing everything, so I know.*

So, every morning, when I do me Wonderwall, I know that you're going to ring. I'm always planning me day so that or that or that could happen, so I'm processing what do I do if that could happen. I'm always planning.

Alan: *It's very impressive, mate, what you do. You're having to put a level of preparation into your day* for what most people just take for granted. Just so that you can get through your day. Whereas the rest of us? If that cup's there when I get in, I'll just say, "Who's left a bloody cup out? Do it yourself, you lazy buggers." And then I'll stick it in the dishwasher or whatever. I don't have to ready myself for that situation, do you know what I mean? Whereas you have to put the prep in, don't you? So that you can deal with it, should it happen. It's impressive.

Arsenal: Yeah. When I used to be driving home from work, I'd be thinking, I hope the house is tidy. The house better be fucking tidy. And then obviously I'd open the door and bang!

Alan: You build yourself up for that, so you're almost there. You almost don't need the trigger. You're looking for the trouble beforehand because you've built yourself up for it.

Arsenal: Yeah. My strategy for that is I have some of my favourite CDs in the car. So, on the way home when that pops into me head – Gary Numan. I put on Gary Numan, so that's a distraction, then.

Alan: When I feel down, I put on David Bowie! It's exactly the same thing, except I won't self-harm if there's a cup left out! And neither do you now.

Arsenal: Some of my other strategies for my social interaction. I'm off every Thursday and every other weekend, so when I'm off at weekends I go into town, Bournemouth Square, and I'll stop strangers and I'll say to them, "Excuse me. Do you know where HMV is?" I know where it is, but for me to stop people and interact... What I do [Arsenal's stammer is getting much worse

during this part of the conversation; he still has
difficulties talking about and considering social
interaction] on a Thursday, I go to a different Post
Office in Bournemouth. And what I do is I get a
second-class stamp.

    And then I'm in the queue and I can't control
that environment, can I? It's horrible. It's like I've
got spiders all over me back when someone's right
behind me. [Arsenal is laughing but shivering as
well. The expression 'a goose has walked over my
grave' was made for this moment.] It's horrible.
And I'll get my autism card out and turn to them
and say, "Listen. Can you just read that for me,
and can you give me a bit of space, please?"

Alan: And are people normally OK when you do that?

Arsenal: Yeah. Normally they're OK. Some of them will go,
and you can see they're not really reading it and
give it me back virtually straightaway. But they
will step back.

Alan: I guess it depends on who you're dealing with?

Arsenal: But on the back of it [the card], it's got about 'I
can show challenging behaviour'. So, if I don't
think I'm being listened to, I'll say, "Can you read
that bit there about challenging behaviour?" And
they'll think, Shit, he might kick me in the head
[laughing], and then they step back. But so, I do
that, and every six weeks I go to the barbers, but I
go to a different barbers all the time.

Alan: You can tell.

Arsenal: It was half day closing when I got this one, I think.

Alan: Did you go to the butchers next door?

Arsenal: So, I go to a different barbers because again, it's
that social interaction, with different people.

Alan:	And, barbers never stop talking to you.
Arsenal:	[Sighs] I know. No, they don't. But I say to them, "If anyone comes in, I won't be able to talk to you."
	And they'll go, "OK." So, at the moment I'm only going to the barbers on a Thursday. Eventually me goal is to go on a Saturday afternoon when it's busy.
Alan:	OK. So, what you are reminding me of is when we had the first conversation to write this book. So, that night, a really lively and busy Friday night, you went to the pub, with a big group of people. Some you knew from work, some you didn't know, how did you manage to do that?
Arsenal:	I went the day before.
Alan:	Did you?
Arsenal:	[In a very quiet and low voice] I went the day before. And I walked all round the pub. [It was a very big pub with lots of nooks and crannies.] But the one thing I never realised, the day before, but what happened on the night, I could hear the barman putting the bottles into a big container. That caught me out. But that's what I try and do, I try and visit the day before.
	Or if I can't I go online and try, and try and look at the building from the outside, so I have at least a build up of it and that's what I do.
Alan:	How did you find that night then?
Arsenal:	Challenging. I couldn't sit down with anyone.
Alan:	No, I know, I asked you to sit down with me.
Arsenal:	I remember, but I couldn't do it. I just felt as though the walls were coming in on me. So, I can't do it, but they're goals for me, aren't they? It's why I'm happy every day now that I think, Right, what

am I going to do today that... Or what's my goal for today?

I'm always learning, so me strategies for me social interaction are: every other Sunday, I go to Nicola's, pick up Alfie, take him to Hengistbury Head for two hours, and what happens then is he sees other dogs and there's always people with other dogs, and people talk to you.

I do that and I go to DAAS meetings [Dorset Adult Asperger's Support] once a month. So, that's meetings for people with autism and that, so I go there.

Alan: And, where are they?

Arsenal: The meetings are based at Bournemouth University. Then once a month I help out at the Kingsleigh School. I do an autism coffee morning. [I check the website out and they are proudly advertising the next coffee morning on Thursday 13th June.] I do that and that's good.

Then, every first Tuesday of the month, I do the autism practise talk at the school [Portfield School, part of Autism Wessex], well above the pool and that and that's all helping with me social interaction skills. And then I did the hug day [more later], wow!

And there's two companies who do nights out in town for people on the spectrum, so I've been going to them, they're good.

Alan: Are they charities?

Arsenal: Yeah, one is called Bournemouth First, and I'm registered to that. They do events all over the year for people on the spectrum or with learning difficulties. Then there's Diverse Abilities. [On their website it says, "Diverse Abilities is Dorset's disability charity, supporting children and adults with profound physical and learning disabilities across the county since 1955."] They do a night out called, 'The Big Night Out'. I go there and it's really good because everyone there is on the spectrum and got learning difficulties.

There's one guy there, and all he does, all night, and I say that's really nice of you, and all he does is walk up and down by the wall, all night long for two hours or three hours. And you know what, he's so happy. And that's what nights out should be like, just let individuals do what they want and because everyone is on that spectrum, they all just... They have support workers and that, but it's really good. You see people in wheelchairs, and you see people on the dance floors and I just go, WOW!

So, the last one—

Alan:	Have you danced yet?
Arsenal:	No. I've been on the dance floor watching people going, "How are their legs moving?" Because I don't get that message from me brain to move me feet. But I watch people, wondering, How do they do that? I'll get there, though.
Alan:	That's a bit like AFC's strikers this year, the message isn't getting to their feet!
Arsenal:	That's true, you're laughing, but it's true.
Alan:	Good for you, mate. It takes bottle, what you're doing.

I'm starting to see the effort required for Arsenal to live his life. Now he knows he has autism, he believes, with time, he can come up with a 'strategy' to deal with every life situation. Can you imagine dealing with a phobia or a real fear just to buy a stamp? That's what he has to overcome, but rather than avoid the situation, clearly described as having spiders crawl over his body, he voluntarily puts himself in those circumstances and forces himself to overcome them. Back to that word again: hero!

> Arsenal: *Another trigger is **directions**. It's just too much information for me. And I get really angry, I can get really angry with it so if we're driving out of Bournemouth, imagine I'm coming off a slip road, and then I see a sign with all the different areas, just overload for me. And then, I come off, and I've not read what turning I've gotta take. So, I'm going round and round the roundabout, you can ask the kids. I'm going round and round the roundabout about five or six times.*
>
> Alan: *And you're trying to work out which one is your turning?*
>
> Arsenal: *And every time I'm going round, I'm getting angrier and angrier and angrier. And where, there's cars beeping me because I'm going from lane to lane, kids are screaming, Nicola's screaming, "You're going to get us killed." And then, I've just got so angry that I'm spitting at the windscreen and stuff because I'm so angry that I've had too much information.*

When Arsenal says he's spitting, he really means he's spitting on the inside of the windscreen. His hands are on the wheel or the gearstick, he's revolving around this roundabout, other people are getting sick of the lunatic all over the road and taking it out on Arsenal and his family, and finally his wife and kids are screaming at him. The only way he could get the anger out without truly endangering them all, by taking his hands off the steering wheel, is to spit. And so, he does!

Arsenal: So, my strategy is for that is [he starts to dig through his paperwork in front of him] when I go up to Bournemouth and I was going to Cambridge, you know what I do?

Alan: You go on the AA website! [He's holding a printout in front of me; I can't read his mind, not yet.]

Arsenal: I print off this and I take Danielle. And she comes everywhere. So, instead of me having to read it all, all she'll say is, "All right, Dad, at the third exit…" Or, "As you come to the end of this slip road you take the third exit…" And you know what, I can go round, and go, one, two, three, and it's so simple. As she tells me, she'll put a tick there and once I'm on it and past it, she'll put a cross. And you know what, it works really well. But then, can you see the start of her ticks getting really big? And no crosses.

And every time we get to Winchester services, always stops, no ticks or crosses. And you know why, she falls asleep. That's why all her ticks are like that, she always falls asleep.

Alan: What do you do then?

Arsenal: Well, from Winchester, luckily enough, that's where Samantha is, so I know me way back from Winchester. But she always falls asleep round Fleet service area. I've gone, "Right, where we going now?"

"Zzzzzzzz." But it works and she ticks it all off for me and that and it's really good of her. And

	just by having that it stops me from spitting at the windscreen.
Alan:	*When you came to my house the other day for the first time, which is quite difficult because it's still not on many sat navs at the minute as it's a new build, I know you don't use a sat nav, but what did you do as you was on your own?*
Arsenal:	*I got lost, I did get lost.*
Alan:	*Well, everyone who comes to ours gets lost at the moment so you're not on your own there.*
Arsenal:	*I looked it up on Google Maps and then I went into work and John at work and he does shifts at Greenways.*
Alan:	*Yeah, it's not far from us.*
Arsenal:	*He said to me, he told me, I said, "Don't tell me any shortcuts, I'd rather go the long way round." So, it's just like even if I got lost, I won't do all that what I said. I think he said, "Pirate Avenue South or North? I was here in about ten minutes, so I wasn't late.*
Alan:	*Well, if you remember what we said? We said come here straight after work so we didn't set a time, so that gave you leeway and you wouldn't get anxious about being late. Which is another of your strategies, set a range rather than an exact time. And you did tell me you had tried using a sat nav and it was just impossible.*
Arsenal:	*It was just too much information for me. The voice kicks in about a hundred metres away from the turn, but that's too late for me. So, that's me strategy for directions.*

The tenth and final trigger on Arsenal's list embodies everything that has gone before in some way or form but it's **football**. Or

more specifically Arsenal Football Club, AFC, the club that
has dictated the course of his life. For years and years, he self-
harmed every time AFC didn't win, even a drawn game would
provoke the most vicious attack on himself. He believed that
AFC should win every single game and if they didn't, he would
for some reason take the pent-up anger inside of him out on
himself.

It was hidden from the family until that too became too
difficult to conceal and before long, his two young daughters
witnessed the devastation of the home they shared, and worse
still they saw the effect it had on the face of their father. It has
impacted on Samantha and Danielle in profound ways and we
will read the full effect on their lives, from their own mouths in
the next chapter. What did Alderney Hospital suggest to Arsenal
in order to cease the abuse from the results of AFC?

They told him to never watch a live game again. Never go
to the ground of his beloved AFC, never watch them run out at
the Emirates ever again; they even told him never to watch a live
game involving AFC on the television again. Arsenal lived for
AFC; his life would be worthless without football.

Alderney explained that he had two choices. Either, it was
stop watching live AFC games or he may lose his daughters. *He
has never watched a live game since!*

But before then it would have been his number one trigger
in terms of frequency.

NUMBER TEN – FOOTBALL – AFC

Arsenal: *Triggers for my special interests were Gary Numan
and football. But I got addicted to football, didn't I?*

Alan: *I want a whole session with you on football. I have
got to be careful because I don't want to upset you
or tip you over the edge. Do you know what I
mean? If it's still a trigger.*

Arsenal:	*Yeah, yeah.*
Alan:	*Because talking about AFC, let's face it, you've not had a lot to cheer about over the years.*
Both:	*[Laughter.]*
Alan:	*You thought I was serious then, didn't you?*
Arsenal:	*It's a good job I poisoned that coffee.*
	Yeah, the football dictated the jobs I had and everything.
Alan:	*It dictated your life, I know.*
Arsenal:	*When I caught me hand in the saw, even though it was halfy, halfy... But, looking back I'd be... Because on the day it happened, it was the first day of the new season.*
Alan:	*Yeah, you did say. You told me you didn't want to work that morning, but they persuaded you as it was extra busy. And it was Liverpool as well, wasn't it?*
Arsenal:	*Yeah.*
Alan:	*It's always bloody Liverpool with you. Is it worse for you when AFC are playing Liverpool rather than any other team?*
Arsenal:	*Hate them, hate them. Absolutely hate them.*
Alan:	*What's the logic behind that?*
Arsenal:	*I think it's just jealousy, I think? In the '70s and '80s they won everything. God, I used to go to school every Monday morning, and everybody would go, "Ha ha ha, I see AFC got beat again." A lot of them didn't even know me but they were just having a go, weren't they? But I think that's what it is. When Liverpool play United, they hate one another.*
Alan:	*I'm from St Helens, as you know, and I'm a rugby man, and Wigan is right next door, about eight*

miles separate the town centres, they border each other, and in the '80s/'90s, Wigan won the Challenge Cup, the FA Cup in Rugby League, eight years in a row. Nobody wins a cup competition eight years consecutive, but Wigan did.

Saints didn't win anything. I hate Wigan. [We both laugh for a while as we nurse our own club's battered pride during these years of dominance by our rivals.]

Arsenal: I remember we were playing Liverpool away, I was in Bournemouth and I never had a ticket but I'd arranged to go and try and get a ticket outside off a tout. But I couldn't get a ticket. I went to the St Albert's Social Club, and they have a big lounge and they have a bar.

So, I went into the bar and Arsenal won 2-1 and we were getting beat actually. We were losing 1-0 and AFC equalised. And I was jumping up and down in the club and that, and everyone thought I was just an Everton fan who wanted AFC to win. Then Robert Pires scored with twenty minutes to go and I was so happy I pissed everyone off. [This could have been October 4th 2003, when Pires did get the winner at Anfield in a 2-1 win.]

A couple of lads must have went to the toilet, and our Simmo was watching the game in the lounge part and I was watching it in the bar part, and we never knew. So, these lads had gone the toilet just before the whistle and our Simmo just happened to be in the toilet. And they said to our Simmo, "All right, Simmo, are you well?" This is on his side, the toilets and they said, "There's an Arsenal supporter in there and he's fucking giving *it all that. We're going to give him a hiding."*

And our Simmo said, "OK." And when he comes out the toilet, it's me!

And he goes, "That's our kid, that." If he hadn't have been there, I'd have been beaten up.

Alan: *I was going to ask you that, because you're so honest and open and straightforward, but football's not like that. I've been to football matches as a Manchester United fan but stood with the opposition fans and not being able to say a word because I know if I speak, I'm going to get battered.*

But you're not like that, are you? You've not got that function.

Arsenal: *I've took some hidings. We were playing Everton. It was the two-legged semi-final of the Littlewoods Cup back then and it was the semi-final and we played Everton in Liverpool at Goodison Park; I think it was 1987. [It was in fact 1988, AFC played Spurs in the 1987 semi and we have looked at that game in a previous chapter.]*

We were playing Everton away first and we won 1-0, Perry Groves [Arsenal has the score and scorer correct, though]. Then on the Wednesday we played them at Highbury, and I think we tonked them about 3-0. [I dig the video out on YouTube and AFC won 3-1 on the night missing a penalty – emphatic, yes, a tonking? Well, Arsenal certainly thought so.]

And all the coaches used to line up in a row and there'd be a gap of about three foot and then all the other coaches. I went up on Barnes Travel, but they were known as the football coaches, so

*they were all Everton fans. And I had my AFC
top on.*

What Arsenal is saying here is that he travelled to London on
a coach full of Everton fans for a League cup semi-final, that
Everton subsequently lost. He then went back to the coach
wearing a football jersey from the team, AFC, that had just
knocked Everton out of the cup. It's close to a turkey going to
the butchers on Christmas Eve.

Arsenal: *I got to the Jolly Miller, that's where all the
football coaches were and I was on coach nine,
so I had to pass eight coaches. The next thing all
these lads are knocking on the window, going,
"What the fuck?! You're fucking dead, you're
fucking dead." And I'm going... [Arsenal makes
the V for victory sign several times, suggesting
he gave back as good as he got.] I got on to me
coach and AFC won but they kept the Everton
fans behind, see. But I'm going on to the Everton
coaches, and I'm in between these two coaches.
I never realised they had a second driver on the
coach to bring it back.*

     *So, I didn't know this and I'm knocking on
this door and the coach driver shakes his head.
And I'm going, "Come on, I've got to get on." But
I've got an Arsenal top on. The next minute there's
a group of Everton fans either side of me and
it's a dead end. I'm banging on the door, saying,
"Fucking let me on."*

     *And the driver's saying, "Get away." He can
see there's going to be trouble. These lads caught
up with me and caught me right on the temple.*

The next minute, phew, I was out cold, out cold.

Then the driver gets off and then I come round and I explain all like that. He says, "Oh no, I'm really sorry, mate, but you've got an Arsenal top on."

I get on the coach and we're about two minutes away from the Jolly Miller to be dropped off, and this steward on the coach, he came up to me, and I was upstairs on the football coach, this steward, and he says [whispers], "All right, mate, the driver wants you. Have you got any bags or anything with you?"

"No."

"All right, then, the driver wants you."

So, I comes down to the driver and he says to me, "At these next set of lights, mate, you're getting off the coach. Even if the lights are on green I'm stopping because all these lads are going to give you a hiding when you get off the coach." So, we get to the lights and they go green and he just stops. On green! The doors open and I'm off and all the scallies from the Wirral are going, "You're fuckin dead."

And I'm going, "Wembeleee, Wembeleee."

Alan: You didn't think to be quiet and get away, did you? You still had to rub their noses in it.

Arsenal: Banter to me, mate, banter. But—

Alan: Some football fans are nasty though, aren't they?

Arsenal: Oh, yeah. It did get bad for a while. I think everyone [all clubs], had their groups. Didn't they? I went to Leicester once and we got ambushed. And they were really really good how they ambushed us. [I'm laughing hard now, as Arsenal believes this *is something to be praised because it was well thought out.] It was really clever.*

They laminated the lampposts saying, "Away fans that way." So, we went into this dead end [Arsenal is laughing now] and they had us all trapped. I got many hidings down the Seven Sisters Road as well against Spurs, but that was just part of it for me.

So, they are Arsenal's ten most popular triggers for anger, self-harm, breaking down and not being able to navigate his way through life. When he makes his 'talks' on living with autism, these are the ten he uses to communicate what it's like living on the spectrum. His words are, "Me strategies to deal with me triggers." His main strategy for dealing with football-related episodes is to avoid football completely, certainly watching AFC play. On the second time I met him on the 8th October 2018, he spoke to me about avoiding AFC.

Alan: *I did notice when I was talking to you last Friday that you knew exactly who was playing whom and at what time kick-off was on Sunday; you knew all the football fixtures. You were all ready for the weekend; you had memorised every single one.*

Arsenal: *Yeah. I've got to leave that alone because it can take over. I'll have a look at the colours what the away team are wearing, who the ref is, where he lives, who his linesmen is; I can get as if I need to know absolutely everything about that match day.*

Alan: *What's your coping mechanism for that? How now, because you do, because you don't go and watch AFC anymore, how do you manage to stop yourself? What do you do to cope? What's your coping mechanism?*

Arsenal: *Err, if I'm on me own, so, I walk into Bournemouth, and then, or I park the car in Bournemouth. Then I'll, if the kick-off is say three o'clock 'til say, five, I'd walk from Bournemouth Pier up to Boscombe. I'll have twenty minutes there and then in the second half, I'll walk, I'll walk back. I cut everything off. And that, that's what I do. I go down to the beach where it's sensory for me. I can hear the waves an' that, that's good for me.*

Alan: *But you know what? Please don't get me wrong here, you've been diagnosed as autistic and I'm not, but this morning what Deb and I did was drive to the beach, park up, walk by the beach for an hour, stopped and had a coffee and then walked back. What you're doing is perfectly normal and something that is completed by thousands of people every single day to help them destress.*

Arsenal: *Yeah, yeah. And if it's a night game, I do the same and then I go down to Bournemouth Pier, go down to the bottom of it, turn round. Then because it's dark, I can see all the different colours of the hotels. And that's sensory again and I can see all the colours, I can hear the waves, and I'll stay there until the match is over. And then I'll get the result. [He's speaking in a voice so low I can hardly pick up what he is saying.] And that's how I do it.*

I always do something; I just keep myself away. I just keep myself away from the telly and everything. And it works. It works for me so it's good.

Alan: *Do you still – and I'm getting side-tracked here from what I wanted to talk about, but it doesn't really matter – do you still watch Match of the Day? I know you mentioned MOTD when you were waiting to watch it when you were fourteen and your mum and dad got married, so do you still watch MOTD?*

Arsenal: *Yeah, yeah. I just have to find out the score beforehand.*

Alan: *You can't watch it if you don't know the score?*

Arsenal: *No. Because then, imagine it's 1-0, and on MOTD it doesn't have any times up or anything. So, I don't know how long's left, so that's out of my control, isn't it? So, then I'm getting agitated because I don't know what the score is. I don't know, do I? So, if the other team score near the end or whatever… FLIP.*

Alan: *Do you not watch live games anymore then?*

Arsenal: *I can watch, as long as it's not AFC. And me strategies for putting the results on, I'm all right, actually, now, I can just get the remote control and get the scores up. But when I first had to do it, it was really hard for me. So, I had strategies. So, I'll tell you what me strategy was, I had the nearest thing to a straitjacket, I could find.*

         What I had to do, I had my straitjacket thing on [Arsenal mimics having a thick belt tied around his arms pinning them to the side of his body just like every adventure movie you've ever seen when the hero gets caught by the bad guys], I'd get the remote control and I'd do that.

Effectively what Arsenal is saying is that he strapped his arms to the side of his body, then picked the remote control up, and turned the TV to the football results while facing the other way, I think we are still in the days of Ceefax here. If AFC had lost, he couldn't hit himself because his arms were strapped to the side of his body. Not so much a coping mechanism this strategy but more a damage limitation one.

> Arsenal: *I'd get the results on and then I'd turn round, put the results on first, then I'd look. Then if they're bad results, because I have me straitjacket on, there's one thing I couldn't do—*
>
> Alan: *You couldn't hit yourself.*
>
> Arsenal: *Yeah. And that's how I weaned it. I'd be like argh, argh. But then it worked over time. Took about, must have took a season. Ha, a season, to get from straitjacket to just looking at it.*

Again, I admire the man's dedication to self-improvement and the betterment of his family. Try and walk a mile in those proverbial shoes. For a year, tie yourself up before you do something you hate in order to stop yourself from overreacting. We all know our own willpower: go on a diet, cut out coffee, go dry for January; it's tough. Now compare it to tying yourself up every time you get a football score so that by the end of the year, you're not hitting yourself in the face until you can't breathe, you're so exhausted. Dedication and strength of character knows no limits for Arsenal. To his credit, he doesn't see it.

"That's just life, mate."

> Arsenal: *But then I always had a, I always had to move on to something straightaway. So, I'd look at the score, and say we got beat 2-0, or whatever, I*

had to have a plan that I could just go and do something else to distract myself. Because if I stay and look at it, 2-0, I'd just be, me head goes and I go, "Why did we get beat by them? They're shit."

Alan: You've come a really long way, haven't you? In a short space of time. If you don't mind me saying.

Arsenal: It's been seven years now.

Alan: But, when I read those letters and reports, and I read how you were seven years ago compared to how you are today... I mean, you've come a long, long way. That's just my observance from a distance.

Arsenal: Yeah, when I see the kids and the kids tell me stuff, I go, wow. But I need to process it and I'll have a little think about it. And then it goes in better, then. But last seas— Last season I was going to say, last year, we played Liverpool, first game of the season [Sunday August 14th 2016].

And I thought, I hate Liverpool. Can't watch that. So, I went up to Winchester to see me daughter [Sam], and I took me other daughter [Danni]. And they go, "We're going to have a girly day, Dad, so why don't you go and watch the football?"

And I went, "OK, I'll go watch the football." And I went.

And I had a distraction, I had me book with me. I was reading the book instead of concentrating on the football. I was reading me book [Paul Merson's book] and we got beat 4-3 but I wasn't aware and me two kids were outside the pub for half an hour going, "I'm not going in. I'm not going in." And they were looking through

the window and they were going, "He looks all
right. He's not smashing anything up. Should we
go in?"

And the kids, they come in, and they walked
up to the table and I went, "Hello, how are yous?"
And they looked like, they just looked like they were
white. If I would have blown at them, they would
have gone over. They'd left because they weren't
sure how I was going to be. It was the distraction
of the book, whereas in the past I would be... I
would just be so focussed on the telly it's like I'm
there. I feel like I'm actually there. And I would
use terrible language and, oh man. So, that's why
I can't watch it because I use bad language and
that and I use bad words, you know, get myself
into trouble.

But I don't mean to, something takes over,
something takes over.

Alan: You say something takes over, but you've
managed to stop it! Are you hoping someday
you'll be able to sit in front of an Arsenal game
and watch it and get beat, or draw, or win, and
be able to enjoy it?

Arsenal: Yeah, I will be, I will be. Yeah, I will do. I know
that, that's a goal for me. "Oh, AFC are playing
today. Should we have a drink and go and watch
the football?" [I can tell that Arsenal has played
this make-believe conversation out in his own
mind many, many times.] That's a goal for me, I
have goals for everything.

Alan: Good. I think that's fantastic.

Arsenal: I have goals for everything.

On another occasion Arsenal talks about how he plans his day and what he has to prepare for on a normal day of his life. He starts by talking about how he knew he had to change his behaviour for the sake of his girls.

Arsenal: *I had to get back on track, didn't I? It's like what you said earlier about an alcoholic, because they've not had a drink for a year doesn't mean they're cured, does it? And that's what I think of every day. Even though I didn't harm yesterday, I have a plan for today and I have a Plan B. So, if Plan A doesn't work, I have a Plan B. So, I have all me strategies and I work out me day, and I don't drink anymore. I haven't drunk since Tuesday 28th October 2014. I can still go into pubs and everything.*

Alan: *I've not drank since about… 10pm last night. See, we can all remember our last drink!*

Arsenal: *I'm getting there, I'm getting there. It just takes time. When I say I'm getting there, I suppose I do, but later on today I'll think about things. Sometimes right on the spot it doesn't register, but it does later on when I do me negatives and positives.*

Alan: *Is that what you call processing?*

Arsenal: *Yeah, yeah, process it. And then if I don't understand anything tonight, I've got me dictionary down there and I'll look it up. Or I'll get the laptop out and I'll type in something and see, "Oh that's what that means." And then I'm getting there then, aren't I?*

I just need time to process stuff all the time. Because I make rash decisions all the time if I don't actually process stuff. I told you when Nicola said, "I want a divorce."

"Yeah, OK." And then, twelve months later when I got the paperwork. BANG! Why did I get a divorce? I don't know. [Arsenal laughs ruefully.] Because I never processed it. If I would have just thought about it, I would have said no. I would have said, "NO!"

"I don't want a divorce. I want to be a unit. I want to be with the kids. I want to be with you." But I didn't process it, did I? And that's what I learn every day, just take that little step back. If anyone asks me stuff, I write it down and say, "I'll get back to you." And that's my processing time.

The final word on coping should be where Arsenal, by utilising all the 'strategies' outlined above, has managed to get himself to. He has others to thank, of course he does, but the only person who has put all the hard yards in is Arsenal himself. I just wish he would realise that fact.

Arsenal: *Everything I ever learnt has been off Alderney Hospital. And they tell me what I have to do. And Samantha tell me and Danielle and they tell me and I go, "What?" I'm amazed by it. I just don't have that information. For some reason I just don't have that ability. I don't get it. Like, I dunno…*

Alan: *Do you sit and watch television, apart from sport?*

Arsenal: *I watch a drama from nine 'til ten each night. And that's when my, that's when me routine starts. So, after nine of the night if I'm on an 8-4 or a day off, I watch a drama nine 'til ten; at ten I do me* kitchen; then at about twenty past ten 'til half ten I sit there and I get my mobile and I delete all me text messages from the day; that's why I lost your address!

Alan: Why do you delete your text messages?

Arsenal: Because that's just an ending to me. Every day is a new day to me so at the end of the day I delete all of them; then I get all me negatives in a little bowl here and I turn them all into positives; then I'll be thinking about the next day and planning it out and what I'm going to do. So, when I go to bed, I've got nothing on me mind at all.

Alan: Put your head down and go to sleep?

Arsenal: Just like that [Arsenal clicks his fingers]. I do now, seven hours. I probably go to bed at five to eleven and five past eleven; I've gone. I get up at five past six every day, and then, I'm so happy, so happy. [His face literally lights up. These are not words someone is spouting, this is a glow that emanates from within and no one can deny that the man sat in front of me isn't euphorically happy.]

I come in here and take a look at me Wonderwall. I look at the date and I go, "A new day." This is what I'm not going to do today, I'm not going to get angry; I'm not going to self-harm; I'll have another look at me Wonderwall and I'll see what I'm doing today and I'm going to work and I'm happy. I am happy, I am.

Arsenal's Wonderwall is the side of a kitchen cupboard that is covered with positivity. At the top is a picture calendar (AFC, if my memory serves), on which is Arsenal's routine and list of things happening in his life, even me. Then there is a drawing from

Danni; a card from Sophie saying how much she loves Arsenal; his iceberg, a self-help diagram from the Starfish Project; a note about his speaking for Autism Wessex – 'How far have I come?'; a card with a picture of a cat on it announcing, 'I am a good person'; a photo card with the theme of 'Second chances'; a pencil – sensory; a Starfish poster – 'Make a Difference'; many other cards he's received praising him for his success and hard work; and finally some photos headed, 'People Understanding Me'.

Arsenal: I'm just happy. Happy.

Alan: That's fantastic, mate. There are not many people that can say that, you know.

Arsenal: What?

Alan: That they can get up in the morning and say they are really happy and looking forward to going to work for the day. Not many people can say that!

Arsenal: I do. Every single day.

Alan: I know you do. I can hear it in your voice.

Arsenal: You know what, I just go somewhere. Just like that. I don't know where I go, I just do. That's why anywhere where I sit in this room there's a positive.

Alan: Wherever you look there is something to see.

Arsenal: Me films, Kes [more later], me rainbows, I love rainbows. There's one on the table, there's one on that top there, another one there and when the weather's nice and the sun shines there's a crystal there that makes a rainbow in the room. There's a rainbow there, can you see it?

    That's when Samantha got me a day out at the track and that's me in the Ferrari. That's me and Danielle at Wembley with the FA Cup in the Royal Box.

Alan:	How did you get in the Royal Box?
Arsenal:	I'm a Scouser, you know, mate! I wrote to Wembley, so we went there. Strolled all round and that. That's the Emirates when I got invited down to the Emirates for a meal. In the stadium.
Alan:	I've been to the Emirates twice, but I bet you can't guess who I saw play?
Arsenal:	Brazil and Argentina.
Alan:	Bruce Springsteen
Arsenal:	So, that's me positive stuff. Sometimes after me talks people send me stuff rainbows and things. *[Arsenal takes lots of hand-drawn pictures out from kids and adults of rainbows. He then gets a poster out from the side of the couch.]* This is me best one.

Arsenal hands me the poster and leaves the room as the doorbell goes.

The poster is a traditional photograph of a sweeping rainbow across a valley and the mist below hides some of the treetops. It's beautiful. Then scrawled across the colours is the statement,

"I'm so fucking happy I could shit rainbows!"

And on that note, we will leave the 'Coping' chapter!

Chapter Fifteen

Samantha and Danielle

1995 to 2019

Whatever brings you down will eventually make you stronger.

Alex Morgan,
Olympic gold winner and
Women's Football World Cup champion

I BELIEVE THAT THE RELATIONSHIPS, STILL-CHANGING relationships, are the crux to Arsenal's life story. I think if they had not been around, Arsenal would still be going to football matches, self-harming and, every now and then, contemplating suicide. It was the need and desire to become a better person for them that fuelled his ambition. Quote: 'I have goals for everything'. The underlying goal was to ensure that Samantha never felt the way she did again and to stop Danielle from ever getting to that state of mind.

After spending time with both of them, it became obvious that they both have very different experiences with their dad.

Sam, it seems, as the eldest bore the brunt of the fastidiousness of Arsenal's autism. Pick that up, put that cup away, lower your skirt hem; if something made Arsenal angry at this time other than football it was liable to emanate from something that Sam had done, or not done.

Danni, on the other hand, was younger. She hadn't reached her teenage years when she was starting to form her own ideas about life and she also seemed to adopt her dad's need for everything to be in its right place. Now today, both Sam and her mum Nicola will say that Danni's the lucky one, as she is getting the best version of dad that Arsenal Whittick can provide.

Alan: *Sam, do you remember anything about your dad's autism when you were growing up as a younger child, a kid?*

Sam: *Obviously when I was a kid, we didn't know he had autism, so anything that was down to him having autism, we didn't know why. It was just when I was older that it was the things, looking back that were out the ordinary, were actually out the ordinary. I've said to other people, that he wasn't the cuddly parent or the affectionate parent; he was the disciplinarian.*

And I thought my friends' parents, one is the strict parent one is the fun parent, so I just thought that's what families are like. And a lot of my friends didn't have two parents anyway, I was one of the only pupils in my school class unit that had both of my parents together. So, I thought, I have a different family dynamic because I have a different family to those other people.

But, obviously, I don't know if it was when I was a little bit older that we started to fall out and stuff and I started to think why is he like this? And it was only a bit later when we got the diagnosis that I was able to look back and see that's why he did this or did that. When I was a kid, I just obviously didn't think too much into it.

Alan: *Can you give me examples of when you look back and you can see what was wrong due to your dad's autism?*

Sam: *Obviously what I can remember best is from when I was over ten rather than when I was younger than that. I don't remember much from when I was younger anyway. Just, mainly things were like… He just didn't hug us! He used to get angry a lot. When the football was on and he would swear and throw things and he would get so angry. But it was because my dad loved football. His name was Arsenal! [Sam laughs but there is no humour in it.]*

I just thought he loves football, I mean it was a weird thing, like his name, for example. I knew his name was Arsenal when I was a kid, thought it was a tiny bit weird but when I started to become a teenager and look back, I'd think, God, that is really weird. It was just as I started to get older and start to think about things, but it was only…

He liked things neat and tidy. He didn't show us affection. He was fun as well as strict, but fun in the fact he liked to take us on trips. He didn't like anything spontaneous. We lived in this street where there was loads of kids and I'd say, "Can I go round theirs?"

And I didn't understand stuff like that when I was younger because my mum would say, "It's next door. We've known these people for years, she's been there before, we know the parents. She hasn't got any plans for today or tomorrow, why can't she just go over there?"

But my dad was, "I need to have it in the diary. If it's not in the diary it doesn't happen." That sort of thing. That's the sort of thing I'd think but... [Sam stops speaking as I believe she's remembering the past and the difficulties her dad's autism caused her.]

Alan: And as a child, when you're not allowed to go next door or go to a sleepover, it breaks your heart, doesn't it?

Sam: Yeah and especially because I could see my mum was also confused. You know what parents are like: "Because I said so!" But my mum was trying to plead with him, but why can't she do that, she's done it before! And it was also obviously confusing as well because if I had said, "In two weeks, I want to go around this person's house," it'll be absolutely fine, and he would be fine about it. Or if we had people over, he would be fine if he knew about it. But obviously he doesn't like spontaneous things and likes things to be planned, which makes sense now but at the time, there was no reason why... I couldn't comprehend why he wouldn't let me go next door for a sleepover. Well, look at my mum, Mum can't understand it so, how can I? How is a ten-year-old supposed to understand it?

Now let's contrast Danielle's answer to the same question. Two girls, both raised by the same parents, but with the exception that for Danielle's formative years Arsenal had been diagnosed and was coming to terms with his autism. Add to this that after twelve months he moved out of the family home as he and Nicola got divorced and you remove the added pressure on everyone of being under the same roof all the time.

Danielle is now seventeen but she was ten when Arsenal got diagnosed.

Alan: *Danni, what do you remember as a child up to your dad being diagnosed, please? What are your memories of his autism?*

Danni: *Well, me and my dad, I've not been like a daddy's girl, but I've been very close to my dad. I don't think we've ever had an argument. We've always been really close and just had a proper relationship. Better than most teenagers do with their dad. I can't remember anything from when me and my sister and mum and dad all used to live together. [Arsenal left the family home in June 2012 when Danni was twelve years old.]*

    I don't have a single memory of what it was like to live there at all, I just know...

Alan: *You have no memories at all up to the age of twelve?*

Danni: *People don't believe me, they say, "You must remember something."*

Alan: *I believe you, it's just unusual.*

Danni: *People say I must be blocking things out, but I don't have one single memory from then, of us all living together.*

Alan: *Where did you live?*

Danni: *[Address withheld.] Where my mum lives now in Bournemouth. I remember living there I just don't have memories of all four of us living there*

	together, as a family. I only have memories of when I was living there on my own with my mum.

Alan: So, your dad has told me, at that house, he had a room downstairs called the 'Arsenal room'. Do you remember the Arsenal room?

Danni: Yeah, I remember. All I remember about that is there was nothing in there that wasn't AFC. There was an AFC clock, scarves decorated everywhere, AFC mats on the table, the lot. And I just remember him being in there a lot of the time and it was only, anyone could go in there but only if they found a reason to, because you know, because it was like his...

Alan: Man cave?

Danni: Yeah. So, you just could go there whenever you want. It was never restricted for us, but it was his, so we knew that, we left it for him.

Alan: But I know what kids are like, even though I'm an old man now, and when Mum and Dad weren't there, you must have had a peep in there to have a look around?

Danni: Yeah, we did, but I can't remember anything from that age. When we were all living there, there's nothing I can remember. [I think I'm getting on Danni's nerves now, how many times can she tell me she doesn't remember?]

Alan: Do you think you are subconsciously blocking that out? I know it's a difficult question to answer.

Danni: I do think that because I know that certain things happened, but I just can't specifically actually remember them in my head. For example, when AFC used to play, and my dad used to watch it, I remember that we all just used to be terrified of the score. *Knowing my dad and being terrified of the score and the way the game would go and how he would react. And I remember [remember?] we would all just, maybe half an hour before the game and my dad was getting ready for it would, we would literally just dart out of the room.*

Go upstairs and be together in me and my sister's room.

Alan: *And were you frightened?*

Danni: *I remember being frightened of how the game was going but never my dad. I remember him getting angry and stuff. I can't remember specific things, but I know that we all used to be in one room away from him. And be scared to know the score and maybe scared of hearing him freaking out about it.*

Alan: *If you were scared of the score, you must also have been scared of what the outcome of that score would be? The consequences of the score.*

Danni: *I was never scared of my dad hurting any of us or anything like that.*

Alan: *No, of course and I'm not suggesting that for a second—*

Danni: *I was always maybe more worried than scared. Mainly I was scared of him hurting himself. I think it was just because we knew it was happening anyway, so I think it was more worry of the consequences of a bad game. Or it didn't go how he wanted then what he would do to himself.*

That's the only thing I can remember from our time living together as a family, so I think I'm blocking things out without just realising. But I have been thinking for years, it's because I've been asked so many times by different people, "What do you remember? How much has your dad changed?" I can't answer that as well as my sister and my mum can. I can only go off how much my dad has changed since he first left, and we got our first place together as to today but no time before that. If that makes sense?

Putting aside for a moment Danni's complete block when it comes to the first twelve years of her life, the difference in the two daughters' recollections and experiences are marked. I think this could simply be put down to where they were in their own stage of development. Samantha was in her formative years, starting to read and understand the greater world and forming her own life opinions. Deciding who exactly she wanted to be.

Danni was still a child. She understood that some behaviours in her household were not what she thought to be the norm but appears to have blocked these out and has a hero worship now of her dad. Which I find hard to criticise as so do I!

We now turn back to Samantha and see if she can remember more of what Danni cannot.

Alan: *So, at the age of ten, do you have any memory of your dad self-harming?*

Sam: *I used to see my dad punch himself in the face and head all the time. Well, not all the time, but he used to go… I can't remember when I first saw anything like that, like I said, the football was a triggering event. He would be in the house watching the football and frequently he would go down to this room that had our computer in, stuff like that. And he would go in there and take himself outside the situation.*

But then obviously if I was in the room when he started, before he took himself out, I would see him, and I just thought he really loves football. He just wants that result. Because I'd seen it, it was just normal to me. And because I'd liked football when I was younger and I would sit in the room and watch football with him; but at the opposite edge of the room, so, then obviously I would see it then, if I wasn't in the room then I obviously wouldn't have seen it, if you know what I mean.

Both the girls use similar expressions to express and discuss their dad's behaviour. Both ask me, 'if you know what I mean'? The honest truth before I started talking to Arsenal would have been, "No, I haven't a clue what you mean." Secondly, they both use similar words – 'Because dad loved football so much' – as if that could be an obvious explanation for their dad's self-harm. They were trying to justify, in their young minds, that what they were seeing was the norm. Finally, they both use the word 'obviously' many times when talking about Arsenal, when his behaviour to others is anything but obvious.

Alan: *I know it's very difficult when you were nine or ten years old, but did you think that other dads did this? That this was the norm? Or did you know it was a little different, but it was your dad, so you went with it?*

Sam: *Probably that one. I don't think I even considered that other people's football-mad dads must do this. I just saw it happen, but because it wasn't a problem, because my mum knew. And we were all there and it was just how he was, it was never, like I didn't feel safe. It was just something that he* did, and I thought he gets angry and that's how he shows his anger.

Alan: And did you ever see him really hurt himself?

Sam: A couple of times afterwards his hand was injured. He'd hit himself or a door or something, the next day... He didn't really have a filter where you would keep something away from, I didn't see him as doing anything wrong really.

Alan: No, of course.

Sam: He wouldn't try and hide it.

"Look at me hand, look how swollen it is." He would treat a five-year-old, a ten-year-old, a fifteen-year-old, a twenty-five-year-old exactly the same. There was no sort of, 'This isn't appropriate for this age'. Just in general he wouldn't try to hide anything.

"Look I punched the wall last night." He didn't think he was doing anything wrong. We knew that he was doing that so when his hand was all swollen or there were cuts to his face or something, then I would see that sort of thing. He wasn't hiding it and I wasn't ashamed.

Alan: So, Sam, what age were you when you believe your dad's behaviour started to impact you?

Sam: Probably when I became a teenager. I was starting to do more things that I wanted to do, like sleepovers and stuff. I wanted to have more freedom, I wanted to do more things. You know, you're less controlled by your parents when you're at secondary school. His sort of behaviours that he had like his, how organised he is, like his time-keeping, how he had to be this and this time and this and this time. As I got older, we began to butt heads about it.

	I was doing my own thing.
Alan:	*You were a normal adolescent.*
Sam:	*Yeah. We always used to go to the Conservative, Con Club, around the corner, there was a family night that they would have. And my dad used to say, "If you're not ready by this time you can meet me there." Which at the time was because my dad didn't want to be late. But I think if I was going to be late for something, depending what it was but, "I'll meet you there."*
	You know, you just show up together because first he'd be like, "Oh, the girls are late," meaning me, my mum and my sister getting ready and whatever. And we would just follow on later because he would be at the door because we'd be leaving at 7pm and he would get so annoyed if it was 7.01pm and we weren't there. But even then, if we had to be there at 8pm, and it took twenty minutes to walk, and we left at 7.20pm instead of 7pm we still wouldn't be late.
	According to him we were late. He used to say, "If you're on time, you're late."
Alan:	*He has told me this.*
Sam:	*That's his phrase. So, stuff like that started to become… Because I started to have my own opinion, as I got a bit older, I would say, "Why do you care so much? We're going to be there. We're going to get there. Why do you care so much just because I've left this here?" I started to think about it as I got older, why does it bother him so much?*
Alan:	*And to be fair, a teenager doesn't make many allowances anyway.*
Sam:	*No.*

Alan:	*But there were no allowances being made for your dad being on the spectrum because at this point, no one knew.*
Sam:	*And I was a typical teenager.*
	"You hate me. You're out to get me. Why won't you let me do this?" I just thought it was all a personal vendetta because my sister wasn't a teenager yet. I was the oldest in the house.
	"You don't want me to have friends. You don't want me to have fun. You don't let me do this. You don't let me do that." I just thought it was him being mean.

It appears that Danni never experienced this side of her dad, or alternatively was too young to take umbrage with him. She describes one particular Christmas as being magical, with Arsenal proving to his girls with little room for argument that Father Christmas had visited early Christmas morning and seemingly leaving quite a mess.

Alan:	*I'm just going to try and prompt a few memories, Danni. Christmas Days, do you remember Christmas Days with your dad?*
Danni:	*Erm... The few things I remember about Xmas is my dad always making it a big deal. I remember me and my sister because we used to share a room, I remember us waking up together and we had to wait to go downstairs until we had been told that we can.*
	I remember going down and we would walk into our living room and there would be presents everywhere and we would all open them together. And everything would be fine and there wouldn't

be any problems. And I remember my dad used to go all out, especially for me as I was younger than my sister. He would decorate the whole house and the garden fully out for me. And I remember that because I always used to look forward to it obviously as a kid.

But I don't remember any specific Xmases, that is just a tradition.

Alan: And what did he used to put in the garden for you?

Danni: It was so funny. Our garden was square and quite big, not massive but it was quite big. We used to have a trampoline, and I remember, the only Xmas year I remember is when my dad put loads of fake snow all over the fence. And he had some parts of Santa's outfit that, to make it look like Santa had jumped off our trampoline over the fence to get away. There were ripped clothes from the trampoline over the fence—

Alan: He had laid a trail out for you.

Danni: Yeah and I remember there were black markings along the walls through our corridor leading up to the garden, so I obviously thought it was Santa's sleigh going through our hallway.

Alan: How cool is that?

Danni: It was a whole house thing. Even in the bathroom there was, my dad always used to put white beard stuff in the sink like as though he was having a shave. Every room had something to show what Santa had done in our house.

I remember, I don't remember any specific Xmas, I remember that one Xmas, whatever year it was, being something in literally almost every room. And I remember I, as a kid, obviously loved it. Yeah, I thought it was great. *[Danni had been on a roll, excited and falling over herself to explain what a great dad Arsenal had been around Christmas time but still at pains to point out to me that she couldn't remember anything specifically.]*

Alan: Fantastic. And what about your birthdays? Did you ever used to do anything special for your birthdays?

Danni: Birthdays? I can't remember any of my childhood birthdays.

Alan: No parties?

Danni: I don't think I've ever had; I don't ever remember ever having any actual birthday parties. I don't think, I think I've only ever had one in my life, was my sixteenth but before that I just don't think I ever had one.

Alan: Did you ever go out for your birthday? Did you ever do theme parks, Chessington?

Danni: I think for my birthday we may have gone to Farmer Palmers one day.

I know we went to Paultons Park one day for my birthday, but I can't remember how old I was or what birthday it was, but I know that we went to a theme park for one of my birthdays, as a family, which I think was maybe one of the last things we did as a family. I think it was but I'm not a hundred per cent sure on that.

While most of Danni's memories are happy and joyous occasions, Sam's memories, more so as she moved into her teenage years, take on a much darker tone.

Alan:	You hit your teen years and it all started getting a little too much for you?
Sam:	Yeah. [Much quieter] Yeah. It was both of us. Because I was a teenager, I had become a massive bitch at this point. It was the hormones, of course it was the hormones, she's a teenager! And my dad, because of the way he was acting just made us clash more, because when I was younger, I didn't have the hormones and went along with everything my parents said. But then when I became a teenager, I started to think for myself.
	I like this. I don't like this. Stuff like that. So, that's when we started to fall out. Before then we were really close, but once I became a teenager, not so much. [Sam appears to want to take a lot of the responsibility for what she is soon going to share with me. She's laying the land for me. But she does stop talking.]
Alan:	Do you want to carry on talking? Can you tell me where you got to eventually?
Sam:	Dad had become impossible to live with. I don't think that's a wrong statement. He might not be now, but I didn't know that, he WAS impossible to live with. When I was fifteen, I think, I had just fell out with all my friends at school.
Alan:	Because?
Sam:	Because this girl started this rumour about me that I had done something with this boy, which I hadn't done, and it made all my friends… She actually made a rumour about another of my friends later on and that's when she realised that she had been lying about her and me and she became my friend again.

We were a group of three or four and it was one of those things when a group of teenage girls, I went to an all girl's school, they were horrified: "Why didn't you tell us?" They thought I'd lied to them about this boy and I don't even... In Year 9 all the girls in our group, three or four of them, they all believed this other girl. And so, I didn't have any friends and it was just a small group anyway. And then the rumour got around.

I would walk in and... [The words dry up.]

Alan: *You were being bullied!*

Sam: *Yeah. At the time my dad may have thought it wasn't bullying as he thinks bullying is being punched in the face by someone. That sort of thing. Whereas I'd go in and people, at lunch people would stand up at lunch and move away from me. That sort of thing and when you're fourteen/ fifteen, all you want is to be liked.*

So, I used to go to the library for my lunch as it used to be too embarrassing on the field, or in the lunch hall, whereas in the library no one's really in there. But you weren't allowed to eat in there, so I'd go and eat my lunch in the toilet. Eat my packed lunch in the toilet and then go back to the library and read.

Alan: *It's tough, isn't it? You feel as though there's no one to talk to, as well.*

Sam: *At school, all I wanted to do was, not be at school. So, when I got home and then me and my dad was arguing all the time about stupid things... Things not being washed properly, him looking at the dishes as I've washed them, saying, "This isn't clean enough." Stuff like that.*

> So, I had no escape at this point because even though everyone goes, "I hate school," with your friends you're OK, you have a laugh together.

Alan: The best days of your life is what everybody told me when I was at school.

Sam: That's what everyone says. So, when you go to school you're together, you're all complaining together. When you're not in a together group and you're just on your own...

Alan: Were you totally on your own?

Sam: I mean, I did have a friend at the boys' school opposite, but I didn't see him a lot as they're different schools. Then I had a boyfriend at some point, but I don't know when he factors into this story.

Alan: Tell it as well as you possibly can, it's OK.

Sam: No friends, no one at home. So, I felt as though I had no one to talk to. And I started self-harming. Not like my dad, I wasn't punching myself, the classic cutting myself. That's why my dad didn't realise he was self-harming because he wasn't cutting himself. You know?

Alan: I can't empathise with that. I can sympathise but I can't empathise. It's not something I've ever done. I've never felt the need to do. So, can you just describe to me how you felt when you were doing it and why you did it? What did you gain from cutting yourself?

Sam: It was just more... I guess I've thought about it since and I... It was just I was controlling it, for me, you feel rubbish inside, so you want, first of all, your pain is changing. So, you're focussing on a physical pain rather than an emotional pain.

You're controlling something and if you're feeling really low like that, I just felt that I wasn't worthy of family like everyone else. My dad hates me! You know that's what I thought at this point. Everyone at school hates me therefore I deserve to feel like this and just like that.

I remember the first time that I did it because I was walking home from school, in a rush, I must have had a bad day. But I had my keys in my hand and as I was walking, I was holding my key in my hand. And I was squeezing it because I didn't want to cry in the street, so I was squeezing it in my hand. You know like people will dig their nails into their hands to stop themselves from getting upset.

I had the key in my hand, and it felt good. Getting the pain out that I could feel inside, feeling it somewhere else that's when I went home, because obviously I knew people cut themselves, so I went home, and I thought this is a way I can...
[Sam doesn't finish the sentence, so I do it for her.]

Alan: *Cope?*

Sam: *Yeah. I started using that as a coping mechanism. I came upon it by accident. In a way I was just holding my key and I felt something that I just wasn't used to.*

Alan: *And where did you cut yourself?*

Sam: *On my arms.*

Alan: *With a razor blade?*

Sam: *Yeah, yeah. There was a time when a glass or a cup had smashed, and I'd kept one of the little shards—*

Alan: *And how badly did you cut yourself?*

Sam:	Not that badly. I don't have any scars. I have tiny little white marks on my arms. Superficial. At first, I was a bit scared and didn't cut too deep.
Alan:	This may seem like an obvious question, but is that because it was more a cry for help?
Sam:	Probably.
Alan:	You said you had no one to talk to but what about your mum?
Sam:	I felt at the time… My mum has changed a lot since then. My mum has, I don't really know how to explain without sounding like a bitch.
Alan:	Just say it honestly and we'll see how it looks when it comes out.
Sam:	She had said to me now, this is the only way I can describe it, since she has suffered with depression, now, that she is so sorry for how she wasn't there for me when I was going through that. Because she, at that time, was very much a 'cheer up' sort of character. My mum never cried, my dad never cried, and I cried all the time. I'm the most emotional person you'll meet. Anything will set me off but I'm sensitive and strong at the same time. I cry at adverts and everything. I've always been a crier.
Alan:	I don't think that the occasional shed tear is any indicator of your internal strength.
Sam:	No, neither do I. Dad would ask, "Why are you crying now?" And that would just make me cry harder. My mum has said now that she is proud that I managed to get through it because now she knows what it feels like to be that down. But at the time I didn't believe I could approach my mum because I didn't think she would understand.

> *Older people don't understand self-harming and I didn't want to upset her by telling her. And I didn't want to cause any further problems between Mum and Dad.*

Sam was a troubled, lonely and confused young teenager who turned to self-harm as some form of solace. She needed support and had no one to provide it. She fought tooth and nail daily with her autistic dad and didn't have the confidence in her relationship with her mum to talk to her about it. Plus (as we have already heard from Nicola), her mum was desperately trying to cope with Sam and Arsenal's toxic relationship, leaving her in the middle and also very alone. Looking back, there were four people living solitary lives under the same roof and the driver was an undiagnosed condition of autism.

Sam: *I was fourteen or fifteen when I tried to take my own life. It had all become too much. Looking back, it seems like a different life because I don't feel like that no more. I can't imagine being in a place now where I'd want to take my own life.*

Alan: *Can I ask you a really straight, honest question?*

Sam: *Yeah.*

Alan: *I know you took some tablets [I'm choosing my words very carefully here], did you really think at the time you were going to kill yourself or did you think you were bringing things to a head? Did you genuinely think that you were killing yourself?*

Sam: *I don't think… Because I left the house to go to a friend's house, I'm not sure if it was him or a new boyfriend, I think it was the boyfriend and then I told him that I'd taken the tablets.*

Alan: *Your dad said it was your boyfriend.*

Sam: Yeah. It makes sense. I'd been with this boyfriend for a few months and he contacted my dad. I left the house because I didn't want to be there, and I was going to my friend's house, but I didn't even make it there because the police picked me up. [Sam has real problems remembering exactly what happened and that's no real surprise.] They collected me from the street.

Not sure what I was thinking of, was I just going to knock on his door at 3am and say what to his dad? I didn't think that far ahead.

Alan: You see it's a strange thing to do if you don't think you're going to be around next morning. To get up, walk out and go and knock on your boyfriend's house.

Sam: Yeah. I'd text him to say I'd done this, but I don't think… I'd read a woman's magazine about the number of tablets to take, but I don't know if I'd taken the right number or not, not sure if I knew? But it wasn't a lot.

Alan: I'm not trying to work out the number of tablets you took, but I'm trying to ascertain the state of your mind at the time. Because I have read the reports, but what I'd like to include in your dad's book is just something a little more personal. This is your dad's story, but your story is intertwined with his and is the reason your dad eventually got diagnosed. In fact, it's the statement that your dad made to me in the pub that made me say, "We've got to get this written down, mate. We have to get this story out there."

Sam: Because people ask me how many tablets it was and it wasn't a lot, it could mean that I wasn't *trying. But I don't think I was... I didn't know what the right number of tablets to take was. I think I was ready for people to realise how serious this was. I remember when I was cutting myself on the arm, I was keeping it hidden, there are pictures of me when I was thirteen with long sleeves on all the time.*

Alan: *How long had you been self-harming before you tried to kill yourself?*

Sam: *I think it was eighteen to twenty-four months. I remember a couple of times I think my sister had seen my arms and that's not what I wanted because she was my younger sister. She would notice more than my parents, but I didn't want anyone to know then.*

Alan: *So, back to the question. Were you really trying to kill yourself or were you waving a massive big red flag to everybody?*

Sam: *Probably wasn't trying to kill myself. By saying it was a cry for help makes me feel that people will think that I wasn't really as down as I was. Probably on that night I didn't want to die but then also I didn't want to live. I wouldn't have been... I wasn't relieved or disappointed afterwards. I was in the middle; I wasn't feeling anything at the time. The fact that it could possibly have been... I wanted. All those times I wanted; I was thinking every day I wanted to die.*

By doing that I obviously thought I wanted to die. But I don't know if that's actually true, it could have been a cry for help. I was feeling so low. My self-worth had dropped to the level where I didn't care anymore.

Alan:	*That's the point.*
Sam:	*Also, do people actually understand how I'm feeling?*
Alan:	*Thinking along those lines, do you therefore think you were perhaps trying to hurt other people by your actions?*
Sam:	*No, because people always say, people who I've spoke to if they know this about me or not, when you kill yourself the only people you hurt are your family and friends, when you're in that state of mind there's no way that you think they care if you die. When you're in that state of mind you don't think, Oh, my parents are going to be upset if I do this.*

Because when you're in that mindset, you're thinking about it so much, you're thinking, They're better off without me. I'm causing all these arguments in my parents' house. Of course, they don't care, it'll be better for them if I'm not here. They won't be arguing. Me and my dad won't be arguing. It's more like that. Obviously now, whether it's because I'm older or it's because I'm not in that headspace anymore, I know for a fact they'd be devastated. Anyone would. I would, if it was one of them.

But when you're in that state of mind, no one cares about you. No one loves you so it doesn't matter. It's a positive for them if you're not around. I personally, and I've talked to people who have tried to kill themselves and read up on the matter, that's the general consensus: "You'll be better off, they'll be better off, if you're not around."

After listening to this several times, my questions now sound harsh, as though I was trying to push Sam into saying something she didn't want to say, but that was not the intention at all. As an inexperienced interviewer, especially on such a specialised topic as mental health issues, I tried to make it a conversation and to make Sam feel as comfortable as she could be about talking to me.

I need to remind myself that this is Arsenal's story, but how can we tell Arsenal's story without Sam? She was the catalyst for two life-changing events, or certainly her actions were the catalyst for both her father's diagnosis and the writing of this very book. Without her, neither would have taken place.

I refer back to the letter from Dorset Healthcare University to Arsenal and Nicola, summarising their then recent assessment of Samantha. The letter is dated 23rd November 2010 and below is an extract, (printed with kind permission from Dorset Healthcare University):

"Samantha reflected on how she has been trying to manage her difficult feelings over the last few years, and openly discussed how last year she was self-harming in the form of cutting and has also made a previous attempt to kill herself. She often feels that she is unsure of what to do when she is having such thoughts and would like further support to do things differently.

"Samantha feels that at the centre of her low mood are the feelings that she is unloved and she often feels as if she doesn't have the one to one attention that she needs. She told me how she cannot tolerate being alone within her home. When alone she questions whether she is loved and whether anyone cares for her.

"Samantha also talked of some of the difficulties within the family home which you Mr Whittick acknowledged.

Samantha explained how she often feels as she is 'walking on eggshells'. This is partly due to your need to have everything in order and for everything to be in its place. She told me that you are very rigid and stick very closely to routines within the home, for example in the morning.

"Samantha explained how having to adhere to such rigid routines and ways of being makes her feel uncomfortable as though she is always doing something wrong. This can leave her feeling low in confidence at a time when she is already vulnerable to this in her teenage years. She also told me how her sister Danielle (nine) also behaves in a similar way which is why she is currently being assessed.

"Based on Samantha's previous experiences it was felt appropriate for her to be offered individual sessions to consider in more depth where her insecure feelings come from, to be aware of the triggers and to find new strategies for managing these unpleasant thoughts and feelings. Samantha would not like any further family therapy at this time but would like her mother to attend some of the sessions with her.

"As you are aware I also met with Mr Whittick subsequent to this session to offer him an assessment with a view to referring him to the Adult Asperger Service for an assessment.

"In the meantime, Samantha and I also spent some time discussing how she would keep herself safe should she begin to feel vulnerable and low in mood once again. Samantha felt that the most helpful thing to do at this time would be to speak to her mum, whom she has a close relationship with.

"Both Samantha and Mr Whittick felt that support for him could have a significant impact on the family *home which as you are aware has contributed to some of Samantha's anxious feelings.*

"Etc. etc. Yours sincerely..."

This is but an extract of the letter which goes on to suggest other coping strategies for Samantha as well as her ongoing therapy sessions, some of which Nicola would also attend. The letter also sets Arsenal off on his own voyage of discovery to his diagnosis.

Danni is also mentioned in this letter as being assessed and now we can return to her thoughts and when she first started to get affected by behaviours in her household.

Alan: *Moving on to your dad's self-harming, that happened both pre and post the diagnosis, I do know that he hasn't self-harmed since 2014, do you ever remember him self-harming and how you felt when he did?*

Danni: *I remember one day after the football, I know it was either half-time or it had ended as it wasn't going on at that minute, we all came downstairs to get a drink, and to see what was going on. My dad came into the kitchen and was making a drink for himself, making a cup of tea. I could see his hand was almost broken. I could see his head; we could tell he had hit himself.*

I remember, being the youngest, not quite understanding what was going on. I had an idea. I remember not knowing what to do because I could see my mum and sister not really knowing what to do themselves. We were just, we used to come together and follow each other every day that the football was on.

Alan:	*How old do you think you were then when you saw this?*
Danni:	*You know I have no idea. I'm so bad at remembering how old I was at certain times. I've no idea but I don't think… I'm so bad with ages.*
Alan:	*Do you remember your mum and dad getting divorced?*
Danni:	*I don't remember the divorce happening in the house. I remember hearing stories about my dad. Before or after the divorce when we were looking at my dad moving out, it was on my sister's birthday, and back then my dad didn't have much understanding about empathy or anything like that. I remember my mum and sister saying to him, "Wait a week before you leave."*
Alan:	*What date's your sister's birthday?*
Danni:	*14th June.*
Alan:	*Yeah, on this list he's given me it says moved into new flat 15th June.*
Danni:	*You can't leave on Sam's birthday, it's too much of a happy occasion. Maybe not so bad for her because of their relationship at the time but I remember my dad not having the understanding: "Why should I stay if I'm not with your mum?" I remember just before my dad moved out when we were all at CAMHS [Child and Adolescent Mental Health] once, me and my sister had been given these booklets to fill out. We were both quite young, so they were trying to find out what we wanted with a separation, in the nicest way, and me and my sister's books were so different.*
	My sister wanted to live with my mum and her boyfriend and her pets and everything. Mine

was like my dad. My book was focussed on my dad; my sisters was all focussed on my mum and not really anything of my dad. Other than that I don't remember going through the divorce, apart from him moving out near my sister's birthday.

Alan: Do you remember how you felt when your dad actually left?

Danni: I don't know. I have no idea how that happened. When my dad first left, I went with him, but my sister stayed at my mum's.

Alan: OK, so let's talk about things that you have a better recollection of. You're seventeen now, a young adult, has your relationship with your dad changed in any way or is it as it always was? I think you have a strong relationship with your dad, that's what I see as an outsider, has it always been as strong?

Danni: We've always had a very strong relationship. We haven't had any problems, any arguments, always been, kind of, always on my dad's side of everything. Just like my sister was with my mum, it was quite divided. Everyone used to mention how it was me and my dad, and my sister and my mum. Never anything else. Me and my sister have always been best friends and really close but my sister and my dad, in the past, never got on at all.

    It never seemed to be anything other than that. Two pairs, me and dad, my sister and mum.

Alan: Why do you think that was?

Danni: I think when I was younger, I related more to my dad rather than my mum. Ever since me and my dad left my mum's, I left with Dad because I wanted to be with him. Since then I've always lived *at both houses. Weekends with Mum, weekdays with Dad. But the first thing I did was be with my dad and then figure out how I could see my mum. Normally when a dad leaves the family house, the kids stay and then go and see their dads at weekends. But I left with my dad.*

Alan: *How did your mum feel about you leaving with your dad?*

Danni: *Me and my mum didn't really talk about things like that. I think she was upset that the whole family was splitting up. She was always upset that I was more on my dad's side.*

Alan: *Today, do you live with your dad permanently or are you back and forth still?*

Danni: *I kind of live between three houses now at the minute. My dad's, my mum's and my boyfriend's. Dad's four days of the week, be at my mum's more so at the weekends, it's changed so many times where I stay at weekends. I now don't spend a lot of time in either parent's houses but spend most time at my boyfriend's.*

Alan: *So what are you doing at the moment, A Levels?*

Danni: *I'm studying health and social care at sixth form college.*

Alan: *OK, thank you. Back to Dad, what changes have you seen in him over the past couple of years?*

Danni: *He's definitely generally more relaxed in life. Having his own place is probably the best thing that could have ever happened to him. I've mostly understood the way my dad has always wanted to live. He wants everything to be really structured and very neat. And I relate to that, a lot, as a child, and my mum and sister didn't.*

He's more relaxed because he can live how he wants and not be on edge all the time. If that makes sense.

When we first moved out and he used to watch the football, it wasn't as bad as when we all used to live together, I never had any problems with him watching it in the house. We used to go out and watch it a lot and there never seemed to be any problem. I could tell he was getting better after the move out. He got to live the lifestyle that he always wanted to have. He also became more open-minded to how other people feel and view things. In the past he would only understand how he thinks.

He's starting to better understand how other people think and feel.

As I'm writing this, I'm starting to think that Danielle's recollections are seen through rose-tinted glasses when speaking about Arsenal. She was at an age when it's easier and better for her to remember the positives and not to spend too much time agonising over the negatives. She sees this definite divide down the middle of the family that the other family members don't see as obviously. For sure Sam moved towards her mum as she and Arsenal started their private battle and Danni believes therefore that it was her and her dad on one side of a family divide. Nicola, Danni's mum, doesn't believe it was that black and white.

Alan:	*Do you feel you have sacrificed your own relationship with Arsenal for Sam's relationship with her dad?*
Nicola:	*I think if we had been on our own, I would probably have put up with it more. Do I leave me*

daughter, or do I leave me husband? And she was literally old enough to pack her things and go, "I'm gunna go," and he was the one in the wrong here, so that was the decision.

Alan: He wasn't in the wrong—

Nicola: None of us were wrong, none of us were right. I know that now, but at that time when I had not a lot of time to make a decision and everything was happening.

Alan: How do you believe it's affected your own mental health? Because you've been exposed to an awful lot of stress—

Nicola: I have a lot of guilt, really, because of where Danielle is involved now. You tried to talk to Danielle at the time and she was, "Don't care. Don't care. Not bothered." You know, that was her way, but she's spoke to me since then and she's opened up over the last year or so, it's affected her massively. Massively. And I'm the reason for the divorce, I'm the one who muted it. Although she understands she doesn't understand in the way that Sam does.

Alan: I don't think either of them blame you.

Nicola: No.

Alan: What Danielle does say, is it was always you and Sam, and her and Dad.

Nicola: You see, for me there was a divide, but it was me, Sam, Danni and then Arsenal. Because we used to have our Friday girls' nights. Me and Sam will sit and speak to Danni and she'll be, "I don't remember." It's almost like Danni is blocking things out as well. And Arsenal has with Danni… [Nicola stops, not certain which way to go with her thoughts.]

Alan: *Danni does say the same thing as Arsenal, almost identical in what she says, "I don't remember anything up to the age of nine." I thought, I've heard Arsenal use those exact same words.*

Nicola: *Yeah. [There is a very long pause here on the tape as Nicola thinks long and hard about what she's about to say next.] I think Danni does as she's been told or thinks. Arsenal uses Danni for certain stories: "Danni remembers that, ask her."*

            And Sam says to me, "No, she doesn't." It's like he's trying to find a reason or an excuse for, "This is how I remember it, it must be like that." But really, it's not, it was me, Sam, Danni. And when the football would be on, we would know. And even the dog, the dog would go, and his ears would go down. And he'd go up the stairs because we all knew all hell was going to break loose. We'd push everything to the side. On a Friday night or Saturday morning we'd push everything to the side of the room where it was less likely to get thrown around the living room.

Alan: *It must have cost you a fortune if you keep smashing bloody things up?*

Nicola: *Things would get broken and stuff, but either he would fix them or get it new. Everything was worked out and sorted out. But I never knew. Because I never opened a letter, you know, until I was thirty-four. Arsenal used to open all of the letters. He used to tell me, bloody hell he used to tell me when my next smear test was! That's how much I never opened a letter, but I was quite happy with that.*

Because I'd get the letter and think, *Don't know what that means.*

And he'd be like, "Do you want me to open that letter?"

And I'd be like, "Yeah." *The mail would be there, and never ever ever would he open it without me.*

And I would say to him, "It's your job, you've been doing it for years. I don't know why you haven't opened it." But every single day he couldn't do it unless I was there.

Alan: He won't open it if it's not got his name on it, but the other side of that is because he was never told anything as a child, because he always felt left out of everything and never knew what was going on, there's also a bit of a control thing there as well, isn't there?

Nicola: Very much so. Massive. The thing about Danielle is, when it was Samantha, we were Mum and Dad; with Danielle he just wanted it to be Dad, Dad, Dad! As he, he didn't work at that time and he was like, "Right, I'm going to be taking her to school." And all of a sudden, he just took over. And whenever a letter came back from school, parent's signature, I remember once putting my name first and never doing it again because all hell broke loose.

Alan: But that's his autism as well.

Nicola: But with Danielle he always needed to be in control. He needed to be in control, definitely.

Alan: And the other side of that is, because he was frightened, that what had happened to Sam would happen again if he didn't change his ways *and behave better, so he may have wanted to be the perfect father to Danielle because he saw what went wrong with Sam.*

He was trying to be a better father.

Once again, people's memories or perceptions don't quite tie up. This can be known as the Rashomon effect, named after the famous 1950 film of the same name in which a samurai has been mysteriously killed, directed by the most famous of Japanese directors, Akira Kurosawa. Four characters give conflicting reports of what happened: the samurai's wife says she was raped by a bandit, fainted, then awoke to find the samurai dead; the bandit says he seduced the wife and then fought the samurai to an honourable death; the woodcutter says he witnessed the rape and murder but stayed out of it; and the dead samurai's ghost says that he killed himself. The true question of Rashomon isn't whose account is correct, however. Instead, it forces audiences to ask if there even *is* a correct version of events.

Of course, a real-world crime would certainly have a single true explanation. In reality, conflicting accounts come down to the unreliability of human memory. In fact, some research has shown that implanting false memories can be as simple as asking someone to recount an event that didn't happen. What's more, every time you remember something, you rewrite it in your brain. If that recollection contains errors, you'll strengthen those errors until you're positive they're correct. That's why even a memory as extreme as fighting a samurai could be constructed out of thin air with the right kind of suggestion.

I have asked several members of the same family similar questions about the same events and the answers in the main have been consistent but just occasionally the Rashomon effect can be recognised, especially when you think how many times they have all been asked questions about Arsenal's autism over the past few years. I'm sure that can be true of all the recollections in this book and the older the memory the less secure it becomes.

We now go back to Danielle and one of the occasions when all the family were invited to a talk at her college.

Danni: *When the talks kind of started, one of the first few, we all got invited to a talk that he did, actually at my college. It was before I started going there. And I remember that being the first, certainly one of the first, that he did. I remember it was me, my dad, my sister and my mum. It was him and my sister that talked and told the story and everything, and me and my mum were there to maybe answer questions rather than talk ourselves.*

Obviously, my dad and my sister have the most to say. And my mum does as well but obviously it's more based on them. I remember going to that talk and going to other events like the hug days.

Alan: *How did you feel that Christmas Day when your dad hugged you and Sam for the first time?*

Danni: *It was really emotional when he hugged Sam. It was the first time and it was so unexpected. Nobody knew what was going on. It was a really nice moment, especially for Sam, is what I think. She appreciated that; a lot.*

Alan: *And what about yourself? He hugged you as well, didn't he?*

Danni: *Because me and my dad never really had any problems like him and my sister, it wasn't such a big deal. I mean it was a big deal but because of the difference in our relationships between my dad and me, and my sister and my dad, the*

	main focus was that he was able to have that hug that he can't really do. Especially with Sam, after everything they've been through.
Alan:	*But it was the first time he hugged you as well, wasn't it?*
Danni:	*Yeah, yeah. It was emotional for everyone and it was really nice, but I feel it was a bit more of a day for my dad and Sam's first hug.*
Alan:	*Did you never feel like Sam did? Did you never feel unloved?*
Danni:	*I can't remember feeling anything that Sam did with my dad because I think partly just because I was a lot younger than my sister when we all lived together, and I can't remember a lot of it all anyway.*
Alan:	*Sam does say you're the lucky one because you've got the best of your dad.*
Danni:	*She does say that all the time to me.*
Alan:	*To be fair, she knows, she did say that.*
Danni:	*She does remind me of that fact to this day. But I just feel that me and my dad have never had a problem. I have had it easier being the younger one. Growing up with my dad, he had already been through so much with Sam and he started to get a bit of help [that might just be the understatement of the last ten years], and she had the worst of it.*
Alan:	*Did you go to the hug day?*
Danni:	*Yes, I did. That was really good. It was so emotional. Everyone was crying. Everyone who was hugging my dad, crying, strangers and friends. I'm not sure how many came in the end, but it was quite a lot. It was really nice when me and my sister got our hugs. I think it was good that people who knew*

my dad came down, obviously because we did it at the uni, we had a lot of students, but when it was people that my dad knew, they were the really emotional ones. It was a really good day.

Alan: I'm going to try and hug him. I was going to try at Christmas, but I thought, No. He's not ready yet. [Twelve months later and I still haven't got to my hug. Perhaps when the book is finished?]

Danni: I feel that as long as he knows it's coming it's fine. People who know him will see him in the street and will automatically go to hug him and there is so much difference between now and the past.

If in the past if someone had just come up to him and hugged him in the street me, my mum and my sister would just freeze in time. We wouldn't want to look because we knew what was going to happen. My dad would freak out. And then looking at the reaction of the other person who would know they had done something wrong but have no idea, it would not be a nice situation.

But now my dad would be better if they hug him straightaway. Although he's not ready for it, his reaction is now not as extreme. He just takes it in, as he can. Which is good, I suppose, that he can do that now.

Alan: I'll bide my time. I won't surprise him with it. I was going to ask him for a Christmas hug, but he had enough going on at the time.

Changing tack, do you remember Sam's problems and Sam trying to take her own life? What you felt at the time? Or were you too young to appreciate what was going on?

Danni: *I don't think I really understood at the time. I don't know what she was going through or the state she was in at hospital. I'm quite glad I don't have a memory of her like that. [It was 2011 and Danni was nine.] I know everything she went through, and I understand today, but I don't remember. I know everyone in the family was so different and it not working out, so we separated. I was too young to be told at the time that it was a consequence of Sam trying to kill herself. When I first found out I was still kind of young [I remind myself that this is a 17 year-old girl saying 'when' she was young], I think back then I thought that maybe I was upset and annoyed at my mum for making my dad just leave.*

But that's because I didn't have an understanding of what Sam was going through because I was so young. I didn't understand why my dad was leaving so I've kind of always been annoyed at my mum because at the time she was just giving up because my dad was the way he was. So, he just got asked to leave and that was that. As I've gotten older and I now know everything that happened it was probably, no, definitely, the right thing. For my sister, my dad, my mum and everyone else. [Interesting here that Danni doesn't include herself in the people that it was 'definitely the right thing' for.]

I was now thinking that Danni had managed to ride the waves of the storm that was her dad's autism and managed to miss many of the rocks waiting to capsize her. While Sam had got herself to such a low level of self-esteem that she thought the world would be a better place without her in it, Danni seemed to have come through relatively unscathed. But I was wrong.

Returning to Sam and the night that she decided life wasn't worth living, I asked her could she remember her exact state of mind and what else from that fateful night.

Sam:	*It was at night, whenever I'd gone to bed. Everyone was asleep and I was in my bedroom. I went downstairs to the kitchen where we kept all the tablets and stuff and took them back up to my bed. I took them in bed.*
Alan:	*And that's when you got up and walked to your boyfriend's?*
Sam:	*I was on my laptop the whole time. I wasn't, like, sleepy? I went downstairs, I didn't fall asleep straightaway because I was on the internet or whatever. Then I just messaged him to say I'd done this, done that.*
Alan:	*What tablets did you take? I know you don't know how many but what were they?*
Sam:	*They would have been paracetamol, ibuprofen, that kind of thing. Whatever we had in the medicine cabinet.*
Alan:	*So, you took the tablets, text your boyfriend, left the house, your boyfriend text your dad, your dad rang the police and the police picked you up on your way to your boyfriend's? And they took you to hospital?*
Sam:	*They took me home and then we went to the hospital together because I didn't need an ambulance. They took me home first because they didn't think I was in need of the hospital, but then I went to the hospital later. To be checked. My dad*

took me in the car and Mum stayed at home with my sister. My dad wanted to drive me, and my mum doesn't drive. It wasn't a decision, it was just practical. One parent needed to take me, and one needed to stay with Danni.

I had some blood tests because at the time I may have suggested a number of tablets or they saw the packets? Something like that. I felt sick but I wasn't sick, so they thought I wasn't in immediate danger. I felt sick but it was not like any other feeling I've ever had before, but that could have been psychological as well.

"I feel sick because I've got all these tablets inside me." I had to stay in overnight while they were waiting for the results of the blood test.

Alan: And they could keep an eye on you!

Sam: I'm sure we went to Bournemouth Hospital and then we had to go to Poole Hospital because they had a kid's ward because I was fifteen. And then, I was staying there overnight, don't think I slept. I remember thinking, I don't want to be on a kid's ward, I'm fifteen. I had cereal so I definitely was there in the morning.

Some sort of doctor, a psychiatrist, came and spoke to me. My parents were in the room. They'd checked my bloods and everything and kept me in overnight, so they just wanted to check the state of mind I was in.

"Why have you done this?" I told them all these things about my dad; I remember telling them about my friends too. Obviously, at this point, I had nothing to lose. They knew that I'd... [Sam still has difficulty in voicing what she had done.] They knew everything, so I told them all these things about my dad.

"We can't relax in the house; it's like living in a museum; it's not somewhere you want to live; he's always angry at us; I can't do nothing right."

So, all these things, and they said to him, "Is that true?"

And he said, "Yep!" And they then just turned their attention to him. And that's when my dad started to be referred to people to see why he was… I went to CAMHS, Child Adolescent Mental Health Services, but we did a family session and my sister went and Mum and everything. Then at last, I had become, not happy but everyone knew. Obviously, Mum had become more like… She kept her eye on me all the time. And was just making sure I was OK all the time.

And then, funnily enough, when I started Year 10 at school… At my school you were split. Four houses and then split into two in Years 7, 8 and 9. I had my classes with everyone in Fry and everyone in Nightingale. In Year 10 you mixed with the whole school because you made your GCSE choices. And there was a girl, in one of the other houses, Brontë, named after famous women, and she was a friend from primary school. We started speaking and we became friends and I made all these new friends through her.

They didn't know anything about what had gone on before. So, in Year 10 I had a whole new group of friends who were inviting me to parties, they were friends with boys, and I felt as though I had a whole new life. I feel as though it all just *happened at once because my mum was being, not that she hadn't been nice before, but she was tiptoeing around me.*

"You don't have to do anything, don't worry about the washing up." She didn't want anything to set me off. So obviously, it was calmer at home and my dad was getting treated. So, at this point I thought, There's something wrong with my dad, NOT me! Insane that my dad had been hard to live with and now I'd got new friends. I was still with that boyfriend and we started to get closer and I thought, It's all turned around.

Alan: *And since then you've never looked back?*

Sam: *I suffered with anxiety, I still do sometimes, in my late teens. It hadn't come out of nowhere, but it got bad out of nowhere. I was at college, aged seventeen/eighteen, and I had to drop drama from college. I loved drama before, but I couldn't think of anything worse than standing up in front of people. So, then I got help for that. Sometimes now I have a little wobble but then I got myself a job that helped as well. But I didn't go to uni until a couple of years later because I wasn't ready.*

From self-harm, being depressed and wanting to kill myself, all that was in the past, but I had this anxiety—

Alan: *And how did that present itself?*

Sam: *I wouldn't leave the house. Because my sister is like this as well and because some people are like this as well, it started off with small things. If I was going to go to the shop, and this is a common thing that a lot of people feel, so it's not a big deal. If my mum sent me to the shop and said, "Go and* get the paper, it's eighty pence," and she gives me 80p, I'm not going to go.

I'll say, "I need a fiver. I need at least... I need more money. What happens if I get there and it's wrong? I would be mortified."

And my mum would try and say to me, "But if it's wrong, it's got the price on."

And I'd say, "It's going to be wrong."

And then she would say, "But if you get there and it says 80p on it and they try and charge you a £1, they're in the wrong, so they're the ones who should feel embarrassed." But I knew I could never do that. I hated going into shops, I was never going to go into a shop and do anything like that. So, at college I had to drop drama. If I couldn't go into a shop I certainly couldn't stand up in front of people. But also, I would have panic attacks.

On bad days, in the old bedroom at my mum's house I had this walk-in wardrobe, and sometimes I would sit in there. I couldn't even leave the house. On bad days I wouldn't leave my room. On very bad days I would lock myself in my wardrobe and just have to ride it out. I wouldn't be able to speak to people for fear of... I would get sweaty hands. Just anything social and everything was going to go wrong. I had always been a little bit shy. I'd always had £3 on me if I was buying something for a £1.

But then it really started to get extreme. I had CBT for it [Cognitive Behavioural Therapy], one of the signs for Generalised Anxiety Disorder [GAD], is you know that your anxieties and fears are not normal, and you know you should be able *to deal with them. That's one of the ways they know you have it; they know that you know that it's not normal.*

GAD is a long-term condition that causes you to feel anxious about a wide range of situations and issues, rather than one specific event. People with this condition are impacted almost every single day. As one anxious thought is resolved their mind immediately jumps to another issue. They rarely feel relaxed.

Symptoms can be:

- feeling restless or worried
- having trouble concentrating or sleeping
- Dizziness or heart palpitations.

It seems it was never-ending for Sam. No sooner had she shook off her depression (not belittling the condition here; I know you just don't shake off depression), when she developed a new condition of GAD. I can only believe that this was yet another impact of Arsenal's autism subliminally affecting his eldest daughter's life.

Sam: *Through the CBT they taught me to train my brain to look at situations differently. They taught me certain coping mechanisms that I don't have to think of now. It's like you have to rewire your brain. But my brain is like that now, but I can still have a bad day.*

    I remember when I was eighteen and I went out for a meal with my dad, and I went up to the bar, I was going to the bar for the first time as an eighteen-year-old, I was with my boyfriend at the time, my dad, my sister, funnily enough the same boyfriend who called my dad [on the night when Sam took the tablets], and my dad would often want other people to go up and do stuff like that, because he didn't like that either, whether because of his stammer or his autism.

Obviously my mum would always do everything for all of us. Anyway, when I was eighteen, my dad was still with my mum at this point, I went up to the bar and every one of them, my dad, my boyfriend, my sister, were all really shocked that I had gone to the bar. I was excited, I was eighteen, I took my ID and they were like, "Happy Birthday."

From then when we went out, I used to go to the bar, I'll get that, I'll order it because I wanted to see if my CBT was working. I think it's part of my personality now that when I'm out with my boyfriend he always orders the food, he'll do it, not that I think I can't do it, but I got so used to other people doing it for me when I was suffering with anxiety that now I've just got so used to it.

I mustn't fall into that habit, though, as I don't want to become too dependent on someone else.

One time I was getting the train and I was about twenty, I was with a friend and I was on my way to meet his friends for the first time and I had a panic attack on the way for the train. We were out of the house on the way and he was like, "Oh my God."

And I said, "Take me back to the house to my mum. She knows what to do."

Alan: *What happens when you have a panic attack?*

Sam: I just can't breathe and I have an inhaler that
         sometimes helps, but most times there's nothing
         they can do. Sometimes it can manifest itself
         in other ways, sometimes I get stomach aches.
         Sometimes I get stomach aches before I even know
         that I'm anxious. Which is just insane when you
         think about it?

         I go to a lot of concerts, so I don't have a thing
         with crowds or people. But then the other day I
         was at a concert and I started to get a stomach
         ache and obviously suddenly I started to feel
         nervous that I was in a big crowd. I never get
         nervous in crowds and then it just passed. So, it's
         just weird stuff like that.

         So, at the time of the train, my friend took
         me home and he didn't know what to do but my
         mum and my sister knew what to do to calm me
         down. I remember that time being shocked it had
         happened again because I was twenty and thought
         I was over it. So, occasionally it can still happen.
         The last panic attack I had was... I might have had
         one more recently, but I was going to work. XXX
         rang them up and explained what had happened
         and, the people who I work for now don't know that
         I suffered with this, because why would they? They
         didn't need to, from my point of view.

         If I have a panic attack now, it's stress-induced.
         I have so much uni work to do; then I have to go
         to work and something else happens that might
         stress me out and it happens.

Alan: How do you feel when you have a panic attack?

Sam: It feels like I'm having a heart attack. A real
         shortness of breath. It definitely is circumstantial

because I know if I have a lot on at uni and work, I need to chill out. I know now when things are getting too much for me. My mum and one of my friends have told me that if I could tell 'Past Sam' some of the things I'm doing now, Past Sam wouldn't have believed me. They knew me when I wasn't leaving the house.

I'm now a supervisor in a shop, telling people what to do and I never used to be able to walk into a shop. It seems again as though I've lived different lives. I feel that there's a part of my anxiety that will always be with me but many people who don't know that about me say how brave I am for colouring my hair green.

And I'm like, "That's not brave. Brave is speaking to people." So, it's weird how some people see things. But I feel that with age – I say age as though I'm ancient, I'm only twenty-three – now I'm living a more adult life, and I'm in control of my life, I don't have issues with anxiety any more, but I feel it's always going to be part of me. It's never fully gone.

Alan: So, this is a really personal question, and you can tell me to mind my own business, but since that night when you took those tablets, have you ever, ever felt the need again?

Sam: No, I don't think so.

Alan: Everything came to that point and since then you've been getting better and better every day. Better control of your life.

Sam: Even when I had anxiety and I had less control of my life, I wanted to do things. My friends were learning how to drive, get jobs. There was no way I *could learn how to drive or get a job, but I wanted to. Whereas before when I was in that low place where I wanted to take my own life, I was thinking what is the point? No one cares about me. When I had anxiety, I had a better relationship with my mum, better relationship with my dad, had a good boyfriend, so I wanted to go out, see my friends, get a job.*

I could still see a future, I wanted to move forward.

Samantha was encouraged by her mum, Nicola, to see someone about her anxiety, which she did, and is now about to finish her third year at university, where she has been studying a Law and Criminology degree. There are light years of difference between her lowest point with depression and her ability to cope with her more and more infrequent anxiety attacks. She has moved from not wanting to live to planning for her future.

In 2010, Sam tried to take her life and then in 2011 she offered her mum the ultimatum, "It's him or me. I can't live in this house."

Spare a thought here for poor Nicola. Her daughter has just tried to kill herself, her husband – who she still loves dearly – has been diagnosed as being on the spectrum and then she is forced to choose between them. Her marriage or her daughter? We now know she sacrificed herself for them and I cannot think of a more selfless decision to have to make in life. The final part of the decision was she didn't want Danni to follow her sister's route through depression and the conclusion that may entail.

Arsenal will still say that the reason for the divorce was because he has autism, but Samantha knows that to be a falsehood. The divorce came about because of Sam's ultimatum, coupled with the fact that somewhere on this journey Nicola was told that Arsenal cannot change. Arsenal has also proved that to be a falsehood and is a different man from the one who first walked into the hospital in 2010.

Now that Sam doesn't live with Arsenal, her relationship with him has improved and she now has the relationship she always wanted with her father. She could make choices about when they met and where, he could keep to his own routines and structures within his own flat, structures that seems to suit Danni as much as they used to rub Sam and her dad up against each other. To quote Sam, "We have managed to rebuild our relationship on our own terms." Nicola and Sam joke about how lucky Danni is as she is getting a better version of Arsenal than they ever knew existed. His strategies and coping mechanisms and the simple knowledge that he knows he can do something about his condition has made him a better person.

Arsenal's girlfriend Sophie is also benefitting from the newer, improved Arsenal and again Nicola jokes, "I wish he had changed for me before he left." The problem then was he didn't know he could change. In 2012, Arsenal and Nicola got divorced and by 2015, Sam left her mum's home and moved to Winchester, where she goes to university. She has now moved in with her boyfriend and, while starting university a couple of years behind other people, shows no repercussions of her attempted suicide. To me she seems a likeable, well-rounded and grounded young woman, who is happy with where she is in her life and, more importantly, looks and sounds very happy.

As suggested earlier, Danni too has had her mental health problems.

> Danni: *I had similar problems to Sam. In my last year at school [aged fifteen/sixteen] I was in hospital three times. I was depressed and suffering with anxiety. From stories that my mum told me when I was*

younger, I always used to feel… I never remember feeling good, I always wanted to be alone. I was constantly in a bad mood. As I've grown up it has developed into actual depression.

It was in my last year at school when it came out to my family that I was struggling. I kept it inside because it wasn't an easy thing to tell. I was struggling at school. I didn't have a specific reason why I didn't want to go; I was trying to isolate myself from everyone. No one knew why I actually didn't want to go or that I had mental health issues.

I remember one day when no one was listening to me. I know most kids don't want to go to school and are a bit lazy, but this was more than this I was really struggling, and no one was listening to me. This wasn't just normal stuff.

Alan: *And how long ago was this?*

Danni: *The last couple of years. [Danni is seventeen when I interview her, so if she's talking about the last year at school, she's referring to the last twenty-four months.] Because I've always known about my sister and what she's done. No one knew what I was going through, they just thought it was a teenager playing up. I remember I used to leave the house on my own in the morning, when no one was looking. I remember once my dad went in the bathroom and I just legged it. I didn't want to go to school.*

My dad found me and took me to school, I couldn't express how I was feeling, people just thought I was acting up. Until one day when I took some tablets. Not many, not a lot, but a few more than you should take in a day. There was actually nothing wrong with me, but I was just sick. Nobody knew why I was sick because nobody would think that I would do something like that. At that stage no one knows I have any mental health problems. I thought to myself if I'm physically sick then that's the only time my parents won't send me to school.

I knew if I was physically sick, they won't send me in. This was my way of telling people this wasn't just me playing up, that something was seriously wrong. I was told at school that my parents would be fined if I didn't go in and that just made me worse. I don't even know to this day if anyone knows that was the first time I took tablets. I don't think I've told anyone about that.

I blurted it out in front of my mum because she said to me, "You've only been in hospital three times."

But I said, "I've only been in hospital three times, but I've taken tablets four times." I didn't take that many first time because I didn't want to die but I didn't want to be up and well either. I was seeing what I could get away with. The second time I took tablets but the first time to everyone else, I took tablets on the way to school but then took myself to the hospital because I knew I felt rubbish, I knew I'd taken a lot so needed to be seen.

I wanted help. I was asking for help by taking tablets and not having to say it. It was the first time people recognised the depth of it. I stayed in hospital overnight because of my age and I had to see CAMHS. They had to see where I was at. I started going to CAMHS for one-to-ones and that helped me. The second time I took tablets was June 2016 and my boyfriend and his mum took me to hospital for that one.

I didn't want to tell my parents I'd done it again. I wasn't fussed about being in hospital, I wasn't at school. I didn't have to deal with the real world if I was in hospital. The fourth time was bad. First time – under ten tablets, I was testing the water. Second and third times – twenty to twenty-five tablets, paracetamol and ibuprofen. The fourth time I took over twenty prescription tablets – Solpadol. That time I was kept in because I needed to be kept in.

Alan: What were the triggers that made you take these tablets?

Danni: There were no specific triggers, nothing particularly going on in my life. I was constantly generally unhappy.

Alan: Have you been diagnosed with depression?

Danni: I haven't clinically been diagnosed but when I was seeing CAMHS they told me I'm not depressed but I have depressive episodes. I wasn't put on medication or diagnosed as clinically depressed. I've not been in hospital for over a year and a half. I've been seeing counsellors, on and off for years, since my parents split.

Alan: How do you feel now?

Danni: I feel fine now, but my opinion is that if you have anxiety and depression you always have that dark cloud at the back of your mind. For Sam, she's a different person. I'm not a hundred per cent over

	it. I feel that if I have a bad day it can come out in me again.
Alan:	*Do you think your depression is what causes you to not remember the first nine/ten years of your life?*
Danni:	*Maybe. I'm not sure. Perhaps I'll never really know. Have I blocked everything out? I've never thought about it. I'm glad I can't remember those bad times when as a family we were at our worst. One day I wouldn't be surprised if it all came out and I sat down with someone and everything came out.*

It's not for me to say, but Sam is well on the way to recovery, but I worry about Danni. It seems acknowledged that Sam tried to take her own life but – thank God – failed. Danni has put herself at risk four times, even if they are described as cries for help. It would have only taken her to misinterpret the really dangerous level of tablets required and she may have been in a worse situation than Sam.

Nevertheless, both girls are strong and capable young adults now with the common sense to ask for help. In our modern society, the quest for help regularly comes as it is just too late.

Chapter Sixteen

The Unspeakable

Circa 1971 to 2019

> *Truth is tough. It will not break, like a bubble, at a touch; nay, you may kick it about all day, like a football, and it will be round and full at evening.*
>
> Mark Twain

THIS NEXT CHAPTER HELPS TO EXPLAIN MUCH OF WHAT HAS gone before. We hear from Arsenal and Sam, interviewed together and sharing their own awful experiences with each other for the first time. I won't offer editorial comment; their words explain everything. This is their testament taken on the 4th June 2019. It was a very emotional evening, especially for Arsenal, who shed many tears.

> Alan: *What I want to talk about tonight is something you have both been through – abuse.*
>
> Arsenal: *I've never spoken to Samantha about this, ever. But we're going to speak about it tonight.*

Sam: Da, da, daaaaa.

Alan: But you knew what we were here to talk about?

Sam: I know this is what we're talking about, but I don't know any more than that.

Alan: OK. I just thought it would be an eye-opener for both of you, and the way I intend to write this is just use your own words. I don't intend adding any comment myself apart from the time and date, etc. I thought it could help if you could talk to each other about it and see where the conversation goes. It will be what it will be. There's no agenda for this. I thought about writing a list of questions and then decided against it. But I thought, Arsenal, we would start with you if you want to? Can you remember back to how old you were when it first happened?

Arsenal: I think I was eight or nine.

Alan: And so it was round about the time you took on the mantle of Arsenal?

Arsenal: Yeah, yeah.

Alan: And what happened?

Arsenal: Wow. Here we go. I lived in a council house and there was a row of about ten houses like that. And opposite there was a row of garages. And right opposite there was a garage where a guy from further down, he repaired cars, in there. And there was about four of them worked there, I think.

          There was the guy who owned it, XXXX; there was another guy called AA; and then I think Mr BB and another guy called CC. That's all I know the names as, so… And I used to do a bit of cleaning up in the garage for them. And then one

Saturday, I was definitely in the juniors because I knew, I used to wear shorts all the time.

So, that's how I knew I was in the juniors, not the seniors because I remember the shorts like the brownish-type tartan shorts, so I remember that.

Alan: Juniors when we were at school used to go up to the age of eleven.

Sam: So primary school?

Alan: You call it primary now, but it was up to the age of eleven back then. And you went to secondary school after that.

Sam: Which is what we—

Alan: We had at the time, infants up to seven, then juniors and then seniors. Anyway, you were nine or ten, or thereabouts.

Arsenal: And Saturdays it was only this one guy there called CC. So, that's the only name I know him by because he wore blue overalls and his head was like a XXX, so everyone called him CC. He had like a van; it wasn't a van it was like today's version of the 'campervan'. But it was a—

Alan: Like a Volkswagen van?

Arsenal: A Bedford. It was a Bedford, with the sliding doors.

It was light blue, that's what I know. And then, wow. Two seats at the front, and then in the middle I think the engine, in between the two seats, and they had a big cover over it and carpeted it. Don't they?

Alan: Uh huh.

Arsenal: I was in there one day with him, ha ha, and next minute, all I remember... [Arsenal nervously looks at Sam and cannot find his words. He clicks *his fingers several times and puts a slide in his projector.]*

I'm lying, well. I'm on this, where the engine is. And I'm lying down and next minute he's playing with me. So yeah, he was just playing with me. And then he said—

Alan: *Was you frightened?*

Arsenal: *I don't know, mate; I really don't know. I just remember him saying, "We can go to Southport Fair." And so, I remember that. I remember when it finished, I went in, and I know it was a Saturday, because, what was on? Swiss Family Robinson was on, Saturday morning. I remember going in and just watching that. I don't know.*

Alan: *Did you tell anybody?*

Arsenal: *No, no. I've only told Alderney Hospital and yous two. That's it. And then another time, we went over to St Albert's field, and the school's there and the field's here, but all this side is cordoned off with panels just like outside. But there was gaps through all the panels where people would come out the woods and cut through. And we were sitting down, and he was trying to touch me there but there was people coming through.*

              And he just said, "It's too busy, but we'll do it another time."

Alan: *And did he ask you to meet him there?*

Arsenal: *I have no memory, mate. I only have the memory of the two of us sitting down there and two of us in his van. I don't know how I got there or anything. Gone.*

Alan: *Well, it's your subconscious blocking it out.*

Arsenal: *Yeah, but I remember it being a Bedford van! Yeah. I remember it being a Saturday. And me* having me shorts on. *That's all. And when I go to Liverpool, don't ask me why, but XXXX has a garage. He's got a garage on the corner. And whenever I go, I don't know why, but whenever I go up north, I go and see the garage. That's what I do.*

And then, I just, back then I seemed to be like no one. No one knew who I was or anything or where I was. I could be out all day, and no one would bother. I remember us playing football on Saturday the 8th May 1971 and that's when I went in goal for Arsenal. And that's when everyone, I turned round and it was nineteen on one side and just me in goal.

Then they all just called me Arsenal. Then I kept hold of the ball and one of the lads went, "Arsenal!" So, I threw him the ball and then that was it then. Every time I got the ball everyone shouted, "Arsenal." That was it then.

Alan: *This is a really difficult question for you to answer—*

Arsenal: *No, go on, it's all right.*

Alan: *Do you think you took on that persona of Arsenal because you wanted to forget what had happened? Or is that, you were only nine—*

Arsenal: *I would never have thought like that.*

Sam: *It was your subconscious, maybe? You weren't getting attention from your family, and like you said, you were no one, so no one you know, you had a big family, so then maybe you were taking on this other sort of identity, that makes you stand out. Rather than just, you've got loads of brothers…*

Arsenal: *I remember kids used to knock at the door, and go to me mum and dad or whoever, "Do you know that boy who has that ball all the time? Is he in?"*

         And me mum would go, "Yeah."

         And then I'd get called and I'd come out and they'd go, "Do you want to come out and have a game of footy?" Because everyone knew that I had a ball, but no one knew who I was. They would actually knock and say, "The boy with the ball. Does he live here?"

         And me mum would go, "Arsenal, can you come out and play?"

Alan: *And then you became Arsenal. Even his mum was calling him Arsenal at this point and it wasn't long afterwards that his mum would shout 'Arsenal' to him.*

Arsenal: *So, that's the way it was then, if anyone called me by me real name, I ignored them. But, looking back, it used to make me angry. I used to get really angry.*

Sam: *Maybe you, I mean I'm no doctor, but maybe you... That stuff that happened to you didn't happen to Arsenal. So, when you created this new persona it was like you were a new person. So, anyone who called you by your old name, you weren't that boy who that stuff had happened to so that was him, not you. So, you made a new—*

Alan: *That's exactly how I see it.*

Arsenal: *And since me mum died, me dad sends me a card, he puts, for some fucking reason, me real name, and it goes in the bin.*

Alan: *I know on the copies of the emails that your dad has sent you about the writing of this book you've blacked out the name at the top of it.*

Arsenal: It just makes me angry.

Alan: Do you think you can get over that anger? Because that's a really important part of what I'm trying to do as part of this book with you.

Arsenal: Tomorrow, I've got to ring, I've got it on here actually, the Truth Project.

Alan: What's the Truth Project?

Arsenal: It's a government thing, what they started, this year, or maybe last year. It's about people who've been abused in the past. And you can actually ring up and talk to people about it. So, that's what I'm doing. Then that, I'm hoping that can release that anger. So—

Sam: I just think—

Alan: That's fantastic, Arsenal.

Sam: Yeah, that is good. The name thing, people don't, people don't mean any harm, your family, by doing it. I think it can be quite funny from my point of view, because you didn't call me Sam up until, I don't know, the last couple of years. You wouldn't call me Sam even though everyone else did.

Alan: You always used the full name, Samantha?

Arsenal: Yeah, always called her Samantha.

Sam: I know you said to me, "That's your name." But how can you, of all people, say that, that I sort of chose a name for myself, and I wasn't really choosing, it was just a natural nickname, that most people have if they have a longer name. And then you wouldn't call me it.

            And then, if your parents call you by your old name, isn't that the same as you calling me—

Arsenal: No, I never thought of it. I never ever thought of it.

Sam:	*They've named you a—*
Arsenal:	*I couldn't even spell Samantha, could I?*
Sam:	*No, he spelt it 'er' a couple of times.*
Arsenal:	*There's a couple of photos on Xmas day, and in the background, it's got, 'Happy Christmas Samantha'.*
Sam:	*And he's spelt it 'er' instead of an 'A' at the end. Samanther.*
Arsenal:	*Samanther!*
Sam:	*It's quite funny. Yeah, it sounds easy for you now, but—*
Arsenal:	*Nothing's easy for me. But yeah, that's all I remember, but, yeah. Got to ring the Truth Project tomorrow.*
Alan:	*Don't tell them too much, mate. We've got a book to sell. You might be hitting your book sales if you tell them too much. [Laughter all round.] What about you Sam? Do you want to talk about what happened to you?*
Sam:	*Yeah, like I said last time, I don't remember too much. I might have blocked it out, like you was saying. I don't remember anything about before or after. I don't know what I did that day, obviously. But I was eight. Look at us, matching.*
Arsenal:	*Yeah, yeah. [Eyes full of tears.]*
Sam:	*Matching tales. We, you and Mum were out.*
Arsenal:	*We went to a wedding, A wedding in June.*
Sam:	*I don't know if it was in June.*
Arsenal:	*Yeah, June. 8th June.*
Sam:	*I didn't know that, but why would I? That means I was almost nine.*
Arsenal:	*Because I only realised, about two years ago, maybe two years ago. Every time I went past the Royal Bath*

Hotel, I always wanted to walk in the water and kill myself. And whether I was driving, every time I seen the Royal Bath, I always used to think, I'll park the car, go in the sea, and walk. And I used to go sometimes there, I'd get to the end and I'd be going, "Do I strip off? Do I take me shoes off? Do I hold me nose? What do I do?" And I couldn't, I couldn't actually work out, actually, what I had to do! I know it sounds stupid but that's how I, I just used to stand there. [Arsenal clicks his fingers and puts slides in.]

And then it was only two years ago, I think I was talking to someone—

Alan: *You were talking to me, in my house. That's what I'm trying to tell you. It was November last year. You were in my house and you were talking me through. Because you told me, for the first time ever, and we'd been talking and talking and talking for months, and then he tells me that, as we're talking about football, that he tried to kill himself. And he hadn't told me that. And then, we were talking about the Royal Bath and he started talking about you, Samantha.*

I remember, it's in the book. I remember you saying, "I have to write that down. And now I know why!" So, it was in my house on the couch in the front room—

Arsenal: *Yeah, yeah. Because the date it happened, June 2003, Saturday, it was a wedding, and where did we go, the Royal Bath.*

Sam: *Yeah.*

Arsenal: *So, every time I never made that connection, reminded me of... Well, it didn't, but I never got that connection until—*

Alan:	You knew something was wrong, every time you saw it.
Arsenal:	I used to think, I'm going to kill myself. And then I remember being at yours, yeah, wow!
Alan:	You need to read this book called, A Boy Called Arsenal, mate, you'll find a lot out about yourself. [Everyone laughs for a while.] Back to you, Sam.
Sam:	Oh yeah, so, I don't think about it much because I don't remember the details, but if I do try to think all I remember is, I was on my bed, in the evening... [The words dry up.]
Arsenal:	It was a trio bed, wasn't it?
Sam:	Yeah. I had the top bunk and the bottom bunk was a double bed, so the top bunk was a single.
Arsenal:	Single on top, double below, and there was a gap then and Danielle in a cot.
Sam:	I, because we had that bed for years, didn't we? Because I remember when I was older, and Danni had it. And if you stood on the bottom bed you could lean in, like me and Danni. Yeah, that's what we used to do. I remember I was in, I always used to wear little crop tops and matching little sets. You know, crop tops and knickers.

I was sat up in the bed, not tucked into bed but sat in the middle of the bed. And he, the babysitter, was just stood on the bottom bed, so he was the same height as me and just started to explain. You see the most vivid thing I remember is him explaining sex to me. [Arsenal is now not looking at Sam but away from her and over my right shoulder as I sit facing her. He can't engage with either of us through his eyes, which have tears spilling over onto his unshaven cheeks. But he is listening intently.] |

	And basically, he was explaining what his parts were and what my parts were and how, explaining sex. If we do this, you know. And I remember backing away with the covers, trying to cover myself. I didn't feel, obviously beforehand I didn't feel uncomfortable going to bed in my knickers and crop top because—
Alan:	*That's what you always did.*
Sam:	*And to me, it didn't even have the concept of that being innocent or not being innocent because it was hot, I was just going to bed. But he was just saying things to me like, "We'll try again in the morning." Because he was trying like, I just remember... I remember me and my reaction, but I don't remember what he was doing to make me do that? I was covering myself because he was explaining to me what I had.*
Alan:	*You were just shying away from him?*
Sam:	*Yeah. And covering myself. I felt I wanted to cover up now. So, he was saying we would try again in the morning and him saying, "You mustn't tell anyone about this. They'll kill me." I knew at that point that I was going to tell someone because I knew it wasn't right, you know. I don't remember thinking it wasn't right but there was no way I wasn't going to not tell someone. Because I had this feeling it was wrong. There was just something not right. And whether that was because why, I don't know, I imagine so many kids would have been OK. [Sam is getting confused as she tries to recollect her feelings on that night as an eight-year-old girl.]*
Alan:	*You did well, though, to defend yourself, didn't you?*

Sam: Yeah. So, "We'll try again in the morning. Don't tell anyone. I'll get killed or shot." I think he said 'shot'. I remember sitting up in my bed all night like this [mimics holding her covers up to her chest], no sleep, waiting. And the door in this flat to the bedroom, if I was sat up in bed, if it was open it'd be facing me. It was shut. And I remember sat there, I'm sure the door was open, I can't sleep now, technically I was scared.

Alan: And was Danni in the cot on the other side of the room?

Sam: I assume so. I don't specifically remember Danni being there because this was… She would have been. Where else would she be? So then, don't remember going to sleep, don't remember falling asleep, I don't remember telling them, my parents. But I know I did.

         I remember being in the morning, waiting for the morning. You know when you have no concept of time when you're a kid? Whether they would have come home, if they came home at 1am in the morning that was foreign to me, so I don't know if they're there, if he stayed over, they're going out, I have no concept of that sort of thing.

         So, in the morning, he said not to tell anyone, but I've got a weird feeling.

Alan: [To Arsenal] So, you came home from your wedding and – was the person's name XXXXX? [Arsenal nods] – and XXXXX was still there minding the girls, you saw him out the house and went to bed and didn't know anything about what had transpired until the next morning. Is that what happened?

Arsenal: There was two of them. His mum went at twelve, he stayed 'til we got home at ten to four.

Sam: But I have no concept of her being there at all. I don't remember anything about being outside of that bed. She's not part of my memory.

Arsenal: We got home at ten to four.

Sam: Look at you, ten to four!

Arsenal: He was there, he was awake. I asked him how everything was, and he said, "Yeah." I asked him if he'd had anything to eat and he said, "Yeah." So, I gave him some money for a taxi, and he went home. Then next morning, must have been about twenty-five past seven—

Sam: That's a specific time.

Arsenal: That's when you said to me, "I need to talk to you."

Sam: I don't have any recollection. I remember being in the bedroom. I guess today's here, it's time. Because I didn't know if he was still here. No concept of the time. They were back, like he said. But I don't remember saying, "Can we sit down and have a word?"

Alan: Do you remember being frightened about leaving your bedroom or knowing when to leave your bedroom?

Sam: Yeah, because I didn't know if he was still here. What if he's here? I'll wait until he's gone. I waited for the morning.

Alan: This was June as well, so it would be coming light about four in the morning. It would have been light for a long time before you ventured down.

Sam: I don't remember going to sleep but I remember thinking I couldn't go to sleep and sitting up. This

	is weird. I don't remember waking up, just getting out of bed. Thinking, now's the time.
Alan:	*And afterwards, Arsenal, you got some photos done?*
Arsenal:	*Yeah, I did a poster campaign.*
Sam:	*I remember you doing that. You know when adults don't think kids know things, but I overheard you talking with D and he went mental.*
Alan:	*Sorry, who's D?*
Sam:	*D was my mum's sister's partner. So, my cousin's dad. He was my uncle, as well. He handled things differently to you.*
Arsenal:	*I remember us being in the pub, The Bell, getting pissed and he was saying, "Come on, let's go and do it now."*
	And I was going, "Listen, we're pissed, mate, we'll get caught."
Alan:	*Is he—*
Arsenal:	*He's roaming free. I believe he still lives in [Arsenal proceeds to give me a full postal address].*
Alan:	*I don't think I can put that in the book. In all seriousness, this is the part of the book when I'm going to have to seek legal advice.*
Arsenal:	*He works in XXXXX in XXXXX, and I went in one day—*
Sam:	*That would be so weird if I went in there.*
Arsenal:	*And I had me camera ready and—*
Sam:	*When was this?*
Arsenal:	*That must have been 2004, maybe 5.*
Sam:	*So he might not work there now?*
Arsenal:	*Oh no, when I took the picture, but I went up because I'd heard on the grapevine he was working there. I went up to him and I went, "XXXXX," and*

when he turned, I went, click, and got his picture. And the picture was amazing. It looked like he's got ghost paint on, honestly, and that's where I got the picture.

And then I done me poster with that picture on and saying, "This is where he lives, where he works."

Sam: I'd heard that XXXXX had had things happen to him as a child and that's why he was the way he was. But trying to convince me and my mum and we were like, "Look, you're talking to the wrong people."

Alan: How do you both feel about, as you both rightly say, Sam, you've probably been more open than your dad over the years, about what happened to you? How do you both feel, potentially, because it doesn't have to be in there, about your stories being out there in a book that anyone will be able to pull off a shelf and read?

Sam: I mean me personally, because from that day I told my parents, it's never really been a secret to the people around me. So, if people know me well anyway, they'll already know. So, it'll just be everyone else. Whereas you've got every single person. [Sam is obviously referring to her dad.] But the thing is when I look at why am I, why would I, be nervous about people reading it, I actually can't pinpoint why. It's not like, the roles are reversed, I've got nothing to be ashamed of!

Alan: Of course you've not and—

Sam: That's why if people were to read it no one's going to feel any sort of negativity towards me, only towards him. So, I don't have any anything,

anything to prove, it's just something that's part of my life and if someone reads about it then—

Alan: But what you're sharing with me – which I really do appreciate so thank you – whether it goes in the book or not, but what you're sharing is a very intimate story that a lot people wouldn't necessarily want people outside close friends and family knowing about. That's all I mean. I would like to use your exact words, though, almost transcribe this part of the book.

What about yourself, Arsenal? How do you feel about it going in the book?

Arsenal: To me? I see it, if you're doing a book of my life, then it's my life, end of! Simple to me, that's how simple it is.

Sam: Also, for stuff like this, I'm very much a, not that anyone is going to read this and become inspired by us, but I'm very much an advocate for... If you've been through something and you share it, there's a slight possibility, that someone who reads it has gone through the same, and it might just help them. Not even come out and say, "This has happened to me." Everyone might know or no one might know. They might not have shared it, but there's just the idea that someone else doesn't feel alone. And that might not happen if someone reads the book and goes, "That's a shame." But I just want, the idea of not keeping something secret might just help them.

Alan: I truly believe that you will inspire people. I think your dad's story in its entirety will inspire people. I describe him in the book as a hero and I stand by that. I've said it to his face, Mr Shy over there, look at him. I genuinely mean it and I've written it into the book on a couple of occasions. And I think it will be inspirational to people. And I think this part of it will be inspirational as well. What you're telling us today.

But Arsenal, you say as far as you're concerned it's pretty black and white as we're writing a story about your life and its part of your life, so therefore it's in there. But you never told anybody else up to this point?

Arsenal: No.

Alan: Not even your closest family.

Sam: Why do you think that is?

Arsenal: [A very long pause as Arsenal processes the question posed by his daughter.] I don't know. I don't know. I haven't got a clue.

Maybe because I'm Arsenal now, and it didn't happen to Arsenal. [And in this sentence Arsenal sums up his entire life story.]

Sam: That's what we said. Because I think I've told, I'm not sure how many people I've told, people like XXXXX. We met around the same time and we've been friends ever since, not as close as we were. I've moved away but we still have time for each other.

I've told, and this might be different because of genders, but in every relationship that I've been in, I've told. Not that I don't think it does affect me now. Sorry about this [to her dad], sexual way, it doesn't but I think I'm quite a, not pushover when it comes to men.

I've always been quite feminist in my outlook. If someone has tried to buy me a drink, I'm like,

"This is just a drink." If I'm not interested, I'll be blunt. I think that's stemmed from me being eight and saying, "No, thanks." [Sam holds her hand up in front of herself, palms outwards in the accepted 'back off' gesture.] And I think I've told people I've been in a relationship with just in case one day, imagine I had a freak out, and wasn't able to explain, "Oh, sorry, I had this major flashback," which has never happened, or anything like that.

Alan: But also, as I said earlier, it's an intimate story, and if you are going to have a relationship with somebody, it almost seals the deal. The fact that you're going to tell this story to somebody.

Sam: Yes, exactly.

Alan: This is how much I trust you; I'm going to trust you with this story.

Sam: Exactly.

Alan: Not story—

Sam: I know what you mean. [Turning to her dad] Maybe it's different for you because, I don't know, you're not like… I don't know, how do I say it? If you were a gay man, maybe it would be different? Do you know what I mean, because this could have made me scared of sexual relationships with men, whereas you have sexual relationships with women, therefore you probably didn't put two and two together as, you didn't tell my mum, for example.

          There wasn't a fear. Whereas, because I'm a woman being—

Alan: You never told Nicola?

Arsenal: No. No. Never told no one. In Alderney Hospital, Doctor XXXXX, the clinical psychologist, the only one. That was the only one.

Sam: *And now us.*

Alan: *You said something, about five minutes ago, which I wrote down: "That happened to someone else, not Arsenal."*

Arsenal: *That's how I feel.*

Alan: *And that is why, I thought it would be the case, but I'm an accountant, not a psychiatrist, but it doesn't take a genius to spot that you created Arsenal because what happened therefore happened to somebody else.*

Sam: *When people go through a break-up; they cut their hair, that sort of classic thing. They want to be a new person. New year, new me. All that stuff. And often when, I know this from watching so many Criminal Minds, but when little kids start to act differently, it's, 'What's happened to them', that sort of stuff. When people change their style, it's like you're disassociating yourself.*

Alan: *You are trying to become someone else. After a break-up, you are right, you cut your hair, you buy yourself a new suit, try to lose a bit of weight, go to the gym or whatever—*

Sam: *You separate yourself from the events that caused you to be this way.*

Alan: *But it happened to you at the age of nine, Arsenal, there is no way you went through that thought process at the age of nine. It was your mind subconsciously working for you. I don't know.*

Arsenal: *I wouldn't have thought of that, would I?*

Sam: *You were just probably, felt like you were in the background of your own life, being left at the beach by your own family, etc. All this stuff and then this happened to you, didn't tell anyone*

	because you didn't feel like it was important, and then you get noticed by people your own age by being Arsenal. This is a better version of me, I'm going to go with it.
Alan:	*Plus, how many people in the world are called Arsenal? I only know of one. How many people in Liverpool walk around with an AFC top on? I only know of one. How many people write Arsenal on walls and think that nobody will know it's him because they can't see him as it's dark? I only know one. [Arsenal is laughing now.]*
	But it's not a funny topic what we're talking about, I know it's not, but how did you stop it? How did you make sure it never happened again? Did you just avoid him like the plague or…?
Arsenal:	*I've got no memory. I've got no memory. It just didn't happen again, didn't happen again. Don't know why, can't answer that. He touched me the first time and second time he couldn't because there were people coming through the fences, the holes in the fences, so—*
Alan:	*Do you remember him still working at the garage as you grew older? Was he always there in the background or do you just not remember anything at all about it?*
Arsenal:	*I've got no memory, got no memory. But, when I go to Liverpool, for some reason, I don't know why, but I go to XXXX's garage.*
Alan:	*Which is on the same site as it always was?*
Arsenal:	*He worked for XXXX. XXXX had the little council garage but over the years he got bigger and bigger and now he's got a big garage on the corner.*

Alan: *OK, I don't really have a lot more to ask you. I thought it would be good for you both to talk together about it and that's how it will be in the book. How do you both feel now? Sam, what about you listening to what your dad had to say?*

Sam: *Obviously I knew that he knew everything about me because I'd told him. Very interested to know how that conversation went. Do you remember? What I said to you? I can't imagine me as a child saying [Sam puts on a deep voice], "We need to talk about something."*

    And you being [puts on a lighter happy voice], "OK."

Arsenal: *Yeah, you came to ask me. You asked me to come in the living room.*

Sam: *That sounds right, because when I had a bad dream it was always you I'd talk to.*

Arsenal: *[This is very difficult for Arsenal.] Went in the living room and you just said, "Last night." Firstly, you said, "I've got something to tell you about last night." Then, you said, "XXXXX come in." You never mentioned all that bit, basically you was straight to the point, you said [Arsenal takes deep breaths to control his stammer and speaks very slowly, enunciating each word carefully], he come in, he pulled the duvet down, and he asked you to take your knickers down. And you said, "But Dad, honestly, I just kept hold of them like that." [Arsenal mimics someone holding on to the top of their pants so they can't be pulled off. This is too much for him and he desperately starts clicking his fingers and trying to put 'happy' slides in his projector. Tears roll down his cheeks. Sam jumps in.]*

Sam:	Well, I don't have any recollection of saying that. I have recollection of talking to people at the police station, and me being embarrassed using the words that he used, I was like, "I can't say these words."
Arsenal:	ZZ was his name. The child protection officer.
Sam:	I remember being like, "Do you want me to say the actual words?" Because I was embarrassed. I love eight-year-old me. She's brave; she's fierce. Got more balls than twenty-three-year-old me, that's for sure.
Alan:	I don't know about that. I don't know. I really don't. I think you're both incredibly brave.
Arsenal:	I remember the police coming and that—
Sam:	All I'm glad for—
Arsenal:	There was a delay of arresting him, which I couldn't understand, but then ZZ, child protection officer, he rang me up and I was in work and he said, "Listen, I was supposed to arrest him today, but I can't. Where are you now?"

I said, "I'm in Westbourne."

He said, "Can you come up to the station?"

So, I went up to the station, and he said, "Listen, the reason we can't arrest him today is because over the weekend there's been a big incident and it involved a young child. I know it's bad what happened to Samantha, but this is an incident where the child has actually been touched."

And he explained the reasons and I was, "OK."

Then they arrested him, he denies it, but then he told ??? it was him. |
| Sam: | His ??? Or my ??? |

Arsenal:	Your ???
Sam:	His ???.
Arsenal:	Yeah.
Alan:	*That'll come across well on the tape. That was like a Laurel and Hardy conversation that was! [Tension lifts a little as we all laugh.]*
Arsenal:	*And one day he turned up at Madeira Road Police Station at 9am in the morning. And he said, "I want to change me story." Because originally, I did say, I don't know why but I said, "Listen, mate, if you get the help, we're going to stand by you. But deny it, mate, and you're going to get your arse kicked." And then a couple of days later, he went the police station, just after nine, and he said, "I want to change me statement."*
	And they said, "You need your solicitor with you."
	So, he got in touch with his solicitor and his solicitor, funnily enough, was in Winchester.
Sam:	*Wooh. [She now lives in Winchester.] It's like it's gone full circle.*
Arsenal:	*He stayed in the police station from just after nine until four o'clock. His solicitor come, they went in a room, he come out and he said, "My client has nothing to add to his statement."*
	And I thought, You fucking twat. He'd been sitting there all day and it was his solicitor, wasn't it? But they know the words to say, don't they?
Alan:	*So the police decided not to prosecute?*
Arsenal:	*Yeah, because of Samantha's actions.*
Alan:	*Samantha's actions?*
Arsenal:	*[To Sam] Do you remember your bathrobe?*
Sam:	*No?*

Arsenal:	What? You don't remember the bathrobe incident?
Sam:	No!
Arsenal:	Don't you? Your bathrobe?
Sam:	NO!
Arsenal:	And you, what's the thing called that goes around the middle to tie a bathrobe?
Alan:	A belt?
Arsenal:	Do you not remember trying to hang yourself with the belt from your bathrobe?
Sam:	Not then, no!
Arsenal:	Fucking hell! [Real shock that Sam can't remember.] On the trio bed…
Sam:	I don't think you're thinking of the right time.
Arsenal:	So, what am I thinking about?
Sam:	When you came in and said, "Stop it, you're scaring your sister."?
	[Long, long pause.] And I was like, "Thanks."
Arsenal:	So when was it when you tried to hang yourself?
Sam:	When we lived in Avon Mews. Because you came in and—
Arsenal:	Oh, that's right, yeah.
Sam:	Because you came in and you were like, "You're scaring your sister."
	And I was like, "I want to die. I don't care." That was, like, when I was fourteen.
Arsenal:	That's right, yeah.
Alan:	So that wasn't linked to what happened to you at eight, nearly nine?
Sam:	No, that's just when I was being bullied at school. You know, and we weren't getting on, you know.
Arsenal:	I just remember you trying to fucking hang yourself with the rope from—

Sam:	*That was years later. That was something else I was dealing with.*
Alan:	*So, why did the police choose to not prosecute then? It couldn't have been because years later Sam trying to take her own life. Was it just because it was a nine-year-olds word against a grown man's or...?*
Arsenal:	*You know what, I know you're right, because it wasn't Avon Road, but I always remember the Child Protection Officer saying to me that it would do you more harm than good if it goes all the way through. And he was thinking of you because—*
Sam:	*But that could just be—*
Arsenal:	*Because when we moved from Westbury Road, we went to Florence Road.*
Sam:	*The next road.*
Arsenal:	*For about a couple of months. Then we moved to Parkwood Road, and when the child protection officer come in, there was two of them, and they come to Parkwood Road and I remember, you were in the bedroom, and one of them was coming in, because he's kept in touch all this time. He was going the toilet and I showed him the toilet and you came out the bedroom and saw this strange man and fucking screamed.*
	And that's when they moved us to Avon Mews.
Alan:	*Is that because you didn't have to live in the same house as where it happened?*
Arsenal:	*It didn't happen there, the protection officers were still coming around, to check on us. I see him now and then. In Tesco's, we'll always talk.*
Sam:	*They decided it would do more harm than good taking it further as it was unlikely, they... There*

was no physical evidence, it would just be me against him. Only for them to do him for 'almost' doing something. It would be worse for me having to go through it.

Alan: *And he is still free?*

Sam: *Yes. But to me, my life is still the same regardless, not thinking of other people because he is still out there, we didn't see him. We stopped contacting him, we didn't see him. Which would have been the same if he had have got done. To me, he's not in my life anymore so it's just the same.*

Alan: *It would have ended up in court and I don't know, I don't know. Sam, have you thought of ringing the Truth Project?*

Sam: *No, I only knew what it was just then. No not really. I don't—*

Alan: *Feel the need?*

Sam: *No, I don't. Also, the thing is, maybe because of my obsession with true crime, and stuff like that. I don't feel there's anything to say because I know that I had a lucky escape in some ways. Horrible thing to happen, but it could have been worse. I read because of my degree, I read, I have a book in my bag now called My Favourite Murder, I am absorbed with horrible things happening to women, children and men. So, if I was to speak about this I feel like, not embarrassed, but 'get over yourself'.*

Because it didn't go further, I don't feel I have anything to say.

Alan: *You're done with it?*

Sam: *Exactly. I mean once... [Sam starts giggling to herself, seemingly embarrassed.] I was going to say something.*

Arsenal: Go on.

Sam: *It's a whole other thing, I don't know. Once, at the first house party I was at, I got very drunk, woke up in a bed and someone's hands were in my knickers. A boy. And that scared me more than what happened when I was nine. My first house party, I just remember being, "Where's the toilet?" And then, "Is that a bed?" And some guy, I didn't know him, and I was like, "Get off."*

But that sort of thing because I was a teenager and I had just met my boyfriend, at this point, he wasn't at the party, me and him weren't having sex at this point, and that affected me more because I was like, "Nooo." I felt that was worse because—

Arsenal: *Do you remember BBB's party and you rang me up at half one in the morning?*

Sam: *No.*

Arsenal: *And I said I'll come and get you.*

Sam: *Oh yeah, and she slammed the door in your face. Because she thought you was a strange man trying to get into her house, I remember that. I was like, I'm too drunk, that was a different party.*

Arsenal: *Do you remember why you wanted to come home?*

Sam: *No.*

Arsenal: *Because your mate had gone outside with a guy, and you went looking for them. And you found them on the bin, having sex.*

Sam: *Oh, no. Yeah, yeah. I freaked out and wanted to go. I forgot all about that until then. Help me, pick me up, I don't want to be here.*

She still talks about that, the time she shut the door in your dad's face.

Alan: *Thank you both very much. I don't think you realise how brave you both are. You may not think it and you may not feel it, but not many people could sit and talk with their own daughter/ father and a stranger – I'm not that strange but you know what I mean – but I appreciate your candidness and your honesty and I think that if you allow it into the book it'll read well and add to your story.*

Chapter Seventeen

Today

2019

When Patrick Vieira came over from AC Milan to Arsenal Football Club, he didn't know a word of English. We gave him accommodation, phone, car and an English teacher. I talked to Patrick in fluent French and before a game I asked in French, Can you speak a bit of English to me? Patrick nodded and replied, Tottenham are shit.

David Dein, former co-owner of AFC

AND SO, WE REACH THE END. IT'S APPROACHING THE END OF the story but not the end of Arsenal Whittick. He charges forward, continually overcoming problems and setbacks, and making his life and the lives of those around him a better place to be. We have several stories to wrap up and details to recall, sending us away into the night, happy that all is well in the world. Unfortunately, this isn't a folk tale or a fantasy novel, and the ending isn't within my power to dictate and so instead we shall see where our hero has taken us through the reality of his situation.

There is no cure for autism! I believe by this stage of our learning we know and realise the best that anyone can hope to be is held within the constraints of the DNA lottery numbers they have drawn.

Let's go back to Liverpool. Arsenal has a full family, still living in the north-west of England that he rarely sees or communicates with. The odd card here and there, perhaps a visit every couple of years to see his dad or those brothers and sisters that he speaks to. The only one he is estranged from is Mark, who through a football game and then Arsenal's inability to process the fact his brother was going to be made redundant, has meant they don't talk. Mark didn't invite Arsenal to his wedding.

In all, he is one of six siblings: Eddie, Mark, Jackie, Anthony – known as Simmo – and Jeni. He is an uncle and a grandad several times over and Simmo has two sons also on the spectrum. Simmo himself was diagnosed five years ago as autistic.

Arsenal has two grown-up sons in X and Y that since his mum's funeral in 2013 he has also not communicated with, but as he says, his door is always open. Perhaps now is the time to try and mend old wounds; we shall see.

Samantha and Danielle are coping with their own mental health problems that are, on the whole, anxiety-related. Danielle is seventeen and studying at college while Samantha is going back to do her masters. Danni still has anxiety issues but when I spoke to her, she seemed a very switched-on young lady who knew what she wanted from life. She also has a deep and lasting bond with her mother and father, and alternates the time she spends between them.

Sam has moved on from her suicide attempts and has just moved out of Winchester to the suburbs; she commutes in for work and university. She has turned into a strong young woman who knows she has to work hard to keep the black dog at bay. As she says, "It will always be part of her."

Nicola, Arsenal's ex-wife, lives in the family home and has an on-off relationship with her new partner. I feel that her one true love was Arsenal and that was sacrificed for the health of her daughters. Her and Arsenal remain friends and are on good social grounds, as I met Nicola at Arsenal's flat where he and his new girlfriend Sophie live together. I don't know of too many ex-wives who could or would do that, or new girlfriends for that matter.

That leaves us with the star of this particular movie; the man above the title; the flawed hero who against all the odds turns bad fortune into good; the man in white; the man in black; more likely the man in red with white sleeves; the man who once said to me, "I'm not a bad dad, I just have autism."

Arsenal Whittick.

Arsenal could not speak well enough to order a drink at the bar. He now speaks to hundreds of people in halls and churches, explaining how he lives with autism.

Arsenal could not hug his own children. He has held a hug day, raising awareness and hundreds of pounds for autism charities. Please look up the video online. For him it was like walking over broken glass with no shoes on, yet he gave hugs to complete strangers that day until the physical effort wore him out, so he almost collapsed. In 2020 he intends to attempt to beat the world record for the greatest number of hugs in a minute. I still await my first.

Arsenal wasn't educated at school because he was 'special'. He now educates the rest of the world on autism, his current role being Autism Specialist, teaching others to understand.

Arsenal – who self-harmed every day of his life and even knocked himself out with a hot iron because it took him longer than four minutes a shirt – hasn't self-harmed since Wednesday 19th August 2014.

Arsenal – who used to scream and shout and throw things at the wall and smash them to pieces if they weren't replaced where they belonged – now has his own flat where things can be left out, coats left over chairs; his obsession has been overcome.

Arsenal – who would beat himself to a pulp if AFC didn't win every game – hasn't been to a match since 2015.

Arsenal helps people. His new partner has her own list of problems and is fighting for the custody of her son. She has a diagnosis of Borderline Personality Disorder which is giving her problems with alcohol. Arsenal, every day of his eventful life, finds time to help her through her problems. I have never met a more patient man. Sophie is attending classes and counselling to cure her addiction and Arsenal is there with her.

Arsenal has tried to kill himself at least five times; I say at least because every time I speak to him, he surprises me. Now, I have never met a more positive man.

"Every day is a new day; and every day I wake up happy."

I asked him, with everything that is still going on in his life, how does he manage to get up and go to work and cope? He said, "Tomorrow is a brand-new day."

One night at Arsenal's we are having a discussion and Sophie has drank herself to sleep in the bedroom. We're joking and I say to Arsenal, "Don't worry, mate, I have a dream of you and I on *The One Show* discussing our best adapted screenplay at the Oscars."

Arsenal replied, "I have a dream that the lady in the bedroom next door is going to be OK." I have never felt more put in my place and it wasn't even meant that way.

Samantha said of her dad, "Every day is a new day for him, and autism actually helps him deal with Sophie's issues. Everything to him is normal. He doesn't panic. Plus, he has an incredibly positive outlook on life."

This is a man who couldn't speak until the age of seven; had a stammer that meant he couldn't hold a conversation properly until he was forty; was chosen at school to help the janitor as he couldn't be educated; at the age of fourteen found out that the person he called Dad was not his biological dad; at the age of forty-nine was diagnosed as autistic; at twenty-three he changed his name by deed poll to Arsenal – in Liverpool; who self-harmed for the best part of forty years; who has two daughters, both with mental health issues, one of whom has tried to take her own life twice and the other who has taken overdoses; who was abused as a nine-year-old child and then finds the same thing nearly happening to his eight-year-old daughter.

What does this man do after diagnosis and the most traumatic life imaginable?

HE DEVOTES HIS LIFE TO HELPING OTHERS!
One of the first times I met Arsenal for this project, he described the hug day that he undertook for charity; bearing in mind the only two people he has ever hugged are his own daughters on that memorable Christmas Day, we can only imagine what his life has been like.

Alan: *I watched the hug video.*
Arsenal: *Oh, did you? Hardest day of my life, that.*
Alan: *You can see it in your face.*
Arsenal: *Bloody hell, yeah. Just after one hug, it felt I'd ran a marathon. I was so drained, I was. I was really drained. Then I was doing it from 9am until 2pm. I don't know if I told you this. I don't remember what I tell people so...*
Alan: *It's OK.*
Arsenal: *It's why I can't lie as well. Ha ha. I can tell you the same thing today; something that's happy for me. And then I can tell you the same thing tomorrow or in a month, exactly the same thing and I'll still get the same buzz.*

Alan: *That's fantastic, though.*

Arsenal: *So, in my world, every day's a new day. Wooh hoo! On the hug day I was doing it from nine 'til twelve, at twelve o'clock I said to XXX, "I've got to stop."*

     And she said, "OK. It's your day." And I told her why I needed to stop because when I was hugging people, mentally, it was getting harder and harder for me. And about midday—

Alan: *Can you describe that to me? Why was it getting harder and harder? I would have thought the opposite. The more you do it, the easier it gets.*

Arsenal: *No, it was getting harder for me. I went to a really bad place. That's why, when you watch the video, the longer it gets, the hugs are virtually, it's a proper hard hug.*

Alan: *And you're walking and then running into them. They became like rugby tackles, you almost knocked one girl over.*

Arsenal: *Yeah, yeah. Because I was looking down as I let go, they didn't have no skin. I know that sounds stupid, but I could just see inside them because they had no skin. Woah, what's happening there? And then it was getting darker and darker, and I gave a girl a hug, it's on the video. And when I hugged her and pulled back, you see me go, "FUCK!" Like that. Because I can see her hanging. And I started seeing all these really dark images. And that's why I went, fuck, like that, because I could see her hanging. Then I told XXX, "Something's happening in me head?"*

     And she said, "What?"

     "I'm seeing people hanging."

     "You'd better stop." [No shit, Sherlock.]

And then Samantha rang me, and she had an exam that day in Winchester and she'd just finished so she was on her way down and she said she was going to be a good hour. I said OK, but I never processed it, did I? What I should have done is just stop for an hour, but I didn't, I carried on.

But then, after about half an hour I said, "I can't do it." And that's why there is no video of me and me daughter hugging. I had hugged her on Xmas Day 2014. That was the first time I ever hugged her, but I didn't hug her on hug day.

Sam has a different recollection of the day. She was late to the hug day because she was on her way back from a holiday in America and was completely jetlagged. She also says that her dad did hug her as well as her mum, sister and her boyfriend. Arsenal has no recollection of this, but as he suggested, he had gone to a very bad place.

Please google the video on Autism Wessex's Facebook website; I promise you, you will not be disappointed.

At the end of every day Arsenal runs through his routine. He tidies his kitchen; he watches an hour of drama; he takes out his bowl and turns all his negatives into positives surrounded by his positive images on the walls of his living room; anything he doesn't understand he looks up and learns something new; he looks at his Wonderwall and plans his next day: "Oh, look, Alan is coming round to do that book."

His head hits the pillow at 10.55pm and within ten minutes he's fast asleep and if anyone deserves a good night's sleep, it's Arsenal Whittick.

He wakes, ready to take on the world again.

"I always wake up happy." – Arsenal Whittick, a true hero.

Epilogue

WE HAVE ARRIVED AT OUR DESTINATION. WE ARE UP TO date in Arsenal's life and times. He carries on working at Autism Wessex, helping others also on the spectrum and educating all as to the colour of the sky in his world. His life is all about family; conditional and unconditional love. I'm not sure Arsenal can differentiate.

Throughout this process and, indeed, his everyday life, Arsenal carries around with him, akin to the Ancient Mariner, his own personal albatross. The abuse he suffered as a child, fleeting though it may have been, has impacted him deeply.

"It happened to someone else. It didn't happen to Arsenal." Speaking about himself in the third person. An ironic English language phrase, as Arsenal is his second person. The first we will never know. Blacked out from Arsenal's mind to protect himself, he can hardly remember an incident from the first ten years of his life.

The deeply disturbing abuse from his childhood would affect anyone, but then put that person on the black-and-white playing board that is the spectrum and you have an increasingly far more complicated scenario. Exponentially so. Arsenal dealt with this by becoming someone else. There are a few family members, his dad and brothers, and old childhood acquaintances in Liverpool who may know his real name.

When Arsenal receives letters or cards from his dad with his birth name written or typed on them, he redacts the name from the document before letting anyone see it. His birth name makes him angry and he once threatened Nicola that he would put his head through the front room window if it was ever said in his presence. Birthday or Christmas cards go straight in the rubbish bin. He cannot bring himself to utter or write the words.

This epilogue was going one of two ways. I wanted to, if possible, for Arsenal to beat the stigma of his abuse. He has turned his life around. I wanted him to be able to say to the world, "You have thrown every kind of shit at me and I've risen above it and come out the other side a bigger and better man. My name was XXXXX, but it doesn't matter anymore. I am not that person. I have beaten this false shame and anger and a couple of words do not matter."

Throughout the process of writing the book we have returned to this topic. Arsenal has always been consistent in telling me he can do it. We can finish with his real name. What does it matter anymore? But he has never told me. I rise on the morning of the 27th June to go to work. Arsenal and I both work for Autism Wessex and we grab the opportunity to meet when the busy work schedules allow.

I have told him the first draft of the book will be finished on Friday 28th June. We are both very excited. I have also told him the epilogue, just like his future, is still unwritten. I don't know how it will end, neither does he.

At exactly twelve noon on Thursday 27th June, I receive the following text:

> Arsenal whittick texting. i
> was born friday 27 april
> 1962 at 12.06am, I was
> named kevin paul flynn,
> feeling very strange and
> sick at the moment in my
> chest, but can't let it ruin
> my life as am in control
> now

I go to see Arsenal; he's struggling a little but feels he's broken it. I couldn't be prouder of the man. He talks about Sam and Danni, Sophie and Nicola, how he's doing at work.

The words are out there now.

There is a chapter much earlier in the book called, 'Becoming Arsenal Whittick'; that 'becoming' is still happening but today is a statement day. Time to go and let him get on with his life, and let's leave him with the last words: "All I ever wanted to be was Arsenal Whittick."

Alan J Hill lives in Christchurch, Dorset and is a semi-retired finance professional after working in the industry for over forty years. Moving from the corporate industry into the charity sector, Alan worked for Autism Wessex as a Finance Director, which is where he met Arsenal. This is Alan's first non-fiction book after having published three books in a young adult series.